Melbourne 1820 – 1875:
"A Diary of the Various Occurrences which have taken place &c &c by John Joseph Briggs FRSL"

Edited by Philip Heath.

Published by the Melbourne Historical Research Group in association with
Derbyshire County Council and South Derbyshire District Council, 2005.

The Diary is transcribed from the original manuscript (ms. no. 4607) at Derby Local
Studies Library and is published by kind permission of Derby City Council.

ISBN 0-903463-78-4

Cover Photographs:	Front:	J.J. Briggs in later life
	Back:	Elms Farm, home of J.J. Briggs
Endpapers:	Front:	King's Newton in 1790, from Bailey's plan of the Parish of Melbourne.
	Back:	King's Newton in 1882, from the 1st edition 25" Ordnance Survey.

Designed by Mono Design Ltd. Derby

Foreword

We are delighted to contribute a foreword for the publication of this fascinating diary, and to commend the co-operation of so many people and organisations who have worked together to make it happen. Without the efforts of all these people, and especially of Philip Heath, South Derbyshire's Heritage Officer who has edited it, it is doubtful that this valuable record of a past way of life would ever have reached a wide audience.

Publication of this diary will help to ensure that its contents are preserved in our folk memory. It is thought-provoking to reflect on the slower pace of life in Briggs's day, and makes us wonder whether there is a lesson to be learned from it, to make our quality of life better in the future. Nevertheless, it is surprising to note the frequency of visitors to Melbourne and travels made from Melbourne at such an early period, and to read what a busy place it was.

One of the reasons that the District Council employs a Heritage Officer is to promote the appreciation, understanding and enjoyment of local historic records and of the historic environment. The County Council's Library Service also has an important role in recording, preserving and promoting the history and heritage of Derbyshire. We hope that you, the reader, will feel that this publication furthers those aims.

Councillor Jean Mead   *Chair, South Derbyshire District Council.*
Councillor Bob Janes   *Cabinet Member for Cultural & Community Services,*
                          Derbyshire County Council.

Acknowledgements

Many people have been involved in the preparation of this book. First and foremost, it would not have come to fruition without the help of fellow members and friends of the Melbourne Historical Research Group. The manuscript was typed by Adrian Earp, Barbara Foster, Philip Heath and Howard Usher (group members) and Marilyn Hallard, Peter Hollins, Shirley Luckett and Debbie Russell (friends). Group members Roy Dunnicliffe, Gordon Foddy, Jean Grimley, Richard Heath, Howard Usher, Lindsay Usher and John Wesson have all given valuable assistance in various other ways. The photographs from the original manuscript were taken by Keith Foster (friend). Marjorie Calow (friend) assisted with the proof reading.

At Derby City Council, Linda Owen, Trish Kenny and Paul Hudson (past and present librarians of Derby Local Studies Library) and Bernard Haigh are thanked for putting the document onto microfilm, giving permission to reproduce it, and assisting with illustrations and questions.

At Derbyshire County Council, Ruth Gordon (Matlock Local Studies Library) and Robert Gent are thanked for their practical help and encouragement in getting the transcription into print and sourcing some illustrations. The County Council has also provided the lion's share of the finance required, as a partner in the project.

South Derbyshire District Council, the third partner in the project, is thanked for its support, particularly by allowing some editorial time for the work within the editor's paid employment as the Council's Heritage Officer.

Our grateful thanks are also due to Melbourne Civic Society, Derbyshire Record Office, Nick McCann of Heritage House Group Ltd, Nick Tomlinson of "Picture the Past", Irene Brightmer, Penny Heath, Lord Ralph Kerr, Sue Murfin, Mick Shaw, Bruce Townsend and Gill Weston. Emlyn Harris and Dennis French are thanked for information on George Wombwell, and Simon Chadwick and Keith Sanger are thanked for information on Patrick Byrne.

Additional illustrations, not included within the original manuscript, have kindly been provided by the following organisations and individuals:

By courtesy of Derby Local Studies Library: pages 20, 21, 24, 48, 76, 104, 114 bottom, 135, 141, 159 bottom, 164 top, 178 and 220.

By courtesy of the Derby Evening Telegraph: pages 84 and 186 top.

By courtesy of Derbyshire Countryside: page 16.

Derbyshire County Council via Matlock Local Studies Library: pages 25/183, 54, 116, 130 top/200, 170 and 189 bottom.

By courtesy of Glasgow University Library: page 65.

By courtesy of Melbourne Baptist Church: page 85.

By courtesy of Melbourne Civic Society: pages 9, 67, 68 top and bottom, 80 bottom, 154 and 156.

Melbourne Historical Research Group collection: front cover/page 164 bottom and pages 29, 42 top and bottom, 49, 60, 73 top, 79 bottom, 80 top, 136 (taken by Richard Lane), 145, 148 bottom, 184, 225 top and 234.

By courtesy of Museum of English Rural Life, University of Reading: page 83.

By courtesy of The National Trust Photographic Library: pages 206/223 top.

South Derbyshire District Council collection: pages 34 and 111.

Notes on the Transcription

Briggs' diary covers, in varying degrees of detail, the period from 1820 to 1875. In transcribing it, care has been taken to make as few changes to his original text, spelling and punctuation as possible, so that the reader can get as close as possible to a sense of the style and flavour of the original.

Picture captions. Where illustrations have been reproduced from the original manuscript no further captions have been added, unless their position within the manuscript has been altered, in which case a caption has been added to record this fact. All pictures from other sources have captions, thus enabling the reader to distinguish the pictures included in the original manuscript from the editorial insertions.

Use of square brackets and italics always denotes editorial additions and comments. Where Briggs himself uses brackets, they appear in this transcription as curved brackets thus: ( ), regardless of whether Briggs used square or curved brackets in the original manuscript. Briggs' own (very occasional) use of italics has been omitted in the transcription to avoid confusion, but is indicated by footnotes .

Paragraph breaks. Some additional paragraph breaks have been added to assist the readability of the text.

Index. In the original, the index was located after the entry for July 2nd, 1861. The pages following the index, commencing with June 17th 1862, were not numbered and Briggs never made an index for them. For this transcription, a new index has been compiled and Briggs' own index has not been used.

Illegible or uncertain words. A few words are difficult to decipher. Where the letters are unclear, the doubtful word (or part of it) has been indicated in square brackets thus: [ ] in italics, with inverted commas and a question mark. Where Briggs' intention is a mystery, the word has been placed in brackets with the missing letters, or the whole word, replaced by dots, followed by a question mark, again in italics. In a small number of cases, Briggs left blanks, clearly with the intention of filling them in later. In the transcription the blanks are indicated thus: *[space left for missing word/words]*.

Briggs often missed words out unintentionally. The intended words are usually obvious from the context, and are indicated in footnotes.

Punctuation has followed Briggs' original text, even where there are cases of clear misuse.

Spelling. The spelling of certain words appears odd to modern eyes. In certain cases this is simply the result of changed normal practice (e.g. the use of "Cronstadt" instead of the more modern "Kronstadt" and "shewed" instead of "showed"). Other, repeated, non-standard spellings include scite, vegitation, dessolate, neucleus, controul, Bredon, lightening, evedent(ly), aweful, sweede, gass and buisness. There are numerous grammatical and spelling errors noted thus: *[sic]*. In entries, or consecutive entries, where Briggs repeatedly uses a non-standard spelling of a word, it is noted thus: *[sic]* after the first appearance only. Where the modern name of a place or person is very different from that current in Briggs' time, or where he appears to have made an error in a proper name, the current or "correct" name is included in square brackets and in italics.

In accordance with the style of the time, Briggs made far more use of capitals when starting improper nouns than we do today and his practice has been followed wherever the original manuscript makes his intention clear. Sometimes it is difficult to distinguish lower and upper case letters.

Insertions. Finally, the manuscript includes a number of drawings, photographs and (particularly in later years) various articles and other printed ephemera. Some of these have been photographed and are included as illustrations; others have been transcribed in full. Where the insertions are neither photographed nor transcribed, they are described and quoted from to a greater or lesser degree in editorial notes in square brackets.

Abbreviations.

DLS	Derby Local Studies Library, Irongate, Derby
DRO	Derbyshire Record Office, New Street, Matlock
MHMR	Melbourne Hall Muniment Room
PRO	Public Record Office

Introduction

Melbourne

Melbourne lies about seven miles south of Derby, just south of the River Trent which forms the northern boundary of the parish. Before the Swadlincote urban area began to develop in the early 19th century, Melbourne was the largest settlement in the current administrative district of South Derbyshire.

Melbourne is best known for its important Norman parish church, the picturesque Melbourne Pool, and Melbourne Hall with its rare survival of an early 18th century formal garden. The town itself also has plenty to offer. Highlights include the attractive streets of the town centre such as Potter Street and Church Street; large houses in landscaped grounds on Penn Lane; artisans' housing on Blanch Croft, and the memorial cottages built in 1890-91 by Thomas Cook the travel agent on High Street.

The parish includes the village of King's Newton where Briggs lived, which has a distinct character of its own. Its main street, with a variety of timber-framed and stone-built houses, is ranked in Pevsner's "Derbyshire" (1978) as "one of the most attractive village streets in Derbyshire". Its western end is presided over by the Hall, whose destruction by fire in April 1859 Briggs describes so vividly.

• *Main Street, King's Newton: "one of the most attractive village streets in Derbyshire" (Pevsner). A photograph by Edward Martin (d1921).*

Briggs regarded himself first and foremost as a King's Newton man, though Melbourne's jurisdiction over King's Newton affairs was rarely called into question. One such occasion in 1832, concerning road repairs, is described by Briggs. Today, Melbourne and King's Newton are virtually joined together by modern development, but a strong separatist tradition survives.

Mediaeval Melbourne had been a place of some consequence and was a Royal manor. The population in general was not particularly well-off, but in addition to the church there was also an unfinished Lancastrian castle and a secondary seat of the Bishop of Carlisle, which is now Melbourne Hall. The castle, fortified at great expense between 1311 and 1322, was destroyed shortly after James I's sale of the manor and castle in 1604. A small area of foundations or basement walls, with masonry of excellent quality, remains exposed on private land on Castle Street.

Melbourne seems never to have achieved the critical mass necessary to sustain the weekly markets and annual fairs granted by Royal charter in the 13th – 15th centuries. By the mid 16th century its objects of pride, including the hunting park, castle and Bishop's palace, were fast fading and deteriorating. Documentary evidence suggests that Melbourne in the 1590s must have had an air of abandonment. Bishops and Kings no longer came. There was no fair or market, the Bishop's house lay vacant and derelict, and the decaying Castle was soon to be demolished. The Parish Church, too large for Melbourne's population, seems also to have been in decline, as it was said to be in great ruin and decay by the 1630s, when extensive alterations and repairs were carried out.

- *An early view of Castle Square, Melbourne's original market place, probably taken in the 1880s.*

Against this background, a number of local families nevertheless rose to prominence and relative affluence, including the Hardinges, Cantrells, Raggs, Bewleys, Wilnes, Dawsons and Rivetts. The houses of the first three still survive in King's Newton. But in a national context the area was not prosperous. When Sir John Coke the Younger proposed to make Melbourne Hall his home in 1635, his father warned him of the problems of living there:

"You shal plant yourself in a town where there are manie beggars, most poore & but few good livers".

He continued with a warning that the Melbourne folk will

"ingage you into debates and sutes wherin little is to be gotten but vexation & troble to no end"[1].

Until the late 18th century, Melbourne remained an agricultural village and the pace of change was slow. Modern Melbourne is largely a product of the Industrial Revolution, and the greater proportion of the buildings in its principal streets date from the late 18th to mid 19th centuries. The population of the parish almost doubled during the 19th century, from 1,861 in 1801 to 3,580 in 1901. The rapid growth seems to have begun around the 1770s, before the availability of census figures, when Melbourne became an outpost of the East Midlands framework knitting industry. There was an initial emphasis on woollen hosiery, later switching to silk gloves and shawls. In the early 19th century framework knitting in Melbourne was still a cottage industry, but by the middle of the century it was largely factory-based.

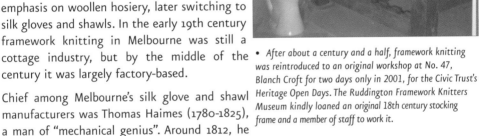

• *After about a century and a half, framework knitting was reintroduced to an original workshop at No. 47, Blanch Croft for two days only in 2001, for the Civic Trust's Heritage Open Days. The Ruddington Framework Knitters Museum kindly loaned an original 18th century stocking frame and a member of staff to work it.*

Chief among Melbourne's silk glove and shawl manufacturers was Thomas Haimes (1780-1825), a man of "mechanical genius". Around 1812, he discovered for himself the method of making figured warp fancy goods, as produced by the French, and introduced the manufacture of these goods to Melbourne:

"His success was complete. The articles produced from his manufactory were of a texture so much superior, and of a brilliancy so far surpassing those manufactured by the French, that he maintained a competition with that country, in the fashionable world, for a period of fourteen years, with much benefit to himself and those connected with his establishment .... Many a mechanic rose from a state of dependence to one of comparative wealth and affluence; a new impulse was given to other branches of traffic, and probably never did this spirited town present such a busy and flourishing aspect, as during the greater part of this gentleman's short, but truly useful life" [2]

During the middle of the 19th century, Melbourne became notable for its market gardens and the production of fruit and vegetables. Briggs noted the rise of market gardening, which he sometimes referred to as "spade cultivation", several times in his diary. This industry remained important for generations, before dwindling during the third quarter of the 20th century.

A writer in 1904 noted that "Melbourne ... seems a thriving little place, whose market gardens are overshadowed by the chimneys of boot and hosiery factories"[3]. Factory-based boot and shoe making began in Melbourne in the 1860s and Briggs died while the industry was still in its early days, so it does not feature in his diary. Shoe making, like textile production, has only ceased in Melbourne within the last few years.

1 British Library Add. Ms. 69870, C124/10.
2 <u>Melbourne; a Sketch of its History and Antiquities</u> by J. J. Briggs 1839, pages 27-28.
3 <u>Black's Guide to Derbyshire with Sherwood Forest</u> 1904, South Derbyshire section, page 14.

While Melbourne transformed itself from a sleepy farming village to a bustling little town, King's Newton remained little changed. The amount of 19th century development there was very small and the village retained its time-honoured mix of gentry, farmers and labourers. A cynic would say it was stagnant, but to others its unchanging state made it a venerable piece of "Merrie England" – feudal, solid, stable and therefore, somehow, naturally superior.

As far as we know, no one in King's Newton ever openly said that Melbourne had become a vulgar manufacturing town, but one cannot help thinking that some of them thought it. And they would not have been alone. J. B. Firth's "Highways and Byways in Derbyshire" (1908) says:

"Melbourne is a curious medley, of which part is as distressingly commonplace as any newly-built country town. This we may ignore. The other half, including the church, the Hall, and the great pool, is altogether charming ...."

• *Derby Road in the late 19th century. "Distressingly commonplace...This we may ignore...".*

This writer's assessment might be justly challenged, but he was at least right to notice the contrasting characteristics that made Victorian Melbourne such a fascinating place. A diverse mix from all walks of life has persisted even to the present day, giving the Melbourne community a vibrancy, buoyancy and "togetherness" that is the envy of many towns of larger size.

Briggs could not have the historical perspective on his life that we can apply to his work today. But he knew that he was chronicling Melbourne during times of great change, worthy of putting on record for future generations.

The Briggs and Rivett families of Elms farm

• The Briggs Family [4]

John Joseph Briggs was born at Elms Farm, King's Newton, on 6th March, 1819. His father ("Old Mr. Briggs", 1777-1864) married his cousin Mary Briggs of Hemington (c1790 - 1870), so when she changed her state her name remained the same. John Joseph used both of his forenames, perhaps to distinguish himself from his father who was also called John, as were his grandfather and great grandfather before.

The Briggs family was anciently seated at Alvaston, but Briggs' great grandfather lived at Thulston in the parish of Elvaston, where the family had owned land for generations. His grandfather John, of Alvaston, farmer (c1746 – 1815), took to Elms Farm through his marriage to Katherine Collyer (1745-1842) in July, 1773 [5]. Katherine was one of the co-heiresses of John Collier and Elizabeth his wife (nee Knifton), who were married in 1736. The Collyers are recorded as tenants of Elms Farm under the Hardinge family at least as far back as 1711 [6].

J. J. Briggs recalled conversations with his grandmother Katherine, who retained a remarkable memory to the last. One of her stories, handed down by her mother, concerned the fear of Melbourne residents on hearing that Bonnie Prince Charlie's men were set to come through Melbourne on their way south from Derby in 1745:

"the inhabitants of Melbourne and King's Newton hid their plate, money, and most valuable clothing in ricks and barns, or buried them in the ground" [7].

There was great relief when the soliders failed to show, having turned back at Swarkestone Bridge.

Although Elms Farm was large by Melbourne standards, the Briggs family augmented their holding by renting land from other landlords as well. A mid 19th century memorandum book (DRO D5238/8) shows that John Briggs paid £283 per year to the Melbourne Estate, £86 per year to the Donington Estate and £47 to the Rev. Joseph Deans, Vicar of Melbourne.

• Elms Farm and the Rivett family

Elms Farm was one of the most substantial farmsteads on the Melbourne Estate, and was anciently the home of the Rivett family who sold it around 1670 [8]. The Rivetts also owned other houses and cottages nearby, including one "at the elm tree", which was perhaps the old cruck-framed house replaced by the present "Crown Cottage" (No. 46, Trent Lane) in 1888-9.

---

4   For sources on the Briggs family history see DRO D4627/2/2; 4627/11/17 and 18; DLS Glover's History of Derbyshire 1831-3, Grangerised by J. J. Briggs 1869, between pages 338 and 343; DLS DA921 Mss (28491); DLS deed collection nos. 740 and 2939; "John Joseph Briggs – a Memory" by Llewellynn Jewitt in The Reliquary Volume 17 (1876-7), pages 49-54; "John Briggs of King's Newton: A famous Derbyshire Naturalist" by Hudson Read in The Derbyshire Countryside Volume 16 No 5, Jan-Mar, 1947.

5   Melbourne Parish Registers.

6   MHMR 12/1/15.

7   DRO In D4627/7-12.

8   For other information about the Rivett family in general, see The Rivett family of Repton and Derby 1538-1909 by Douglas Rivett-Carnac (1980, privately printed). This only makes a passing mention of the Melbourne/King's Newton Rivetts, but suggests that all the Midlands Rivetts were from a common ancestry.

The farm clearly took its name from the same source, and Mr. C. W. Robey of Trent Lane recalls that large elm trees were still to be seen in the vicinity after the Second World War. The hedgerow on the west side of Trent Lane, just below Elms Farm, had massive elm stumps in it and there was a large old elm there which eventually blew down and blocked the road. Further down was another large elm in the gardens of No. 50 and 52, Trent Lane.

The Rivetts' copyhold estate at King's Newton had been built up slowly over several centuries. The kernel of their estate, which is likely to have included the site of the present buildings at Elms Farm, can be traced back through surviving "copies of court roll" [9] to their forebears the Elys family who held it in the 14th century. The Melbourne Manor Court Rolls at the Public Record Office, not yet examined, survive from the reign of Edward III (1327-77) and could perhaps take the story back even further [10]. Johanna Elys, formerly the wife of John Elys, took the estate into the Rivett family by her subsequent marriage to John Rivett, who was formally admitted to the estate at a manorial court held on 14th April, 1423. Johanna had already died by this time [11].

- *"At the Elm Tree". This picturesque cruck framed house was pulled down and replaced by the Melbourne Estate in 1888-9.*

As the estate passed down generations of the Rivett family, it was augmented with additional property from time to time, both freehold and copyhold. One important addition, in 1594, was a copyhold estate previously held by George, Earl of Shrewsbury and his servant Roger Sheldon. It comprised two messuages (homesteads) and three and a third "virgates" or "yardlands" of land [12]. A virgate or yardland was nominally 30 acres and was $\frac{1}{4}$ of a hide, which was nominally 120 acres, but in practice the acreages varied widely across the country. In Melbourne, a yardland was about 19 acres.

9   MHMR 9/11/1-50.
10   PRO In DL30/44 and DL30/45.
11   MHMR 9/11/47 and 48.
12   MHMR 9/11/19,20 and 26 (copies of court roll); MHMR 14/10/4 and 5 (deeds).

One of these two houses stood where 27, Trent Lane and the adjacent bungalow now stand[13] , and was rebuilt for William Rivett, junior, and his wife Margery around 1612 [14]. William (hereafter William II) was the second son of William Rivett senior (hereafter William I), who lived at the ancient family home where Elms Farm now stands. William I (died 1626) had four sons altogether. German (c1587-1616/17) was the eldest, followed by William (II), Raphe and Francis. There were also three daughters Marie, Jane and Rebecca.

German, as the eldest son, would normally have inherited the bulk of his father's estate but in 1603, aged about sixteen, he "was stolne (stolen) away and marryed to Mary without any marryage porcon (portion) against the consent & good likeinge of ... his father.[15]" So William I settled part of his estate on his second son William II and his heirs instead. German was not disinherited. By an agreement of 1609, he and his heirs were to have the old family home at King's Newton after his parents were both dead, together with the great close butting on Crowder Lane, the close in West Field adjoining the Marsh, three yardlands of arable land, 6 acres of meadowland and the right to graze 6 beasts in the Marsh. In the meantime he was given a copyhold house in Melbourne occupied by his uncle Roger Rivett [16].

German died in 1616 or 1617 aged only 29. His mother lived until 1645, so it was German's eldest son William (hereafter William III) that inherited the old family house at King's Newton. The estate was now split between the heirs of German and the heirs of his brother William II, and remained so until it was all sold.

William III died around 1650, leaving five daughters as his co-heiresses. They sold the old family farm to Robert Harding of King's Newton Hall in March 1668/9 for "severall competent summes" [17], thus ending an association of some 300 years or more with the property. The transaction does not appear to have been straightforward, as part of Hardinge's payment was still outstanding in 1673 [18].

Meanwhile, William II seems to have moved away with his wife Margery, as he made his will at Ulverscroft Abbey in Leicestershire in 1630. He had died by May 1631 [19]. Nevertheless, he asked to be buried in Melbourne Parish Church, and gave his lands at Melbourne to his son Theodor. Theodor "of Newton" was buried at Melbourne on March 5th, 1657 [20] leaving a daughter, Jane, as his heiress. In 1676 or 77, Jane married John Berrisford junior of King's Newton, yeoman, and the couple sold three messuages, a cottage, closes, land and two beastgates [21] in the Marsh to John Coke Esq. in 1677 for £300. The houses were described as a capital messuage where Thomas Mugleston dwells (presumably the house built for William Rivett II and his wife Margery c1612, which would rank as "capital"), a messuage "beinge neere the Elme Tree" occupied by Jane Bucknall, widow, a messuage in the occupation of Robert Draper, and a cottage occupied by John Birch [22].

---

13   LRO DE658/8 folio 42 (copyhold survey, 1623); MHMR 9/11/4b (copy of court roll, 1631).
14   MHMR 7/7/3, 7/7/4, 9/9/1 and 9/9/2 (marriage settlements).
15   H. J. Usher, The Rivetts of Kings Newton, unpublished typescript 1984. This draws mainly on documents in MHMR Boxes 52 and 54 (formerly E2 and E4) and probate records at the Lichfield Record Office.
16   MHMR 7/10/14.
17   MHMR Box 9, Bundle 6.
18   MHMR 7/7/2.
19   PRO PROB11/159 file ref. 474. See also MHMR 9/5i/2 for a probate copy of the will.
20   Melbourne Parish Registers.
21   A "beastgate" or "cowpasture" was the right to graze an animal on a communal pastureland.
22   MHMR 6/9/13, 14 and 19.

In the 1670s, John Riley was tenant of some of the former Rivett property purchased by Robert Hardinge. As this included the occupancy of "Rivetts house", it seems clear that Riley's holding was Elms Farm [23]. This makes sense, as Katherine Briggs (nee Collier of Elms Farm) was descended from the Rileys. Her father John (baptised 1698) was the eldest son of James Collier who died in 1734 and is recorded as tenant of the farm in 1711. James Collier had married Elizabeth Rylie in September, 1696. It is likely, therefore, that the tenancy of Elms Farm passed from the Rileys to the Colliers by marriage, just as it was to pass from the Colliers to the Briggses after the marriage of John Briggs and Katherine Collier in 1773.

Between the 1690s and 1720s, the Hardinges of King's Newton Hall and the Cokes of Melbourne Hall exchanged property among themselves and with others [24], but in 1735 the Coke estate bought the Hardinge estate [25]. The deeds and papers of both parts of the Rivett estate consequently came together in the Muniment Room at Melbourne Hall, where they remain to this day. Elms Farm remained the property of the Melbourne Estate until 1919, when a large portion of the estate in Melbourne, King's Newton and Derby Hills was sold off at auction.

- *A painting of Elms Farm in the early 19th century, as reproduced in "Derbyshire Countryside" Volume 16, No. 5 (1947) from an original which cannot now be traced.*

Briggs variously claimed that his family had lived at Elms Farm for three centuries and for seven or eight centuries, but the latter extravagant claim must surely be a fanciful and romantic notion, and Briggs offers no evidence to back it up. Surely, as a chronicler himself, Briggs would have recorded the solid evidence if he had any. Nevertheless, if blood links can ever be demonstrated between the Rivetts and the Rileys, it would indeed provide Briggs with a very impressive documented lineage at King's Newton reaching well back into the mediaeval period.

23 MHMR 9/8/1-4.
24 See, for example MHMR Box 7, Bundle 4; MHMR Box 14, Bundles 11 and 12; MHMR Box 15, Bundle 1.
25 MHMR 13/3/12 and 13.

It is interesting to note that one of the Rivetts' houses at King's Newton was occupied in 1605 by Humfrey Ryley [26], while a Robert Ryley was servant to William Rivett I and witnessed his will in 1626 [27]. Intermarriage at some point between the Rivetts and Rileys in such a small village is not unlikely, so Briggs' claim that his family had lived at Elms Farm "from time immemorial" could be correct.

• The "very dreadful and wilfull fire" at Elms Farm, November 1800.

Today the farmbuildings at Elms Farm are converted into dwellings. The house and buildings are substantial, but date only from the early 19th century onwards and do not betray the farm's long history. The absence of old buildings on a large old farm can often be explained by an expansion in acreage in the post-Enclosure period, with an associated need for improved accommodation and better quality buildings. But in the case of Elms Farm the explanation lies in the total destruction of the house and buildings by an arson attack in 1800. "A very dreadful and wilfull fire on our own premises on the 17th of Novr. in the year 1800", wrote a sorrowful John Briggs in his notebook [28], "in the 23 year of my Age. On a Monday night they did it"

The previous entry in the same notebook records a similar catastrophe that occurred just two months earlier, although in this case there was no malicious cause:

"A very dreadful day of Thunder and lightening on Wednesday the 3 day of Septr. 1800 by which means part of Mrs. Leedam's Buildings where consumed and two lives lost".

What grievance did the culprit at Elms Farm bear against John Briggs? The answer lies in the stoppage of imported grain from the continent during the Napoleonic Wars. As a result, demand for English wheat was great and prices were correspondingly high. Farmers were seen to do well at the expense of the less well-off and were frequently accused of profiteering. The poor were driven to desperation and madness by the high price of staple foodstuffs, and the situation was at its worst in 1800, when the average price of wheat reached 128 shillings per quarter-hundredweight [29]. Elms Farm was but one of many casualties across the country, and the Derby Mercury of Thursday, November 20th, 1800 records the incident as follows:

"Monday night last, between 11 and 12 o'clock, some daring villain or villains set fire to the out-premises of Mr. John Briggs of King's-Newton, in this county, which in a short time communicated to the dwelling-house. The flames raged with such fury, that the whole of the premises were destroyed, together with a quantity of thrashed barley, some straw, &c. Fortunately, by assistance from the neighbours, the corn stacks, hay stacks, and most of the household furniture were saved."

The farmstead was rebuilt for John Briggs by the Melbourne Estate in 1801-4 [30]. The handsome farmhouse, commanding good views, has been little altered since and is now a Grade II listed building. It is curious that J. J. Briggs never refers to the incident which destroyed the family farm. Did he regard it as irrelevant, or could it be that some truth in the allegations of profiteering made the subject taboo among the family?

---

26 MHMR 9/6/1 (unexecuted enfranchisement deed).
27 Lichfield Record Office.
28 DLS DA921 Mss (28491).
29 The Crowd in History by George Rudé (Serif, 1995), page 39.
30 Melbourne Hall Muniment Room (hereafter MHMR), annual volumes of estate accounts.

"Winter Nights is not past therefore your person shall not go home alive – or if you chance to escape the hand that guides this pen, a lighted Match will do eaqual execution. Your family I know not But the whole shall be inveloped in flames, your Carkase if any such should be found will be given to the Dogs if it contains any Moisture for the Annimals to devour it..." (A chilling note, typical of threats sent to farmers and millers in the Napoleonic Wars, quoted in The Making of the English Working Class by E. P. Thompson (Penguin, 1991), page 69.)

• Elms Farm before the Fire

What was Elms Farm like before the fire of 1800 destroyed it? We know little of it, but it was clearly a substantial house and may well have contained mediaeval fabric. We know that the hall and parlour had panelled interiors and glass in the windows when William Rivett I died in 1626, because he bequeathed the panelling and glass of those rooms to his grandson William III [31]. Panelling, glass and floorboards were all regarded as movables instead of fixtures at that time, which is why old panelling often shows evidence of being cut about and altered.

The inventory made on the death of William Rivett I in 1626 lists the following rooms: house (or hall, i.e. main living room), parlour, maids' parlour, old buttery, milkhouse, entry, painted chamber, malt chamber, two other store chambers, kitchen, larder, buttery, menservant's parlour, coalhouse and chamber over, stall, barns and oxhouse. So it was indeed a substantial property by the standards of the time.

The hearth tax returns for Melbourne in 1662 have been published, giving valuable evidence about the social hierarchy of the parish, as the number of hearths in a house was related to the status of the occupants. 125 householders in Melbourne were eligible to pay tax, while a further 52 were exempt. Out of this total of 177, only 12 had three or more hearths, inluding Melbourne Hall (14 hearths) and Newton Hall (11 hearths). Jane Rivett is listed with three hearths, which presumably belonged to one or other of the two principal Rivett houses, i.e. the ancient house where Elms Farm now stands or the house built for William Rivett II c1612. William Rose is listed with 5 hearths. A King's Newton gentleman of this name took a seven year lease of some Rivett property in 1653 [32], which he perhaps renewed for a further term. It is impossible to say, at the moment, whether the five hearths belonged to the other principal Rivett house, or Rose's own.

• Some Local Traditions

John Briggs lived at the farm for a further sixty years after it was rebuilt, and lived a life deeply rooted in tradition. John Joseph noted that "he kept up as long as he was able the festivities of Christmas and the jollity of Harvest Home, and, as ever had been the custom of his family, at his father's death he gave a dole of bread, and paid a mortuary" [33].

These customs deserve some explanation:

Harvest Home was the bringing home of the last wagon load from the fields, decorated with branches, flowers and ribbons. The horses pulling the wagon were also decorated and the front horse would often have a ring of Pack Horse bells round his neck. On top of the load, women

---

31 Probate records, Lichfield Record Office.
32 MHMR 9/5iii/9.
33 The Reliquary Volume 17 (1876-7), page 49.

and children would sing songs. The tradition was kept up on the Briggses farm until 1869, when the wagon overturned. So many were injured that the practice was discontinued [34].

Briggs also records the local harvest custom of whooping "All's Down": "When the corn is all cut, all the persons on a farm gather together on some prominent hill or knowl near the house and stand in a cluster. One with broader lungs and deeper voice than the rest, at the top of his voice calls out three times distinctly "whoop""whoop""whoop": then the whole party make a loud "huzzah". Then the leader "whoops" again & again the "huzzah" follows, three times. This custom is resorted to to let those on the neighbouring farms see how harvest is progressing."[35]

A dole of bread was the custom of giving a loaf to every poor person in the village, following a funeral. The loaves were each worth about 10d and were marked with the initials of the deceased person. The custom was much valued by the poor who often did not eat the loaves, but kept them as long as they would keep.

The custom of paying a mortuary is again best described in John Joseph Briggs' own words:

"When the head of a family died it was usual to give the Undertaker a guinea enclosed with a papers, stating when deceased had died, and this was given by him to the officiating minister who buried the corpse. This was called a "Mortuary" fee and the minister entered a notice of the same in the Register Book belonging to the Church... My grandfather John Briggs of Kings Newton had one paid for him at his burial in 1816 [sic, should be 1815, Ed.] and my father had one paid for him at his burial in 1844 [sic, should be 1864, Ed.]" [36]

"Here's a health unto our Master, the founder of the feast
And I do wish with all my heart his soul in heaven may rest
That all things may prosper that he do take in hand
For we are all his servants & all at his command:
Then drink boys, & drink boys & see that you do not spill
For if ye do ye shall drink two, it is your master's will"

A favourite harvest home song as recorded by Briggs in his Grangerised copy of Glover's Derbyshire, 1869, opp. page 262.

---

34 DLS <u>History and Gazetteer of the County of Derby</u> (Glover), Grangerised by J. J. Briggs, 1869, opp. page 262.
35 ibid, opposite page 261.
36 ibid, opposite page 260.

John Joseph Briggs (1819-1876)

• Early Years [37]

John Briggs' deeply traditional life did not prevent him from realising the value of education. At the age of eight, the young John Joseph was sent to school in Wymeswold under the charge of Mr. Thomas Rossel Potter. Briggs and Potter got on well, and remained friends in Briggs' adult life. Briggs recalled him as "a kind-hearted, generous, amiable man, who treated me firmly but kindly".

In an autobiographical sketch, Briggs tells a story of himself and other boys throwing stones at a cog in a windmill near Wymeswold, in an attempt to upset the machinery. The miller "issued forth in a towering passion and vowed vengeance upon the first boy he could lay of". He pursued the boys a long distance, occasionally letting forth "terrific volleys of oaths", until he caught a panic-stricken Briggs by the ankle while crossing a stream. He was dragged to the mill "like a martyr to the stake", fearing a terrible fate, but the miller simply procured a batch-bag and dusted him as white as a sheet! Briggs was caught while stealing back to his room to change clothes, and was made to learn 100 lines of Latin from the 2nd Book of Virgil to do penance for his crime.

Briggs was at Wymeswold five years, followed by two years with the Rev. Solomon Saxton (c1796-1859) of Darley Dale [38]. Briggs made himself content there, but was less fond of Rev. Saxton than he had been of Mr. Potter. Rev. Saxton was a man of rigid piety, and Briggs claimed that he learned very little from him. With his education completed, Briggs went home while some employment was arranged for him.

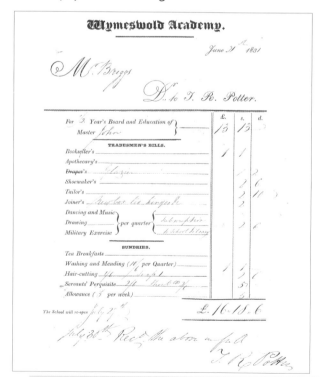

• Master John's schooling bill, 1831.
   *Derby Local Studies Library DA921
   Mss 28491.*

---

37 This material is from "a sketch of my life" DLS DA921 Mss (28491). A fragment of autobiography now at the
   Derbyshire Record Office (DRO D4627/2/1) seems to be the piece that is missing from the document at Derby.
38 See DRO 4627/1/24 for a note of his death.

• An Unhappy Apprenticeship

Briggs' school years were followed by an apprenticeship with Mr. Bemrose, printer and publisher of Derby, but the relationship was not a successful one. Briggs had made his own choice of career, but found that the trade disagreed with him and was injurious to his health.

Briggs claimed to like his work at Bemrose's, and to like living in Derby. But one suspects that he said these things for the peace of mind of his parents, who no doubt hoped the apprenticeship would secure his long term benefit and happiness. Briggs' letters are not specific about his ailments and his statement that "I never feel to have that energy and flow of spirits as when (sic, word left out) the country" points to a general depressed state of mind about his circumstances. "I shall have been a [sic] Derby 4 year on 1st of January next", wrote a sorrowful Briggs in a letter to his mother, " – and shall have to stay 1 year from March 5th next. What am I to do after that time? Go to London ? What?"[39]

• *Irongate, Derby, with decorations to celebrate the end of the Crimean War in 1856. Bemrose's premises are prominent in the view.*

It was a good question. Briggs confessed that "To employment of an agricultural nature I had from infancy a great aversion" and he had seen farmers stay in the same financial state while tradesmen using less capital and less exertion rose from a state of dependence to a state of comparative affluence [40]. Briggs loved to observe nature and to live among it, but he had no wish to control it by managing a farm.

In the Spring of 1837, Briggs was released from his apprenticeship. Mr. and Mrs. Bemrose treated him kindly over the matter, but said they must ask £10 as a year's wages for a replacement member of staff. Briggs offered, in a letter to his father, to pay the £10 out of the money his father allowed him for clothes [41]. Later in life, Briggs gave typhoid fever as the reason for leaving his apprenticeship, and said it took three or four years under the care of Dr. Shirley Palmer of Tamworth to restore him to health [42].

• Farm and Family

Dr. Palmer considered that a return to town would be fatal. So, back in King's Newton, Briggs settled into life as a bachelor gentleman farmer in the bosom of his family. The farm was clearly prosperous enough to allow for Briggs' inability to take a full role in the management of it, and to allow him a privileged lifestyle with plenty of time to indulge his leisure pursuits. Moreover, his father remained active on the farm well into the 1840s, so John Joseph's stated

aversion to a career in agriculture was not such a problem after all.

Surviving letters reveal an affectionate relationship with his parents [43], and he must have become all the more precious to them when he became their only child to achieve the age of 25. Seven other children died. Four of them died in infancy and childhood, and the other three died in their twenties, during the Spring and Summer of 1846. Marianne (also Maryanne, Marian and Mary Anne) died in May aged 24. Sarah died in July aged 22. Joseph died in August aged 20.

Briggs wrote about the final illnesses of Marianne and Joseph in some detail [44]. He describes how Joseph's decline into solemnity and ill-health began after a dream he had, when he wandered full of high spirits into a churchyard and encountered a crowd there.

• *A youthful J. J. Briggs, painted around the time that his first History of Melbourne was published in 1839.*

40 DLS DA921 Mss (28491) "a sketch of my life".
41 DRO 4627/1/2.
42 DLS DA921 Mss (28491) "a sketch of my life".
43 DRO D4627/1. See item 10, for example.
44 DRO D4627/2/3-5.

He soon realised that they were standing round an open grave. When Joseph asked "Who is it for?" the answer came: "For you".

• Travels

After his liberation from Bemrose's Briggs never looked back, but he maintained a close friendship with his old colleague Dewe, who was a frequent companion on his travels for several years afterwards. But Dewe eventually emigrated to New Zealand in 1848 [45], Briggs having first given him a calf to take as a present. Having arrived in New Zealand in September 1848, Dewe wrote

"my dear Briggs I wish you every success in Old England as you stay there but I do not regret leaving it".

He added that the calf was thriving well.

Briggs travelled widely. After a visit to Fountains Abbey, he wrote boastfully to his mother, saying "I have seen almost all the ruins of England but these surpass them all" [46]. Closer to home, he described a visit with the eminent Dr. Bateman to the henge monument of Arbor Low as "the happiest day of my life" [47].

Towns seem to have held less appeal for him. In 1841 he described Birmingham in a letter to his sister:

"Imagine to yourself some thousand streets (each like Walker lane in Derby) for filth & dirt intersecting one another with here and there a tolerable good Church and perambulated by mean haggardly, miserable wretched looking mechanics & polluted women with a few gentlemen & some genteel ladies mixed with them and you have Birmingham precisely — In fact it is the most disagreeable, disgusting, beastly town I ever visited in my life without exception". [48]

A budding engineer or industrialist would probably have been more stimulated by the place.

• Briggs' First History of Melbourne, 1839.

Although Briggs abandoned printing and publishing as a career, his links with his old employer were useful to him in his new direction as a poet and as a writer on antiquities and natural history. All three of his histories of Melbourne were published by Bemrose (i.e. William Bemrose, later Bemrose and Sons), and the Briggses and Bemroses remained on friendly terms throughout Briggs' life.

Briggs describes how his first history of Melbourne came to be written: "To amuse myself during the hours of sickness, being unable to undergo a more laborious occupation, I began to write a little work upon the History and Antiquities of Melbourne. It was published in 1849 [sic, means 1839] & about 400 copies were soon sold." [49] People continued to enquire about it, so Briggs carried on collecting material for a new edition and by 1847 he had begun to collect the names of subscribers to his revised work. In reality the second edition was so different from the first, and so much larger, that it may be considered as a wholly separate work.

---

45 DLS DA921 Mss (28491) letter from Dewe to Briggs 1848; DRO D5238/2/2.
46 DRO D4627/1/70.
47 DLS DA921 Mss (28491) "a sketch of my life".
48 DRO D4627/1/4.
49 DLS DA921 Mss (28491) "a sketch of my life".

• Briggs' "Second Edition" History of Melbourne, 1852.

Briggs' second edition, which finally appeared in 1852, has become time-hallowed and revered. It was regarded as the authoritative work on Melbourne for almost a century and a half, and in the 1970s the loan copy at Melbourne Library was still in high demand. Even now it is only superseded by a scattering of small works instead of a single large one. Briggs would probably be surprised at the long currency of his book, as he thought the lavish praise of it was rather inflated.[50]

Alluding to the book in a fragment of autobiography, Briggs says: "I had searched thro nearly 800 volumes manuscripts original letters and Rolls ... and although from the Patent and Close Rolls temp. K. John I gleaned some good extracts and had obtained some pretty, gossiping letters from Melbourne Hall ... I was disappointed upon the whole to be able to gather so little information about the history of the place"[51].

In his researches concerning the historic owners of Melbourne Hall, Briggs was assisted by the Hon. Mrs. Caroline Lamb, widow of George Lamb (1784-1834) and sister-in-law of Lord Melbourne (William Lamb, 1779-1848) the Prime Minister. Born Caroline St. Jules, she signed herself "C. G. Lamb" i.e. Caroline George Lamb, to distinguish herself from the notorious Lady Caroline Lamb, wife of George's brother William Lamb. When newly married, the two Carolines were known as "Caro George" and "Caro William" to avoid mixing them up, even before any stigma was attached to "Caro William" as a result of her outrageous behaviour.

SHORTLY WILL BE PUBLISHED, ROYAL 8vo., PRICE NOT EXCEEDING 7s. 6d.

DEDICATED BY PERMISSION TO THE RIGHT HONOURABLE

LORD VISCOUNT MELBOURNE,

THE

HISTORY AND ANTIQUITIES OF MELBOURNE AND KING'S-NEWTON,

SITUATED IN THE COUNTY OF DERBY,—

(Including a selection from the Unpublished Papers at Melbourne Hall, written during the reign of Charles I.,)

BY JOHN JOSEPH BRIGGS.

Second Edition.

CONTENTS OF THE WORK:—

Situation of the parish—extent—early history under the Britains—Romans—Saxons.

The Manor of Melbourne—ancient proprietors—changes in it—extracts from a survey in 1586—Robin Hood, said to be born in the Manor House at Chellaston.

Derivation of the name of the town—early traders—condition of the place during the Civil Wars—Sir John Gell—skirmish at Swarkeston Bridge—complaint about the Parliamentary Troops—Prince Charles Edward—Rebels at Swarkeston Bridge—Rural pastimes—hawking.

Natural features of the parish—Donnington Park—old oaks—deer—cliff—Melbourne Pool—River Trent—allusions to it by Milton, Scott, and Shakespeare.

Agriculture—soil—rotation of crops—farm-buildings, Lord Melbourne's Estate—improvements—field-gardening, allotments, &c., &c.

Description of the town—number of inhabitants—trade—manufactures—inventions—notice of the late Mr. Haimes,—Court Leet—schools—institutions, &c.

The Castle—the possessors of it—John Duke of Bourbon a prisoner there—officers of the Castle—present state.

The Church—description of it—Vicarage House—List of the Vicars—curious latin note—registers.

Chapels belonging to different denominations—schools—John Wesley preaching at Melbourne—Rev. John Pearson.

Palace of the Bishops of Carlisle—Chantry of St. Catherine—Hall and Gardens—noble fir trees—fountains—grotto—recent additions—the pool—Baxter the Divine at Melbourne Hall.

History of the Cokes—Life of Sir John Coke, Secretary of State to King Charles I.—George Coke, Bishop of Hereford—Sir John Coke, Knight—Thomas Coke, Esq., M.P.—Colonel Coke—Right Honourable Thomas Coke, Vice-Chamberlain to Queen Anne.

Pedigree of the Melbourne family—Honourable George Lamb—the late Right Honourable William Lord Viscount Melbourne, &c., &c.

Selection from unpublished Letters of Sir John Coke—Thomas Coke, Esq., M.P.—Bishop Coke, &c., written during the reign of Charles I.

The Hardinges, formerly of King's-Newton—Sir Robert, Knight—George Hardinge, Esq.—George Nicholas, (Naval Hero)—the present Right Honourable Lord Viscount Hardinge.

King's-Newton—curious incident—King Charles at Newton—the Hall—Holy Well—Cross—families—Cantrell—&c., &c. Skirmish at King's-Mills between the Royalists and Parliamentarians.

Appendix—charities—monuments in the Church—catalogue of pictures at Melbourne Hall, &c., &c.

The Work will be neatly printed and bound, and embellished with one or more Engravings.

As a limited number of copies will be printed, Subscribers are particularly requested to forward their names as early as possible, either to the Author, King's-Newton, Swarkeston, Derbyshire, or to the Publishers. It is intended to print a List of Subscribers with the Work.

DERBY: WM. BEMROSE AND SON, IRONGATE.

• An advertisement for Briggs' "second edition", pasted by him into his own "Grangerised" copy of the second edition. Derby Local Studies Library Ms 4606.

---

50 DRO D4627/2/1.
51 ibid.

George and Caroline lived at Melbourne Hall for about ten years prior to George's death. Mrs. George Lamb took a particular interest in the "Stone House" opposite the parish church. Her name appears on the well head in the garden, and her initials "CGL" are borne on a plaque over the front door. She later moved away, but her local knowledge and approachability made her a valuable contact between Briggs and the Lamb family.

Having received her subscription copy of Briggs' second edition, Mrs. Lamb wrote to Briggs from Brighton on 1st February, 1853:

"My dear Sir

I have received the book quite safe, I think it makes a very pretty & interesting work. I am only sorry you have left in, so many of my stupid & ill written remarks, I felt quite ashamed & shy when I saw them in print, and thought you would have extracted what was worth in them, & clothed them in better language. Luckily you do not mention my name. I feel I have been very careless about them and should have revised them with more care ..." [52]

420 copies of the second edition were produced. 300 were subscribed for, and the rest were disposed of within a few weeks. Briggs notes that the book "was noticed by 14 local papers which gave it more praise than probably it deserved." Later, in 1870, Briggs published a sixpenny "Guide to Melbourne & King's Newton".

- *The front cover of Briggs' 6d guide to Melbourne and King's Newton (1870). From a copy at Matlock Local Studies Library.*

[52] DLS DA921 Mss (28491).

• Briggs' Legacy

During 1875, Briggs' health began to fail. In September, the Vicar of Melbourne noted in his diary that "J. Briggs has given up farming and is to move into his own little house at the Cross"[53], thus ending his family's historic association with the farm. In a letter to his friend Llewellynn Jewitt in February 1876, Briggs wrote:

- "...his own little house at the Cross." Briggs moved into his own house, now known as "Cofton", upon surrendering the tenancy of Elms Farm.

"As for myself, I shall be obliged to relinquish a vast deal that I had cut out, and consider myself somewhat of an invalid for the rest of my life, and must content myself with collecting books, and amusing myself with my little garden, by growing tulips and roses, and such like little treasures"[54].

Within three weeks, Briggs had died. His old friend Jewitt wrote a warm obituary[55], though he was lukewarm in his comments on Briggs as an antiquarian and historian. He said: "Natural History was his forte... Antiquarian matters were a pleasure to him; he loved nature for nature's sake ... ; and poetry was his natural gift". One of Briggs' daughters, in her later life, had a more caustic assessment of her father: "If he'd paid more attention to farming and less to natural history, it might have been better for his family"[56]. Whatever view we may take of Briggs' life today, one thing is certain. As a farmer he would not have been remembered, but as a writer he secured himself a niche among the recorders of Derbyshire's heritage, and Melbourne's in particular.

53 Diary of Joseph Deans, Vicar of Melbourne, 1872-82. Unpublished photocopy, with draft transcription by Nigel Harding, MHRG collection
54 The Reliquary Volume 17 (1876-7), page 54.
55 The Reliquary, Vol 17 (1876-77), pages 49-54.
56 "A Derbyshire Naturalist: John Joseph Briggs" by H. J. Wain in The Derbyshire Advertiser, 18th January, 1974, page 4.

His published books were not numerous. Apart from the three histories of Melbourne and King's Newton, they included: "The Trent and other Poems" (1857, enlarged and reprinted 1859); "The History and Antiquities of Hemington" (a slim but lavishly-presented volume of 1873, of which only twelve copies were printed); and a series of chatty sketches reprinted from "The Field" and called "The Peacock at Rowsley" (1869). Briggs contributed numerous articles to newspapers and Journals, including "The Zoologist", "The Field", the "Derby Reporter", the "Critic", the "Sun", "The Reliquary" and the "Journal of the British Archaeological Association". He was also a Fellow of the Royal Society of Literature.

Two ambitious works were in an advanced state of preparation at the time of his death but remained unpublished. One was a Natural History of Melbourne, King's Newton, Weston Cliff, Swarkestone, King's Mills, Sinfin Moor, Stanton-by-Bridge, Foremark and Knowle Hills. This work was passing through the press at the time of Briggs' death, and some illustrations had already been prepared for it by George Bailey, a well-known Derbyshire engraver. Some proof pages survive, but the work was abandoned when Briggs died.

NATURAL HISTORY OF MELBOURNE.

1843.

CTOBER 13th. This morning early a small fall of snow took place, the first this season. On the distant hills of Charnwood and the Peak snow was visible, and persons who came from near the latter said that it lay on the ground to the depth of six inches.

October 14th. Observed an individual of the yellow wagtail (*Motacilla Rayii*), an unusual occurrence, inasmuch as the birds usually depart early in September. It was probably an inhabitant of the north on its way to the south. House swallows (*H. R.*) still continue here, lured probably so late by the fine autum. Although the air is keen and cold, these birds

The other, entitled "The Worthies of Derbyshire", survives as a collection of material recently transferred from Derby Local Studies Library to the Derbyshire Record Office (ref D5363/1-6 and D5709/1-6). The Local Studies Library still possesses many of the manuscript and Grangerised volumes from Briggs' "Derbyshire Collection", including the diary that is the subject of this book.

- *A proof page from Briggs' unpublished Natural History of Melbourne &c, pasted into Briggs' diary after the entry for 9th July, 1872 q.v.*

• Briggs' Melbourne Diary

Briggs' historical works, particularly his 1852 History of Melbourne, were well received at the time but, as his good friend Llewellynn Jewitt noted, Briggs was not a man of deep research as an historian or antiquary [57]. Natural history and poetry were his chief talents, but he has failed to secure enduring fame in either sphere. The study of natural history has moved on greatly since Briggs' time, while the Victorian sentimentality and exaggerated imagery that infuses his poetry seems painfully outdated to the modern audience.

Fortunately for us, Briggs left behind this diary, a locally important, unpublished work of history that remains fresh and appealing today, with much to tell us. Briggs never intended the work for publication, yet it is clear from his prophetic introduction that he wrote it for the benefit of future generations:

"Many of the notes I am fully aware may seem uninteresting and unworthy of record and yet I cannot but imagine that even the most trivial in distant years must be found useful for oftentimes a small well-authenticated fact tends most materially to forward a great end. Improvements are in progress and we like to see the state of objects before such were effected - Times and manners change & man loves to contemplate how men lived & acted before him - We live in a changing age and I conceive that half a century hence we shall view the present time with as much amusement as we now look back upon that which is past -"

The diary spans the years 1820 – 1875, but the entries for the early years are very sparse and are written retrospectively. The recording of events as they happened appears to begin in January 1845, when Briggs was 25. His coverage of the next thirty years is inconsistent. Events that fired his enthusiasm and imagination are naturally described in considerable detail, while others are passed over briefly. There must have been periods when Briggs was unable to devote much time to his diary, causing him to pass over events that he would normally have recorded. The diary trails off noticeably after 1867. There are no entries at all for 1869 and only a few thereafter. Briggs' late marriage in 1868 at the age of 49, and the subsequent birth of four children [58], no doubt provides at least part of the explanation for the tailing-off.

The poignant final entry in the diary is dated January 4th, 1875:

"There has been a hard long continued frost : thermometer standing at 10°. Trent & Melbourne Pool thick with ice. The snow has also been very deep. It broke up about the 4th . A good deal of wild-fowl about amongst which was a splendid Goosander shot by the Earl of Loudoun. The Birds have had a terrible, hard, time of it. Almost all kinds of work have been suspended."

The suspension of all kinds of work was fated to include Briggs' own diary.

In his will [59], Briggs left his "Derbyshire Collection" to his infant son John Joseph, perhaps in the hope that he would inherit his father's interest in antiquities and natural history. But it was not to be. In 1913, when the Bemrose Library was for sale, it included 35 manuscript volumes of the late J. J. Briggs [60]. These are almost certainly the same "Derbyshire Collection" bequeathed by Briggs to his son. They would have included Briggs' Melbourne diary, explaining why it was bound by Bemroses after Briggs' death.

---

57 The Reliquary, Vol 17 (1876-77), page 50.
58 Briggs married Hannah Soar of Chellaston (born 1836). Their four children were Mary (or "May") Elizabeth Briggs (born 15/3/1869), John Joseph Briggs (born 13/3/1870), Alice Soar Briggs (born 23/12/1871) and Avena Maude Briggs (born 21/6/1874).
59 DLS Deeds Collection, no. 740.
60 DLS BA027.4 CUR (Reprint from the Derbyshire Advertiser October 3rd, 1913, re the Bemrose Library, which is for sale. It includes "35 volumes MSS. collections of the late J. J. Briggs, of Melbourne.")

• *The back of Briggs' own house at the Cross in King's Newton. The people are unidentified, but may well include members of his family.*

The Bemrose Library was bought by Derby Borough Library, but the buildings had to be extended to house it, and the Melbourne diary was not formally accessioned into the Borough Library collection until 1925 [61].

A chance search by the editor in the "old" library catalogue of Derby Local Studies Library brought the manuscript to light again. The index card in the library catalogue referred to Briggs' History of Melbourne 1852 with notes and additions. It seemed that no one, the editor included, had bothered to request the item. There were several copies of Briggs' 1852 history easily available at various local libraries on the open shelves, and it was quite common for them to contain marginal notes and a few inserted items. Their content was usually predictable.

One day, with a few moments to spare before leaving, the editor decided to put in a request to see the item. He was surprised when two items, instead of one, arrived on the counter. The first one was indeed a copy of Briggs' History of Melbourne, but it was his own copy and the insertions and additions were substantial. The second, wrapped in brown paper and firmly sealed up with sticky tape, contained the long-lost diary.

The diary was too delicate to be photocopied. Linda Owen, the librarian at the Local Studies Library, therefore kindly agreed to have the manuscript microfilmed so that a print-out could be made by the editor, for transcription purposes. A number of members and friends of the Melbourne Historical Research Group then undertook to type sections of the diary, which were afterwards seamed together as a single document by Mr. Peter Hollins.

61 ex inf library staff.

The final proof-reading, introduction, editorial notes, footnotes, cross-references and up-dated index are the work of the editor, who accepts all responsibility for any errors. Every care has been taken to provide a trustworthy and reliable transcription and we hope you will enjoy reading it.

Philip Heath, Melbourne, January 2005.
(Chairman, Melbourne Historical Research Group;
Heritage Officer, South Derbyshire District Council)

The
History of Melbourne

being a continuation of
the 2nd Edition

Brought down from the year 1820
to the present by

A Diary

of

The Various Occurrences which have
taken place &c &c

by

John Joseph Briggs FRSL
1870

A Collection of Notes,

Having reference to the weather, natural phenomina [sic], local occurrences, changes in the occupation of land, deaths of individuals, local improvements and various other things connected with the Town of Melbourne and also its Parish in the County of Derby.

Commenced in the year 1832: by

John Joseph Briggs.

"Melbourne"

The Notes contained in this volume will consist of remarks upon Local Occurrences, references to families - the weather - Roads - and incidents whch have taken place in this Parish - It is my intention to note them down correctly and add such observations of my own as may appear to me desirable in order to illustrate the subject. Many of the notes I am fully aware may seem uninteresting and unworthy of record and yet I cannot but imagine that even the most trivial in distant years must be found useful - for oftentimes a small well authenticated fact tends most materially to forward a great end. Improvements are in progress and we like to see the state of objects before such were effected. Times & manners change and man loves to contemplate how men lived & acted before him. We live in a changing age and I conceive that half a century hence we shall view the present time with as much amusement as we now look back upon that which is past.

Vol. 1.

1820

In this year died Mr. Thomas Dugmore, a somewhat remarkable and eccentric character. He was descended of good family and received his education under a clergyman of the Church of England. He was born at a small place called Ouston or Houston [62] near Rolleston not far from Burton-on-Trent. In religion he was a Roman Catholic. For many years he resided at Melbourne and kept a small Inn there [63] and he was most methodical and exact in all his dealings with his customers.

If a party went into his house and called for a gallon of ale he would draw the quantity in separate pints to shew that full measure was given. If one of the household put on the teakettle to boil and was absent when it boiled he allowed it to boil over and waste to the last drop before he would take it off conceiving as he observed "that he had no right to interfere with the buisness [sic] of another". A person met him one morning and accosted him, "Good morning Mr. Dugmore a fine morning - "Fool" said he "don't you think I know it"

- *Potter Street in 1991, showing the former "Bull's Head" on the right.*

Beneath a crude shell however lay the pearl of a good understanding which he exercised for the public good. On one occasion Lord Melbourne stopped up a footpath which Mr Dugmore conceived he had no authority for doing. He saw this circumstance would prove a great annoyance and inconvenience to the people of Melbourne and at his own cost entered an action against his Lordship who upon further consideration did not come to trial and the footpath remained open.

---

62 This place name is unfamiliar. Could it be that Briggs, seeing the name written down somewhere, read it as Ouston or Houston instead of Marston (on Dove), Derbyshire, a hamlet situated near Rolleston on the opposite side of the River Dove?

63 The Inn concerned was the former Bull's Head on Potter Street, eventually bought by the Melbourne Estate in 1851 and converted into cottages. It had been sold out of the Dugmore family in 1848, by Thomas's grandson William Dugmore, who was an innkeeper at Finsbury Square, London. Thomas Dugmore was 81 years old when he died (Information from title deeds to the Bull's Head in the Muniment Room at Melbourne Hall, Box 263, Bundle 343k).

He wrote a work called "Observations on Inclosing the Manor of Melbourne in the County of Derby: with some remarks upon the Act of Parliament obtained for that purpose" [64]. This pamphlet shews how well he could wield the pen and even at this day (1859) [65] the work is interesting to the Inhabitant of Melbourne on account of the allusions to persons and places. Mr Dugmore died in 1820 and was buried at Melbourne [66].

After the 1832 court case [see entry for 1832, below] Melbourne and Newton remained separate, as far as road maintenance was concerned, for many years.

Mrs. Bunty Ernill of "The Limes", King's Newton has in her possession a Survey Book of the Highway Accounts for the Hamlet of Kings Newton for 1846 – 1858. The roads in the township are named, and the expenses listed. These include 8 shillings paid annually to Repton and 10 shillings annually paid to Melbourne for the rent of the lock-up in Melbourne. For the road repairs, William Chambers supplied stone and John Briggs supplied the bricks, William Barton repaired the Pinfold for 19s.11d. and a new shovel was supplied by Mr Ratcliff of Derby for 2s. 6d.

Spreading gravel, forming the roads, scraping the roads and mowing thistles were carried out by Day Labour in 1846-7 at a cost of £7.12s.11d. Team Work in the same year came to £20.8s.0d. and included 16 days work by Mr. Briggs in Marsh Lane @ 9s.0d. per day, 6 days by Mr. Newbold in Wards Lane. etc.

Mr. George Sims was confirmed as the Surveyor of the Parish (sic!) of Kings Newton from March 30, 1846 to March 29, 1847. The total cost for the year was £48.15s.10d.

At a meeting of the inhabitants of the Hamlet of Kings Newton assembled in the Pack Horse on the 27 March, 1847, the above account was allowed and Mr. Wm. Taylor and Mr. James Newbold were elected as Surveyors.

Howard Usher.

In this year a dispute arose between the Parish of Melbourne & the township of Kings Newton respecting the roads [67]. After causing much dissension [sic] and unpleasant feeling it was finally terminated at an Assize Trial before Judge Baily.

1832

---

64 John Farey alluded to this work in his encyclopedic General View of the Agriculture and Minerals of Derbyshire (three volumes, 1811-17). At page 79 in Volume II (1813) he says: "When at Melborne, I purchased of Mr. Thomas Dugmore a large Pamphlet written by him, which details several most extraordinary proceedings of the parties concerned in that Inclosure: some of which, it might perhaps be worth while to guard against the recurrence of, in any revisal of the Act containing the general Clauses in Inclosure Acts". Two copies of the pamphlet itself can be found at Derby Local Studies Library.

65 Briggs clearly added this entry after he had written the title page of his diary stating that it began in 1832.

66 A similar version of this text was used by Briggs in his Worthies of Derbyshire Volume 5, page 565 (DLS). However, in the "Worthies" version, Briggs adds the following: "Mr. Dugmore died in 1820 and was buried at Melbourne after his own fashion with a green turf placed upon his breast and a penny clasped in his right hand. At his death he possessed several rare and curious manuscripts having reference to the parish of Melbourne and the district surrounding it but they appear to have been lost".

67 See also Derby Local Studies Library Letters Book A920 Acc No 16500 p75 (letter dated 2nd June 1830, about Messrs. Hazard and Fox's appointment as surveyors of the roads in Melbourne).

1832-1843

The question was "whether both villages joined in the repairs of the Roads in the Parish of Melbourne or whether each repaired its <u>own</u> portion of the Roads in the said Parish? Melbourne contested that both joined – Newton that they were separate - Melbourne Plaintiff - Newton Defendant - Council for Melbourne - Balguy & Clark - Council for Defendant - Adams & Hill. Newtons Expences £222:3:4. Melbournes a larger sum but what I cannot ascertain. Verdict for the <u>Defendant</u>.

1836 This year the Parish of Melbourne joined the Shardlow House of Industry as required by the New Poor Law Act - The first Poor Law Gardians [sic] were Henry Fox Esq. & Mr John Briggs Senr who each served the office three years -

1837 The Parish Register of Baptisms for the year 1837 contains 339 or 298 more than the previous one. In 1837 the New Poor Law Act came into operation in this neighbourhood and many poor people (who had neglected to have their children baptised) getting a mistaken notion that this law would deprive them after a certain period of that right flocked to the church in large parties to have it performed. This will account for the extraordinary number in that year -

1843 In the Spring of this year the old Vicarage House belonging to the living being in a very dilapidated state was taken down and a new one in the Elizabethian [sic] style built upon its scite [sic] - This building was designed by Mitchel of Sheffield who estimated for the work at £750 - The money was raised in the following manner - £600 were procured from Queen Annes Bounty (upon 5 per cent interest for 30 years) £100 from Lord Melbourne and £50 from the largest land holders and land proprietors in the Parish - Besides the £750 a considerable sum was laid out by the Rev Joseph Deans the Vicar –

• *The font in the parish church, before it was moved to its present position in 1931.*

1843/1845

• *A view in Church Close, with the Vicarage built by Joseph Deans on the right.*

In the Summer, Wordworths [sic] (the Poet Laureate) visited Melbourne Gardens and recorded his name in the Vistors [sic] Book -

Rev Joseph Deans published a History of the Church, an elaborate and beautiful work with plates by Mitchel - **October**

The labourers when cleaning Melbourne Pool found a Cannon Ball 6 lb in weight -

Many observations upon the remarkable season of 1844 will be found in another volume of mine entitled "Journal relating to the Natural History of Melbourne &c" 4to and also some remarks about the weather in the years 1842 & 3. In future all remarks upon similar subjects I shall note down in this volume. **1845**

A number of workmen are engaged in taking down the most saleable trees in Donnington [sic] Park which now presents a most dessolate [sic] appearance. It is said that during this season and the next timber will be fallen to the amount of £10,000. Jan 7

The family escutcheon which has hung over the entrance door of Donnington Hall on account of the death of the Most Noble the Marquis of Hastings is now removed - It has remained there a year. Feb 28

1845

Mar 25   Mr Hemsley the silk glove Manufacturer has entered upon a farm on Melbourne Common comprising 100 acres which he purchased for £10,000 of Mr. Beard of Dalbury Lees [68] -

Mar 25   Mr John Briggs Senr resigned the office of Church warden of Melbourne Church which had been held by him for 36 years - His successor is Mr Hasard of Lodge Hill farm [69] -

Mar 28   So little rain has fallen during the last 12 months that much inconvenience is felt in many parts for want of water - Some wells, usually plentiful in water are dry and others are failing.

April 3   One of the best authenticated instances of the truth of Mesmerism occurred near here. A short time ago Lady Hastings came to reside at Donnington [sic] Hall. In her household was a young woman who was much afflicted with toothache, to relieve which her noble mistress had often thrown her into a mesmeric sleep when she remained unconcious [sic] of any pain. As soon however as she regained her usual feelings the pain re-appeared & much troubled her.

- *Donington Park, from the article pasted in Briggs' diary after the entry dated 11th October, 1872, q.v.*

A neighbouring surgeon (who I knew well and related to me the case) was sent for and in his presence the young woman was mesmerised. In this state he extracted from her mouth two teeth which he assured me required more than ordinary force, and from the calm manner and seemingly quiet ease with which she bore the operation he had no doubt whatever that she felt quite unconcious of any pain - this she asserted when she awoke and was surprized and delighted at what had been done. The Surgeon said he believed that he could have taken off a limb without her feeling any inconvenience - Without I had heard this incident upon the most undoubted authority I should not have ventured to record it.

April 7   Throughout last Summer (owing to the extraordinary shortness of fodder and almost entire failure of the hay crop) fears were entertained that during the last Winter and present Spring hay would be unusually dear. The reverse is however the case and it is a curious fact that whilst in June last this article was £8 per tone [sic] yet during the last Winter I have heard of none hereabouts selling for more than £7 and for some time past it has only reached £5 & £5"10"0.

---

68 The farm concerned is now known as Highfields, on Cockshut Lane, adjoining the former Melbourne Common.
69 Now known as Melbourne Park Farm. The farmstead was built on Lodge Hill in Melbourne Park between 1834 and 1840 (Melbourne Hall estate accounts), to replace the old home farm buildings at Church Close.

At the residence of Lady de Ruthyn (her Ladyships's mother) at Harbledown near   April 9
Canterbury was married the Marchioness of Hastings to Captain Hastings Reginald
Henry second son of Mr and Lady Emiline Henry and nephew to the Duke of
Leinster. The Noble Duke - Lord Fitzgerald - the Baron and Baroness de Robeck - Mr
& Miss de Robeck - Miss Henry Miss C. Balguy and several other persons were of
the bridal party.

On April 2nd Lady Hastings left Donnington [sic] Park for Canterbury the place   April 12
arranged for her marriage with Captain Hastings Henry. After the celebration on
the 9th, the bridal pair were about to leave England for Paris (next day) and had
proceeded to Dover when Lady Hastings hearing of the illness of the youngest
child she had by her former husband hasten'd home again and arrived at
Donnington Park the same night.

In the possession of Lord Melbourne is an ancient Roll containing the Pedigree of   April 14
the Coke family which held this Estate before the Melbournes [70]. It was found
during a search last Summer amongst some old State and family papers in the

Library situated in Melbourne
Gardens - This Roll gives an account
of the Cokes from the earliest period
- shews their relationship to other
families and whom they married -
describes their possessions and lands
and has the amorial [sic]
bearings of each member properly
emblazoned - thus forming a lucid
and valuable history of the family. It
is many yards in length and altogether
is an Antiquarian curiosity [71].

- The "Muniment Room" or "Library" in
  Melbourne Hall gardens, converted from a
  dovecot by the Right Hon. Thomas Coke in
  1709

A party of about 20 gentlemen met at Swarkestone to try an experiment with   April 19
some Bloodhounds. A man was sent off with a piece of mutton to drag along the
ground, and 3/4 of an hour afterwards the hounds were laid upon the scent.

70 The word "Melbournes" has been deleted in pencil and a marginal note added as follows: "the Lambs. The
    Melbourne family became extinct before the Cokes came into possession of the estate."
71 Howard Usher, co-archivist at Melbourne Hall, says: "This document surfaced again in the 1980s when a drawer
    full of papers was found in the attics at Melbourne Hall and given to the archivists to sort. Box 258 was created
    to store the papers, of which 258/1 was listed as "Cocianae Familiae Stemmata" from Robert Coke de Cokeshale in
    Marchington, his son Hugh Coke, tempus Edward III, to Francis Coke of Trusley his children and Johannes Coke de
    Melburne, his wife Marie Powel and their son Joseph born 11February, 1605. Families mentioned - Odingsell,
    Fitzherbert, Sacheverell, Bonington, Leek, Owin."

1845

The dogs very shortly ran up to the man without once coming to a fault. Several other similar runs were had and it was the opinion of most gentlemen present that by proper training & treatment these hounds might be extremely serviceable in tracing sheep stealers by their footsteps.

April 22 The fallow deer in Donnington [sic] now amount to a very noble herd, I think about 500 head or thereabouts. It is the determination however of the trustees of the estate to thin them. Today 17 have been taken alive. These were sent to London by Railway and sold.

April 23 Last night about 9 o'clock there was seen here a most curious and beautiful meteoreous [sic] phenomenon. The night was dark but about the hour before mentioned it suddenly grew light and the atmosphere shone as clear and delightful as when the moon was in full radience [sic]. This lasted for some minutes - then died away and all was as dark as before - The light emanated from a large brilliant star which seemed to fall down the sky and bring along with it a broad tail of flame which had a fine appearance. This phenomenon was noticed by numerous persons who never witnessed anything similar before.

April 29 Today Wombwells fine collection of animals came into Melbourne to exhibit for two days - It is well worth the attention not only of the Naturalist but the ordinary observer - Such exhibitions are at once pleasing, rational and instructive and have a tendency to enlarge and enoble the mind - Who can contemplate the Rhinoseros [sic], clad in his thick coat of natural armour - the Elephant full of wisdom & sagacity - the various kinds of deer all grace and gentleness - the Lions all might and majesty - the Panthers, growling sufficiently loud to awaken a hundred echoes in their native forests and indeed the whole retinue of quadrupeds & birds without being struck with the beautiful adaptation of each animal to his peculiar sphere and perceiving the Hand of Him who formed the whole -

• *Bostock and Wombwell's Menagerie photographed at Gargrave, North Yorkshire, c1912.*

George Wombwell, Menagerist

Born at Wendon Lofts, Essex, in 1777, George Wombwell moved to London in 1800 and opened a cordwainer's shop in Soho in 1804. His life took an unexpected turn when he heard that some extremely large snakes had been found in a ship at the docks. Buying the two boa constrictors for seventy guineas, George recouped his outlay in a mere three weeks by exhibiting them in local public houses and, spurred by success, he started to acquire more exotic creatures. In 1810, he founded Wombwell's Travelling Menagerie and set off to tour the land with his collection. In subsequent years, Wombwell bred the first lion to be born in Britain; naming him Wallace after William Wallace the Scottish patriot, and he came to national attention with the infamous "Lion Fight" in Warwick.

As a publicity stunt, Wombwell advertised that he intended to test his lion's fighting abilities in a match against bull mastiffs. Two relays of three dogs were to fight Nero, Wombwell's pet lion, who was known for his docility. The lion refused to fight and Wallace was brought into the fray, inflicting such injuries on the dogs that the fight was soon abandoned.

In following years Wombwell's menagerie became the largest and most popular show in the country and included amongst its animals Bengal tigers, elephants, zebras, pumas and polar bears; and "the real unicorn of scripture" – a rhinoceros.

As the show grew, word of Wombwell's husbandry skills reached the ears of Prince Albert, whose harriers were suffering a great mortality. Summoned to the palace, George took one look at His Majesty's hounds and, without hesitation, pronounced that the water they drank had affected their health. Prince Albert had the water changed, the deaths ceased and he in gratitude inquired in what way he could be of service to Mr. Wombwell. George replied "What can you give a man who has everythink?"

A year later, when Queen Victoria demanded that George exhibit his "Elephant of Siam" at Windsor, Albert was waiting with a gift for "the man who has everythink": a brand spanking new oak coffin. George thanked Albert heartily and proudly exhibited the coffin as part of his menagerie, charging an extra admission fee to all that queued to see it.

On his death in 1850, Wombwell's obituary in "The Times" stated that "no one probably has done so much to forward practically the study of natural history amongst the masses"

(From "The Sexton's Tales" © Emlyn Harris, from www.tales.ndirect.co.uk and used by kind permission of the author. For more information on Wombwell's menagerie, see "A Zoo on Wheels" by J. L. Middlemiss, 1987.)

1845

May 18   Mr Hemsley has pulled down the old house on "Mr Beards Farm" and is erecting another on its scite [sic].

• *The house built at Highfields by Thomas Hemsley, silk glove manufacturer, in 1845.*

May 18   The Melbourne trade in silk gloves and fancy articles has, during the last Winter, been rather steadier than usual but the mechanics have got on the whole less remunerating wages –

• *Before the Hemsley brothers built "Victoria Mill" and "Kendrick Mill", the family business was based on Castle Street. This photograph (from the "Derbyshire Advertiser", 1959) shows their premises at "Drab Row", demolished in the early 1960s. Part of Drab Row, fronting Castle Street, seems to have been built as cottages from the start, but this part stood to the rear and has the look of a former factory converted to cottages later on.*

May 18   Last night some thief, or thieves broke into Mr William Peggs house at Melbourne and took therefrom £82"o"o being the money paid to him for assessed taxes by different individuals. They also took away a few articles of plate.

During the last few days heavy showers have fallen - A high flood upon the Brook - An old proverb says

"A flood in May"

"Is a flood on hay" -

May 26

Last night a child met with its death in a singular manner. It went to the Privy and is supposed to have fallen head foremost through the seat and by that means suffocated -

June 4

Mr Henry Orton of Kings Newton was returning home from Derby and coming by Mr Tafts the Wheelright [sic] a little dog began to bark which so frightened his horse that he immediately set off at full speed down Newton. In passing Miss Greaves house he managed in some way to catch the iron which goes round the top of the gig on the palisadoes [sic, = palisades = palings of wood or iron] - Mr Orton was thrown out into her garden opposite the drawing room window - After leaving the body of the gig hanging on the palisadoes the horse galloped at full speed down the street to the Marsh Gate with the shafts and wheels which he smashed to pieces and afterwards got the wheels fast in a trench which threw him down and when the people got up to him he was completely exhausted - Mr Orton was providentially not hurt seriously though his clothes were very much torn -

June 13

A very heavy thunder-shower occurred which flooded the streets in Melbourne and caused a stream to run down them like a brook -

June 15

The grass crops are now beginning to be cut and fall heavily to the scythe with the exception of seeds which being thin last year are not found very abundant. The season, alternating from showers to sunshine has been upon the whole favourable for the growth of vegitation [sic].

June 26

Captain Colvile of the Repton and Gresley Yeomanry Cavalry gives a gold Medal to that member of his Troop, who at the distance of 100 yards can count the greatest number of shots on a Target. Each division (of which there are four) shoots at the Target and three of its best men are chosen to shoot for the Medal. To day the Melbourne and Swarkestone Divisions met at Swarkeston [sic] to try their skill , the Moira and Repton having tried yesterday - The result is as follows - The shots numberd [sic] by the Moira Division 59 - Swarkeston 56 - Repton 46 - Melbourne 55 - The men chosen ["out"?] of the Melbourne Division to shoot for the prize are

June 26

Warren	numbering	8 shots & hitting the Bulls Eye
Hodgekinson	-	7 Do -
Peat	-	6 Do -

George Stevenson Esq - the celebrated Engineer (who designed the North Midland Railway) visited Melbourne Gardens -

July 5

1845

- *A view by the yew tunnel in the Hall gardens*

July 6   To day presented one of the most extraordinary exhibitions of weather and phenomena ever witnessed by any person even our oldest inhabitants. From sunrise to sunset the air was extremely hot and sultry and the most clear and lovely weather prevailed. About 8 o'clock in the evening low, rolling peals of thunder were heard which were kept up continuously for about an hour and almost [..?]*tently*, bright flashes of lightening [sic] illumined the heavens which grew less vivid as they approached the period when they ceased - These flashes were sometimes of a brilliant yellow, at others of a hazy blue and seemed to come every moment for the first two hours but did not die away under three - The last hour they grew less quick but I found upon timing them by a watch they flickered 126 times in 5 minutes.

About 10 O'Clock was seen stretched from East to West a bow in appearance like a Rainbow, but of a misty white which the repeated flashes rendered more clear and sometimes even brilliant and shortly afterwards fell a tremendous shower of rain – pouring in torrents and deluging the lanes - All was calm about 11 -

July 13   Old Thomas Thompson of Kings Newton, labourer, died. He was buried July 15th - He worked with my father for 30 years -

A large Cobble, from Gainsborough, which had been up to Burton passed by   July 30
Weston Cliff, down the Trent. A stiff south breeze blowing at the time made it
difficult to pass the shallows but as soon as she reached the Cliff where the water
is deep, she hoisted both sails and made down for Kings Mills in most gallant style
– About 30 years ago the river was navigable but since that period it has become
in some places almost choked with weed and probably this is the first boat of that
size that has ventured up the river from Gainsborough for the last ["80"?] years.

• Kings Mills stands on the river bank opposite Weston on Trent, in the parish of Castle Donington

The Order of Foresters from Melbourne and the adjacent lodges met at Melbourne,   July 30
paraded the town, & went to Church. They made a pretty show in their quaint and
antique dresses which were principally of green velvet and scarlet trimed [sic] with fur.

The Melbourne Horticultural and Floricultural Society held their annual show   July 31
which was upon the whole very good, but the fruit was later than usual - The prize
for Goosberies [sic] was awarded to Mr. E. Salisbury Melbourne who produced one
(called London) weighing 29gr 7pcs. The next largest were Mr Dalbys (Wonderful)
27gr 15p & the next Mr Fletchers (London [sic, brackets not closed] 27g 7p

The Marchioness of Hastings and Capt Hastings Henry left Donnington [sic] Park   July 31
where they have been staying for their residence at Southampton.

In the middle of 40 foot Lane is a stone bridge, over the brook, which was built in   Aug 4
the year 1834. The brook forms the boundery [sic] between the two parcels of roads
belonging respectively to Melbourne and Kings Newton. When the Bridge was
built, it was considered at the time that Melbourne would reap the most advantage
from its erection and that consequently its Overseers paid the greater share of the
money. The expenses of its erection were divided into three equal parts of which
Melbourne paid two - Kings Newton one and Wilson gave something.

1845

The Overseers of Wilson consented to pay a trifle in consideration of a considerable portion of land belonging to people in the village, lying beyond the bridge, which served them to cross the brook in their way to it. The expenses of Newton on this occasion were £5"16"8 - Mr Thomas Taft and Mr Samuel Tomlinson being the Overseers.

This Bridge has again undergone repair (Aug 5) and Melbourne has paid two thirds of the expense and Newton one third - Wilson nothing

Mr Tagg		Overseers	Mr Briggs		Overseers
Mr Banton	}	of Melbourne	Mr Sims	}	of Kings Newton

Newtons share amounted to £1"5"5 1/2 -

Aug 7   A small flood on the Trent. It is remarkable and has been noticed repeatedly by other people as well as myself, that however wet and rainy the weather may be before and afterwards, yet on the day when a flood occurs on the Trent it is sure to be fine -

Aug 11   Another flood on the Trent. Some few pieces of hay lying near the river were damaged and sanded -

Aug 20   A large flood on the Brook

Aug 20   Flood on the Trent

Aug 20   Corn harvest commenced - oats and barley cut -

Aug 20   Mr William Nicklinson, late of Wilson but formerly of Kings Newton, died at Ticknall, rather unexpectedly after a long series of ill-health -

Aug 23   Mr. Nicklinson was buried at Melbourne -

Aug 23   The water has been turned into Melbourne Pool - The Pool was nearly grown up with weeds and vegitation [sic], which have been cleared out and the bottom deepend [sic] and at the suggestion of Mr. Pontay, the London lanscape [sic] gardner [sic], two Islands placed in the middle - It has been exactly 2 years under hand and it is said has cost £3000 -[72]

---

72   Lindsay Usher, co-archivist at Melbourne Hall, observes that the incentive for this work came from Lord Melbourne's increased use of Melbourne Hall following his resignation as Prime Minister in May, 1841. Between then and his death in November, 1848, he made frequent visits, particularly for the autumn shooting. Except for a new terrace walk (see entry for March 20th, 1848), he did little to alter the famous 18th century garden, but many visual improvements were made to the parts of the estate that could be seen from the house. Lord Melbourne's last letter to his Melbourne agent was dated 9th November, 1848, about plants for the vacant spaces in the parterres of the new terrace in the gardens, near the Mill.

- *An early view of Melbourne Pool from the Intake, perhaps c1865, from a steroscopic slide by James Earp of High Street. The trees and shrubs on the island are still very young.*

Lord Melbourne arrived at Melbourne Hall. The bells rang merrily and the Band was stationed on one of the Islands in the Pool playing several lively airs. Lord and Lady Beauvale accompanied Lord Melbourne who appeared in excellent spirits & looked remarkably well. — Sep 3

In this Railway age, when the whole country seems ["one"?] vast lunatic Assylum [sic], ["as regard"?] railway speculation it has ever seemed to me surprizing [sic] that no project has been started to cut through this neighbourhood so fertile in agricultural produce coal -limestone - lead - plaster - gravel – stone &c. It appears however that now, this project is likely to be undertaken and several Companies are marking out lines through this district. The one likely to prove most beneficial to this neighbourhood is the Manchester and Rugby - It passes Hinkley [sic], Ashby de la Zouch and comes near Calke Abbey within a quarter of a mile from Melbourne and so on for Derby & Manchester. — Sep 8

A Mr Moseley has been visiting Melbourne and adjacent villages in order to get all the Historical and antiquarian information he could, for a work on Derbyshire by Bagshawe which is to be issued shortly. This work is to be completed in one volume and promises to be a good one. — Sep 12

Today there was held at the White Lion Inn a meeting of those persons who take any interest in the newly proposed Railway from Manchester to London by Rugby which touches us. The Meeting was attended by the Mayor of Derby, Mr Blunt the Engineer, and a large number of influential individuals from the neighbourhood. — Sep 13

1845

Mr Fox, Lord Melbourne's agent was unanimously called to the chair when the following resolution was unanimously agreed to;-

"That a Railway from Melbourne to Rugby and so to London and from Melbourne to Derby and so to Manchester is higly [sic] desirable for the inhabitants of Melbourne and its vicinity and that therefore the Rugby, Derby and Manchester Railway which alone of the many projected Railways is proposed to carry through Melbourne, deserves the support of the Inhabitants of Melbourne and its vicinity and that a Petition to Parliament shall be drawn up in accordance with the resolution" -

On this meeting the "Iron Times" of Monday remarks -

"Frederick Fox Esqre Lord Melbourne's agent was in the chair and informed the Meeting, "that the Line had the entire consent and would have the support of his Lordship - Lord "Melbourne's support is of so much importance, that there is no doubt of the line "meeting with the approbation of Parliament under his fostering influence - We hope he "will shortly join the Board of Directors. The Directors instead of disregarding the "feelings of the noblemen and gentlemen through whose property the line is to pass, have "shewn every disposition to meet their wishes and to avoid if possible favourite Parks or "ornamental grounds endeared to their owners - Lord Howe and other noblemen of "undoubted influence will not only give the Line their support but aid in carrying it out – "["our"?] special report will shew the generous reception which the promoters of the "line met with at Melbourne. It must be encouraging to them to find that the more "their line becomes known the greater is the enthusiasm manifested in its behalf -"

• *The original railway station at Derby, built in 1840.*

Lady Beauvale and Miss Cuyler ["*Shlyloe*"?] (daughr of Genl ["*Shlyloe*"?]) appeared at Melbourne Church -

Sep 14

Sir John Crewe Bart unfortunately opposes the Rugby Derby & Manchester Railway and has issued Circulars to his Tennantry [*sic*] and Agents authorizing them to discharge any persons found surveying any part of his property.

Sep 20

The "Iron Times" of to-day contains an advertizement of another Railway, a branch of which will carry close by us. This line is to called [73] the "Grand Trunk Railway" and forms a connecting Line between the Midland and Grand Junction Railways with a branch from Derby to Ashby-de-la-Zouch - This branch will commence at the Derby Station and taking the course of the Derby Canal, proceed to Chellaston where there are extensive plaster works and thence by Swarkeston [*sic*], to the River Trent which it will cross near to the ferry at Weston Cliff and so proceed to King's Newton and Melbourne - From the latter place it will pass by the village of Wilson to Bredon [*sic*] -on-the Hill, where there are extensive lime works and thence proceed by Staunton Harold, communicating by a branch line with the lead lime and coal works there: thence by the Lount Colliery to Worthington Rough where it will follow the line of the Cole-Orton and Swannington Railway until its junction with the first line of the Grand Trunk at or near Pegs [*sic*] Green Colliery and so proceed from thence to Ashby-de-la-Zouch-

Sep 22

An inquest held at the Woodhouses, on the body of George Black before Mr Joseph Sale Coroner. It appeared that the deceased who was a labourer, came home from work, as usual and went down to Melbourne on the previous night - When he came back he appeared as well as usual and went to bed, but in the middle of the night, he groaned much which awoke one of his children, who got up to call a neighbour the child being frightened. Before assistance came he was a corspe [*sic*]. There was not the least mark of violence on the body nor could there be gleaned the least

Sep 23

evidence that the deceased had taken anything intentionally or accidentally. The Jury returned the verdict "Died by the visitation of God" -

Lord and Lady Beauvale came down from Melbourne Hall and called upon my father -

Sep 27

A Sermon preached in Melbourne Church by the Rev. Joseph Deans, Vicar, in aid of the Sunday and National Schools - Collection amounted to the sum of £16-6-10 - Lord and Lady Cowper, Lord and Lady Jocelyn and Lady Beauvale attended divine service - Lady Jocelyn before her marriage was the celebrated and beautiful Lady Fanny Cowper & is exceedingly youthful in appearance -

Sep 28

• *The Reverend Joseph Deans (1803-1888), who became Vicar of Melbourne in 1831.*

73 Sic. There is no "be".

1845

Oct 1   A party of Surveyors came and surveyed the valley of the Trent for the Grand Junction and Midland Counties Railway — It is their intention to cross the Trent by a Bridge at Kincham Eave.

Oct 1   Lord Melbourne gave the Independent Sunday Schools £5 in aid of their funds. His Lordship scarcely ever refuses to come forwards in support of the Institutions of his favourite seat — The following Sonnett [sic] appeared in the papers referring to his Lordship's donation —

> "I am of Paul", the ancient bigot cried
> The nutshell propagandist of a "creed"
> as if humility had only need
> to mumble shibboleths — Not so the tide
> of Thy benevolence: unsatisfied
> If sect thy generosity impede
> Or deeds of nobleness be travestied
> The symbols of the empire laid aside
> ["Nor"?] manacled by customs iron sway
> The real <u>man</u> above <u>viscount</u> shines
> In sympathy that raises and refines
> The youth who are to rule another day.
> Nobility of soul with noble birth
> Combines to scatter blessings on the earth.

Oct 2   Corn Harvest ended -

Oct 7   In this and the neighbouring villages, there is a disease amongst cattle especially cows, in which medicinal remedies seem of no avail - When it once attacks a dairy it generally goes through it — Mr Scott of Newton has lost 5 cows -

Oct 8   People upon getting up their potatoes find that they are affected with a disease like the rot which renders them unfit for any kind of use - This disease prevails to an alarming extent in some localities -

Oct 8   The Rugby, Derby & Southampton Railway is to run near Melbourne-

Oct 8   The Birmingham and Nottingham Railway is marked to run through Melbne. It enters the parish somewhere towards its western boundary and passing on the north side of the village between Newton and Melbourne, takes the valley of the Brook by Ramsley Field and so on by Castle Donnington [sic], Hemington to Long Eaton Station on the Nottingham & Derby Line -

Oct 14   Walnuts this year, here an entire failure, scarce one nut in a 100 being fit for use -

Oct 14   It is an ancient custom which has now almost grown into a right, for the head of the Melbourne family to send to Hardwick Hall, annually for a buck, and at any season of the year which he who demands it thinks proper — The animal is killed by the Duke of Devonshire's keepers, skinned and made fit for use for it is ["sent"?]

1845

Bonfires in commemoration of "Gunpowder Plot" -

Nov 5

Lord Melbourne left Melbourne Hall -

Nov 13

• William Lamb, 2nd Lord Melbourne (1779-1848).

The Rugby, Derby and Manchester Railway Company sent a party of surveyors, to survey that part of the line which runs through Sir John Crewe's estate near Swarkestone – By Sir John's orders (who opposes the line) about 50 persons were stationed on the land to prevent them, but the Company procured about 80 others from Melbourne and elsewhere and guarded by these men measured the line in defiance of Sir John's party. When Sir Johns men saw the opposite party were not to be lightly frustrated, they quietly and very prudently withdrew, thus preventing no doubt a rather serious encounter - The Railway Company gave their men 5/- each for the day and so anxious were they to get them that in some cases they were fetched in a carriage and pair.

Nov 14

The potatoe [sic] disease prevails to an alarming extent and in <u>no</u> instance have I heard [74] a crop which has escaped it within miles of this parish - People get them up & lay them in dry rooms with plenty of air in the hope that that the moisture of the rot will be dried up by such means, others sprinkle quick lime amongst them – others pack them up between straw but all efforts seem of little avail.

Nov 14

Sir John Harpur Crewe Bart. was married to his cousin Miss Georgiana, Jane, Henrietta, Eliza Lovell, second daughter of Captain Stanhope Lovell R.N.K.K. at St Georges Hanover Square, London.

Nov 20

---

74 Sic. Not "heard of".

1845

The ceremony was performed by the Rev H. R Crewe Breadsall - They left town the same day for Calke Abbey and at the Railway Station Derby were met by a number of Sir John Crewe's tennantry [sic] who escorted them to the family seat - At the different villages between Derby & Calke were suspended garlands and festoons of evergreens and many of the houses were illuminated. Public dinners were also served up at Swarkeston Smisby &c in honor [sic] of the occasion -

Nov 20   A party of 150 men went from Melbourne to Swarkeston [sic] to oppose a party that Sir John Crewe sent to discharge the surveyors of the Rugby - Derby & Manchester Railway from taking levels upon his property. The surveying party took the levels but all passed off peaceably.

Nov 21   The ancient custom of ringing the Curfew still appertains here. The Sexton commences ringing it on [space left blank] and ceaces [sic] on [space left blank] and it is tolled every evening at 8 o'clock through the winter season -

Nov 21   There is a circumstance connected with the Crewe family which I think worth noting as no notice whatever has been taken of it that I am aware of it since it occurred - About 50 years ago, the corpse of an individual of the Harpur family (said to be Sir John Harpur) was brought from a distance to be buried in an old Chapel, now in ruins at Hemington in Leicestershire - It was attended by no member of the Harpur family & the only person who accompanied it was an old housekeeper who had promised, to see the deceased safely buried in this Chapel. A grave was dug for the reception of the corpse, but as there was no burial ground to the Chapel and the edifice was in ruins, after much persuasion the Housekeeper agreed to have her charge removed to Lockington where a grave was dug in the church and the coffin put into it, but so negligent seemed those connected with the deceased that the soil was never filled into the grave for weeks & at this day not even a tablet shews the place where he rests -

• An early photograph of the ruined chapel at Hemington, probably taken in the 1860s.

1845

First snow fell this winter - About 8 O'clock in the evening I observed a white bow in the Heavens stretching from N.E. to S.W. – The previous weather had been so mild and genial that I saw a branch of hawthorn (which had been gathered from a hedgerow) in full green leaf and in full blossom.

Dec 3 [or 9?]

The Rugby Derby and Manchester Railway, got their plans into Parliament, but in so imperfect a state that at a general meeting of the Committee in London it was agreed to abandon the Line - 30/- shillings of the deposit money is to be returned again to the shareholders, the remainder having been consumed in surveying and preliminary arrangements &c. As many people hereabouts took shares, of course their loss will be considerable -

Dec 22

Of what profession was Sir Mathew [sic] Lambes [sic] father? is a question that has been frequently asked but until lately never satisfactorily answered - He was a Barrister and resided at Southwell Nottinghamshire - His son married the heiress of the Coke family who possessed the Melbourne Estate and so brought that property to the Melbourne family -

Dec 23

Two parties of singers and musicians came underneath the windows of respectable houses and sang "Christians Awake" and other hymns as is always their custom on Christmas Eve - It is truely [sic] delightful on a calm, still early morning when all is solemnity and repose, to awake from ones sleep and hear the sweet voices of these village minstrels, swelling forth into rich and harmonious numbers, rendered even more enrapturing by the recollection, that they are heard in celebration of that glorious event – the birth of the Saviour of Mankind -

Dec 25

High flood on the Trent.

Dec 30

Miss Orton of King's Newton married to Mr David Bryan of Northampton.

Dec

Very high winds and heavy rains occurred for several days previously -

Dec 31

1846

Jan 3   The Donnington [sic] hounds brought a fox from Oakley Wood, near Loughborough, to King's Newton, without a check. The pace was severe and the riding over the plough very heavy.

Jan 12   Being Plough Monday, parties of men came round dressed as Morrice [sic] - Dancers as is annually their custom -

Jan 24   The season about [75] period has been remarkably [sic] mild and indeed all through the Winter but a few days frosts have occurred up to to-day. Vegitation [sic] is feeling the effects of such unusual warmth. ["many"?] spring flowers as violets, snowdrops and hepaticas having already appeared — gooseberry trees and the honeysuckle are budding and as you wander into the fields and see the fresh green hue of the grass and here and there recognize the delicate form of meadow flower or listen to the sweet song of the thrush, sky lark and other vernal choristers you can hardly help feeling that it is the middle of Spring rather than the depth of Winter.

Jan 24   High flood upon the Trent

Jan 26   There is a well grounded tradition that when King Charles visited the Northern part of his dominions he delayed some time at King's Newton Hall and was entertained by Sir Robert Hardinge at considerable expense. Sir Robert was a distinguished Royalist — had raised a Troop of Horse in the Royal Cause at his own expense — hazarded his life and property in the service of Charles — was the principal opponent of the Parliament and Sir John Gell in this part of the Kingdom and it does not seem surprizing [sic] that his royal Master when journeying through this part of his dominions should pay him the compliment of a visit — [76]

INTERIOR OF KING'S NEWTON HALL IN 1846

• Inside King's Newton Hall, 1846, from Briggs' "2nd edition" History of Melbourne (1852).

---

75   Sic. Presumably Briggs intended to write "about this"

76   There was a pane of glass at King's Newton Hall inscribed with the Latin words "Cras Ero Lux" = "Tomorrow I shall shine". It was said to have been inscribed with a diamond by King Charles II during his dark days in the Commonwealth period, and is an anagram of "Carolus Rex". The Rev. James Bagge, a former tenant of the Hall, said that the pane was still there when his tenancy ended in 1828 (DRO 4627/1/27), but it had gone by the time Briggs published his first History of Melbourne in 1839 (q.v., page 31).

Like the entertainments provided for our present Sovereign by her nobility during her progresses, they seem to have been provided at an enormous expense for we find one which was given to the King at Welbeck which cost [77] Earl of Newcastle £6000 – And it does not seem improbable that owing to the expenditure of raising and maintaining his troop of horse, combined with the hospitality which would be shewn towards the Royal Visitor, that the estate of Sir Robert Hardinge was considerably impoverished, so much indeed, that few years elapsed before it passed into other hands - The King began his progress on the 13th May 1633.

Up up [sic] Feb.9. from my last note the weather continued most unseasonably spring-like. Upon the afternoon of that day a heavy snow storm occurred which vanished before sunrise - Since that period the weather has been warm and lovely like May and all our resident birds are now in full song as in that month - Violets and many flowers are also in bloom - The meadows in the neighbourhood of Nottingham are litterally [sic] purpled over with the autumnal Crocus as they are in October - I have seen a hawthorn hedge in rather a sheltered situation in full green leaf - Feb 16

Considerable interest has been awaken'd in this neighbourhood, by a trial which has just terminated in London between the Right Hon. Washington, Earl Ferrers and Miss Smith of Austrey, Warwickshire - It was a trial for breach of promise of marriage - It appears that the Earl for some time, resided at Austrey, under the care of a gentleman who was superintending his education and had seen but never was at all upon intimate terms with the Lady – Feb 21

- *The Hall and Church at Staunton Harold, Deat of Earl Ferrers.*

1846

The commencement of this extraordinary affair was as follows - After his departure from Austrey, his Lordship received several anonymous letters, written [78] the hand of a lady and breathing for him the most ardent attachment. The first letter however was written not from the lady herself but apparently an indifferent one, recommending to his particular attention a certain other lady who would attend the next ball at Tamworth, advising him to dance with her - to court her society and finally marry her - She was poetically described as dark and graceful as a Spaniard, tall and majestic as a Circassian and beautiful as an Italian – She was to wear a single white rose in her dark hair - His Lordship however did not go to the ball or take any notice of his anonymous correspondent.

This stratagem not succeeding according to expectation it appears that some other letters were forged addressed to Miss Smith and as coming from Earl Ferrers breathing of love and devotion to her – giving her to understand that his intention was to marry her and take her on the Continent &c. It was proved in Court that so far from the letters being Lord Ferrers he never wrote them – that he but just knew Miss Smith never having been in her company and the whole affair was one of fabrication & falsehood got up for the base purpose of extorting money from the pockets of the noble lord – The Lady of course was non suited [sic].

Feb 27	Miss Hutchinson, of King's Newton, died at the house of Mrs Cantrell.
Mar 5	Miss Hutchinson buried. She was laid in the north transept of Melbourne Church near Mrs Cecelia Cantrell in a new vault. Aged 79 years.
Mar 7	Old Joseph Barber died at Melbourne rather suddenly. Although in appearance he looked healthy as usual he seemed for some days previously to his death to have an idea he should not live more than a week and told people he should be buried the next Sunday - He died the Saturday before that time - He was 81 years of age and worked under my grandfather & father at Newton as day-labourer for nearly 70 years who esteemed him highly for his straightforward - honest & industrious character - Buried March 12.
Mar 10	Swarkestone Steeple Chaces [sic] - The sport was good and the day beautifully fine which attracted a very large attendance of the neighbouring Gentry - When the Hunters Stakes was contested 15 horses started and one horse, Red Hawthorn who was third when his rider fell kept his place the whole of the round and without rider and the reins hanging loosely about his neck crossed a brook (with 5 yards of water) and after taking every fence came in the third at the winning post.
Mar 19	Snow and frost.
Mar 20	Snow showers – snow might be seen on the hedges in full ["leaf"?]
Mar 28	Beautiful vernal weather.

---

78 Sic. Presumably Briggs intended to write "written in".

Mr Newbold of Stanton Barns wished to have the 2nd gate on the West Field Lane shifted between his own farm and Mr Briggs's. The question arose "as to whether it was right to shift it at the expense of the Parish, or his own? [79] He agreed to shift it at his own, put down a new gate and keep it in repair.

Mar 28

Although great scarcity was apprehended in potatoes this spring, such has not been the case. The price is even less than it was this time last year - A foreseen famine never happens.

Mar 29

Instances of Longevity -

Mar 29

Elizabeth Buck died and was buried in Melbourne in her 100th year
Mary Blunt died and was buried at Borrowash in her 101st year
Mrs Orgill died and was buried at Smisby in 1837 in her 104th Do.
The above are not recorded in any published work.

Lovely weather

April 1

Heavy snow and rough winterly [sic] weather.

April 4

Very High floods on the Trent.

April 7

Sir Henry Hardinge created Baron Hardinge of Kings Newton, in the County of Derby on account of his late brilliant exploits and distinguished valour on the banks of the Sutlej, India. Such a mark of distinction was never more justly conferred, for Sir Henry has not only displayed on every occasion "the hereditary courage of his race" but also its firmness, moderation and perseverance under difficulties & also its wisdom, ability and discretion.

April 13

Tradesmans token found in a garden near the cross at Newton by Thomas Thompson.

April 25

---

79 The quotation marks are not closed.

1846

April 25 Seed – time began -

May 9 Seed – time finished.

May 9 Disease and sickness very prevalent this year, more particularly consumption. Thirteen cases, have come under my own knowledge, within a month, in this parish -

May 9 Lovely May weather -

May 10 My sister Maryanne Briggs died at Kings Newton. *[see pages 22-23.]*

May 16 My sister Marianne Briggs buried in the churchyard of Melbourne Church at $^1/_2$ past two o'clock. Aged 24 years.

June 9 The past month of May has been exceedingly dry and sultry with scarcely a shower. Wheat is forward and just coming into ear – Barley backward.

June 10 Hay harvest commenced.

June 18 Hon. Mrs. Lamb arrived at Melbourne Hall

June 18 Thermometer stood many days about this period at 136.

June 19 Rain

June 19 Oats came into ear

June 19 About 6 O'clock this evening occurred a most aweful *[sic]* and distressing circumstance. At that time a heavy shower came on accompanied by thunder and lightening *[sic]*. Two persons in Melbourne named Willm Baily (hair dresser) and Hugh Dolman (Baker) were standing in the Potters Street talking together, Baily being in his own garden within a few yards of his own house, and Dolman in the street, just opposite to him. Just at that moment a loud peal of thunder was heard which in an instant [80] followed by a flash of vivid lightening, which struck these poor men, and only a few minutes elapsed before they were both corpses.

- *The unfortunate Mr. Bailey lived at no. 19, Potter Street, the two storey house just visible on the right beyond the string of decorations. The Athenaeum, on the left, was built on his garden a few years later.*

80 sic. Briggs presumably intended to write "was followed".

Baily was taken across the road to his own house and expired immediately and the only mark visible upon him was a small place on one of his cheeks. Dolman lived a few minutes after being struck, his clothes seemed scorched or burnt with the fluid and littorally [sic] kept dropping from him piecemeal as he was carried up the street. His hair, whiskers, & also his shoes were also burnt. The faces of both of them went black and discoloured immediately. Just before Mr Bailey [sic] left the house his wife remarked "I would not go out something may happen to you". He replied naturally enough as many a one has before him "Oh! one knows thunder and lightening to occurs [sic] a hundred times and nobody ever hurt by it" - This circumstance has created a great sensation in the neighbourhood.

> "Blooming in health and strength I gazed
> Where my Creator's lightning blazed;
> Nor for a moment thought that He
> Had such a shaft prepared for me:
> He gave command - the thunder peal'd
> And my eternal doom was seal'd!"
>
> (H. Dolman's epitaph)[81]

Inquest on the bodies. Verdict [blank]	June 20
Hugh Dolman & Wm Baily buried side by side in the burial ground belonging to the General Baptist Chappel [sic] [82].	June 21
A sermon preached in Melbourne Church for the benefit of the "British and Foreign Bible Society" by the Rev. A Brandram, M.A. Secretary to the Parent Institution. Collection £7"o"o. Text. Micah. [blank] Chap. [blank] verse [blank]	June 21

During the course of his sermon the Rev. gentleman quoted many circumstances and anecdotes illustrative of the interrogation Do not my words do good? and in passing paid a pleasing tribute to my late lamented sister (Miss Briggs), whose exertions as Minute Secretary to the Melbourne Ladies Bible Association were almost unremitting.

Fearful thunder storm. A ball of fire descended at a distance of not more than 50 yards from the spot where the above fatal catastrophe took place and entering a house, set fire to a quantity of papers in a room where a sick person was lying and then passing through the chamber entered a lower room. In its passage a portion of a scythe attached to the wall was melted and then entering the chimney carried with it the iron apparatus employed to hang kettles &c upon. The sick person escaped unharmed.	June 22
My sister Sarah Briggs died at 1/4 past 7.a.m	July 6
Wheat cut -	July 23
Judges Patteson and Coleridge were on a visit to the Rev. Thos. Whittaker, Stanton and attended service at Stanton Church.	July 26

---

81 The verse as typed here is transcribed directly off the tombstone. Briggs' version has one or two minor inaccuracies of punctuation.
82 Their gravestones can still be found side by side there today.

1846

Aug 1   Terriffic [sic] Thunder lightening [sic] and rain for 4 hours

Aug 12   Beans finished.

Aug 12   Barley cut.

Aug 13   Heavy Rain – thunder & lightening [sic].

Aug 20   The desease [sic] has again appeared amongst potatoes, which are worse affected than last year -

Aug 20   The fatal disease in cattle continues in this parish. Mr Robinson has lost 16 cows - Widow Cowley 1 - Mr Orton 6 -

Aug 24   No plums this Summer – very few apples – gooseberries – currants - pears or garden fruit of any kind. Blackberries on hedges are very abundant this year which in some measure compensate the poor for the loss of their fruit.

Aug 26   My Brother Joseph Thomas Briggs died.

Aug 31   My Brother Jos. Thos. Briggs buried at Melbourne.

Oct 1   Captain Colvile of the Repton & Griesley Troop of Yeomanry Cavalry presents a gold medal annually to the best carbine shot in his troop. This year it was won by Mr Newbold of Kings Newton.

Oct   Boy drowned at Weston Cliff - He was bringing the boat over and was blown over board by the wind and perished.

Oct   Court Leet & Baron held at Melbourne. It is always held on the Saturday before the Wakes - at the Swan public house at elven [sic] o'clock - Lord Hastings agent arrives about that ["time"?] opens the Court in the following manner. He utters aloud these words which are repeated by the Clerk of the Court, "oh yes! oh yes! [83] oh yes! – all you who owe suit and service to to [sic] Pauline Reginald Augustus Rawdon Hastings draw near and answer to your names".

• An early photograph of the White Swan, probably taken in the 1880s.

---

83   sic. Perhaps the agent and clerk were unaware that the phrase was originally "Oyez! Oyez! Oyez!" (French, = "listen!"). Or perhaps the misunderstanding was Briggs's?

Then the Roll containing the names of every householder in Melbourne and Kings Newton is called over, and if the person is there to answer to his name well and good, but if not he must pay 1d which he must send by some other person - If he neither answers to his name nor sends his penny then he is amerced or fined 4d for neglect.

The next feature at the Court is to swear in 12 Jurymen who are to see Justice done between the Lord of the Manor and the inhabitants of the Manor - Their business is also to walk the Town and correct nuisances - and to be present at surrenders of copyhold property. The person possessing copyhold property and wishing it to be surrendered to another comes to the court, pays a certain fine and it is transmitted to him by the Lord Hastings Agent - Chief Rents are also paid here - The villages of Normanton & Chellaston owe suit and service to this Court and send their deputies annually.

Bonfires - squibs and crackers -	Nov 5
Barley 50/- per qr - Corn Laws off -	Nov 10
Hon. Mrs Lamb left Melbourne Hall -	Nov 17
Beautiful dry weather -	Nov 18
Very hard frost	Dec 14
Trade very bad in Melbourne.	Dec 14
Miss Smith of Austrey has published a pamphlet, in which she makes it appear that Lord Ferrers did promise her marriage - It is very cleverly written and ingenious -	Dec 14
Frost. Trent iced over. John King & I walked over the Trent at Weston Cliff this morning, no one having gone over before.	Dec 16
Snow 6 inches deep – Hard frost.	Christmas Day
Haws being scarce the Fieldfares have cleared all the Holly bushes of their berries so that this year neither the Church nor houses can be decorated with berried holly.	Dec 25
Last night the Trent was quite clear of ice – this morning it is quite frozen over.	Dec 26
	1847
Wheat 100 shillings per quarter -	May 12
A free delivery of letters for K.Newton	May 18
Wheat 107 shillings per qr.	May 19
Fruit trees of all descriptions expand a great amount of blossom and everything promises an abundant yield.	May 20
Flour 4/- pr. stone.	May 20

1847

May 28   Our oldest inhabitants never remember the country to look so beautiful. Everything is most luxuriant & magnificent – Last winter was very severe and protracted -

June 10   New early potatoes excellent.

July 15   <u>St Swithen</u>

A young gentleman (Davidson, son of Mr Davidson Engineer of Ashby de la zouch) drowned whilst bathing in [84] Trent just below the old stone wharehouse [85] [sic] - He & four companions came to Swarkestone for a days pleasure and two went into the river to bathe at the place above mentioned - Suddenly young Davidson reeled backwards ([86] probably having stept [sic] out of his depth and in a moment sunk beneath the water and never appeared afterwards alive - His body was recovered about three hours afterwards near the spot where he went down, with an iron hay rake tied to a boat oar -

Sep 20   Remarkably fine harvest -

Oct 21   Crops found very heavy and well corn'd

Nov 24   Very fine Autumn – weather beautiful -

Nov 25   A Magazine started in Melbourne called the "Mechanics Organ[87] . Sale about 600. Articles furnished chiefly by persons residents [sic] in Melbourne – the public Journals speak very highly of it -

Dec 5   Very high winds -

Dec 7   High Trent flood -

Dec 8   First snow fell this winter – very slight.

Dec 16   The funeral of Mrs Allsop of Barrow-upon-Trent passed through Melbourne on its way to Sheepshead [sic] where her remains were buried - She was the wife of Rev. [blank] Allsop formerly minister of Sheepshead and died at Barrow on the [blank] inst.

Dec 14   Melbourne Pool stocked with five hundred brace of Tench and 300 brace of Carp which had been procured in the neighbourhood -

Copy of a silver coin found near Swarkeston December 12th 1847 -

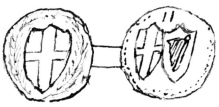

---

84   sic, not "in the".

85   This warehouse of stone and thatch was built by Melbourne stonemason John Chambers in the 1760s. Chambers had a stone sawing mill on the river at Shardlow and built No. 15 Potter Street, Melbourne c1789. The warehouse is long gone, but its site can still be traced including the quay.

86   these brackets are not closed.

87   sic. Inverted commas not closed.

The Influenza has reached Melbourne.	Dec 18
Very High flood on the Trent.	Dec 20
High Winds -	Dec 20
Trade very bad in Melbourne this winter -	Dec 21

The Holly-trees this year are most beautiful, being berried in a very extraordinary manner - — Dec 22

Christmas Day. — Dec 25

Persons came last night under our windows and sang "Christians Awake"

Christmas Day. — Dec 25

Old George Adams the parish Clerk died of influenza at 4 O'clock this morning. He had been clerk to Melbourne Church about 14 years. He was a sober, steady and honest man, but of very quaint manners and eccentric character.

George Adams buried. — Dec 28

Monument put up in the Church to the memory of Sarah, Marianne and Joseph Briggs of K. Newton. — Dec 29

The ground covered with snow-first time this winter. — Dec 30

Very few houses in the Parish have escaped the Influenza and with old people and those sickly it has in several instances been fatal. This disease has visited almost every parish hereabouts. — Dec 31

A Beech Tree has been planted near the bottom of Meeting Lane at the junction of the three roads- — Dec 31

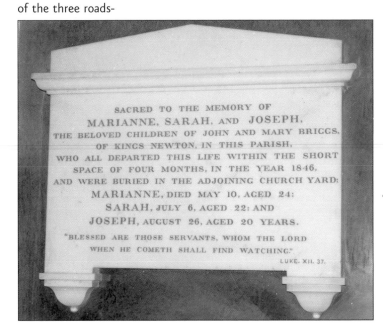

SACRED TO THE MEMORY OF
MARIANNE, SARAH, AND JOSEPH,
THE BELOVED CHILDREN OF JOHN AND MARY BRIGGS,
OF KINGS NEWTON, IN THIS PARISH,
WHO ALL DEPARTED THIS LIFE WITHIN THE SHORT
SPACE OF FOUR MONTHS, IN THE YEAR 1846,
AND WERE BURIED IN THE ADJOINING CHURCH YARD:
MARIANNE, DIED MAY 10, AGED 24:
SARAH, JULY 6, AGED 22: AND
JOSEPH, AUGUST 26, AGED 20 YEARS.
"BLESSED ARE THOSE SERVANTS, WHOM THE LORD
WHEN HE COMETH SHALL FIND WATCHING."
LUKE. XII. 37.

• The memorial to the Briggs children in the south aisle of Melbourne Parish Church.

1848

Jan 2 A day remarkable for its mildness.

Jan 7 Great rejoicings on the neighbouring estate on account of the young Earl of Stamford and Warrington coming of age. At Bredon [sic], Wilson it was celebrated with dinners, dancings [sic], fireworks and all kinds of merriment and bonfires blazed all night on Bredon Hill [88].

• Breedon Hill from the Green, c1900.

Jan 9 First hard frost -

Jan 10 "An Association for Killing Sparrows" commenced.

Jan 10 Plough Bullocks and Morrice [sic] dancers came.

Jan 13 The Influenza begins with a bad cold - chilly skin – headache – sore throat – pains in the limbs and general lassitude and appears to linger long with a person after the worst symptoms are subdued.

Jan 14 Trade very bad in Melbourne.

Jan 14 Very mild

Jan 16 Frost

Jan 17 Soft mild weather.

Jan High cold winds

---

88 The Grey family, Earls of Stamford and Warrington, had their seat at Enville, Staffordshire, and were lords of the manor and chief owners of Breedon.

Berne the blind Irish Harper [89] who played before the Queen & Prince Albert, and   Jan 25
whose portrait appeared a short time ago in the "Illustrated London News" has
been staying at Staunton Hall at Lord Ferrers. He spends his time going from one
nobleman's seat to another, playing his harp, and is always a welcome guest.

• *Patrick Byrne in a remarkably early*
  photograph of 1845, by pioneering
  photographers Hill and Adamson.

About 26,000 Letters pass through Melbourne Post Office annually.   Jan 25

An interesting Meeting held this day in Melbourne, the occasion being the   Jan 26
presentation of a piece of plate to Mr John Earp who during the last six years has
devoted much time and attention to the local affairs of the Parish to the great
benefit of the rate-payers at large.

Six years ago the affairs of the parish were in a very complicated state: Mr Earp
applied all the powers of his mind to restore them to a more becoming position
and succeeded. It was considered that some recognition of these gratuitous
services should be made and after due consideration, a subscription amounting to
upward of £50 was raised and a service of plate presented - It was arranged that
the presentation should take place at a public dinner which was held at Mr
Deavilles White Lion [90], the Rev. Joseph Deans the Vicar of the parish in the chair.

89 i.e. Patrick Byrne or O'Byrne (1794-1863). He was photographed by pioneering photographers Hill and Adamson in
    the 1840s and was a friend of the Shirley family. He made his will at Ettington Park (Warks), the seat of Evelyn
    Philip Shirley, to whom Byrne bequeathed his harp. He requested that it should be preserved in the Great Hall of
    Shirley's house at Lough Fea in Ireland, as a family heirloom. Byrne was the most successful student to emerge
    from the Irish Harp Society Schools, and played only old tunes. When asked to play new tunes, he would say "I
    never learned them, my son". (Information from Illustrated London News Oct 11th, 1856, and from Keith Sanger
    and Clarsach.net, a website dedicated to the Gaelic harp tradition).
90 This building survives, but was converted to a private house when the Melbourne Estate bought it in February
    1867 (Title deeds in the Muniment Room, Melbourne Hall, Box 262, Bundle 343j). It is now known as "Wisteria
    House", No. 49, Church Street. The club room on the top floor survives intact, with its fixed seating.

1848

- *The former "White Lion" is the creeper-clad building in the centre of this photograph, taken by Edward Martin from the church tower c1893.*

The proceedings were enlivened by two bands who are good musicians and songs and glees were introduced. and after the cloths were removed many excellent toasts were given and responded to by the Vicar Mr Earp, F. Fox Esq. (Lord Melbournes Agent) James Dolman Esq, Mr Haimes, Mr Orton & others.

The silver service consisted of Coffee pot - tea pot - sugar basin cream ewer and toast rack very chastely worked in bright and dead silver - The inscription as follows. " Presented to Mr. John Earp by the Inhabitants of Melbourne Derbyshire, in acknowledgement of his long, varied and gratuitous services to the parish. 26th Jan. 1848." It weighed about 70 ounces cost upwards of £50 and was obtained from the establishment of Cox, Savory & Co London. Mr. Earp made some very good observations in his speech upon the duties of parish officers, and endeavoured to impress upon the party assembled, "that it was the duty of every one filling the office of Overseer to take care that the greatest order and regularity prevailed in the management of the affairs of a parish"

Jan 27   Last night snow fell in considerable quantities – very high winds – froze last night the milk in dairies and water in bed rooms. Coldest day so far this winter -

Feb 1   " Mechanics Organ" progresses. The following are the Melbourne contributors and their articles –
"Editorial Papers" – Thomas Pass Druggist
"Thomas Ashton" – Rev. Joseph Deans Vicar
"Poetry &c" – Rev. John Young
"Our Apiary" – John Green Shoemaker
"Notes on Natural History" – John Joseph Briggs Farmer
"Woman &c" – Stephen Adcock Grocer.

- *The premises of Thomas Pass, druggist etc., Potter Street. There has been a chemist's shop on the site continually since Pass's day, but the quaint old premises shown in this photograph were replaced by the present building in 1884-5.*

High flood on the Trent and brook. Heavy rains last night.	Feb 9

Mild sunny weather. **Feb 12**

Mr Nicklinson formerly of Kings Newton who died August 20 1845, possessed lands in Newton called the Chantry Close, Cross Flats, Smithergreen &c amounting to about 40 acres, with a farm house buildings [91], and several cottages and tenements. At his death they went to his only daughter and heiress, Mary Anne Nicklinson who married an Archer, near Ashbourne - He has lately rebuilt the farm buildings, and felled most of the timber on the property. **Feb 12**

A poor woman of Melbourne had her arm taken off at the shoulder at Derby whilst under the influence of chloriform [sic]. The pain she felt was very trifling. **Feb 12**

The "Mechanics Organ" has now a sale of about 1000 per month. **Feb 20**

Influenza has left the neighbourhood. **Feb 20**

Great consternation in Melbourne at the arrival of news that a revolution had broken out in France and that Louis Phillip [sic] had abdicated the Throne. **Mar 1**

Hedges in full bud – some in leaf - **Mar 3**

Gooseberry trees in full bud. **Mar 3**

The month of February just passed has been very wet. **Mar 5**

During some alterations which have been made lately in the Castle Orchard, some men found a large room, built of well-chiselled stone. Some of this stone crumbled immediately to pieces upon exposure to the air whilst other blocks were solid and good and were remodelled by the men into coping stones for a wall - **Mar 5**

---

91 i.e. Chantry House, Main Street, King's Newton.

1848

- *This print of Melbourne Castle was produced in 1733 from an original drawing made in the reign of Queen Elizabeth I, now preserved at the Public Rtecord Office, London.*

Mar 6　News reached Melbourne that King Louis Phillipe had arrived at Newhaven in Sussex with his Queen both in most deplorable condition.

Mar 12　High flood on the Trent.

Mar 13　Mr Henry Orton of Kings Newton has purchased from Mr Archer of Ashborne [sic] all his lands houses and tenements which he held in Kings Newton, amounting in the whole to about 40 acres, for the sum of 4500 pounds.
(See note on Feb. 12. 1848)

Mar 16　Mr Scott of Newton sold off his farming stock on account of leaving his farm

- *A Victorian view of the farmhouse on Main Street, King's Newton that was formerly Scott's. Today it is known as "Four Gables". The roof was thatched until damage by a fire in 1879 caused it to be replaced with tile.*

1848

Mar 20   Mr Scott's farm has been divided and let to different persons. Mr Newbold has the marshes – Mr Vandeleur [92] the Broom Leys and the other parts are to be occupied by smaller tennants [sic] -

Mar 20   Mr Pontay the eminent Lanscape [sic] Gardener has been laying out some ornamental ground about Melbourne. The new Terrace Walk in Melbourne gardens he has planted with choice pines and firs also he has made plantations of evergreens at the back of the Pool and other parts which will add very greatly to the beauty of the place - [93]

Mar 20   Tremendous shower of hail.

Mar 21   Snow. Flood on the Brook and Trent

April 1   Lovely weather – extremely mild

April 3   Oat sowing commenced

April 3   Barley sowing commenced

April 9   Considerable excitement in the neighbourhood owing to large meetings of Chartists in London Nottingham Derby and most large towns - A riot is expected – the Yeomanry Cavalry has orders to be ready at a moments notice -

April 15   Swarkeston [sic] Steeple Chaces [sic]

April 18   Chartists quiet again -

April 18   Very wet weather

May 24   Seed-time finished

May 24   Very dry and fine

June 15   Wheat in full ear.

June 15   Wheat 46 shillings per qr in the market.

Jul ["22"?] Hay finished

July 22   The Melbourne Agricultural Library established.

Aug 6   Potatoe [sic] disease again appeared -

Aug 24   Wheat harvested

Aug 24   Barley cut.

Aug 24   The weather for some weeks previously has been very wet and gloomy and driven the harvest late -

Oct 25   Very wet seed time.

Nov 5   Hard frost – the first this winter – ice half an inch thick.

92 tenant of King's Newton Hall.
93 William Pontey later laid out the roads, garden and planting etc. at Derby Hills House farm in 1861, when the new house there was built for Mr. Barrs (Melbourne Hall Estate Accounts 1861). It seems likely, therefore, that he would have been employed by the Estate on other occasions also.

1848

Nov 17   On the evening of this day there was a very unusual appearance in the sky – The whole heavens and more particularly the east and the west was illumined with rays of fiery red light, very vivid, and the atmosphere was light as day - The night was calm and beautiful and a soft mellowed light fell upon the earth. This phenomenon was first visible about seven O clock and the latest trace of it died away about eleven.

Nov 17   Wheat sowing finished.

Nov 18   On getting up potatoes this year it was found that those on the stiffest red loams and brown marls had almost entirely escaped the disease - Those on high dry light soils were very little affected - Those on wet soils very much - The kind most diseased were kidneys and the various kinds of white potatoes. The Red sorts were decidedly the best and most free from disease.

Nov 24   On this day died at his residence Brocket Hall, Hertfordshire, the Right Hon. William Lord Viscount Melbourne, late Premier of England and owner of this estate - His title and estates descend of [sic] Lord Beauvale his brother -

Nov 24   This morning presented us with one of the most brilliant sights that can be conceived. The sun rose from a sea of gold and the whole heaven was dotted over with detatched [sic] golden clouds -

• Brocket Hall, Hertfordshire.

Lord Melbourne buried at Hatfield - near which Brocket Hall is situated - Lord Broughham [sic] and Sir Henry Ellice are his executors -	Dec 1

[Print of Lord Melbourne, omitted in this transcription.]

The Pulpet [sic] and Hall pew in the Church, hung with mourning for Lord Melbourne -	Dec 3
The weather during the Autumn has been cold and wet and much of the wheat sown, comes up weak and sickly on stiff clay soils a great breadth of wheat remains un-sown and is obliged to be reserved for spring-cropping.	Dec 5
Trade rather revived in Melbourne – Silk-hosiery branch commenced by Mr Haimes.	Dec 5
High flood on the Trent -	Dec 8
During the last few days the weather has been most beautiful and mild. The grass looks green and vigorous, the turnips growing fast on fallows, the bat may be seen alert in the evening and in the morning the wild varied voice of the Song Thrush may be heard as clear and distinct as when ushering in the daylight in May - High winds however have prevailed for many weeks -	Dec 11
Clear mild weather with high winds.	Dec 14
Very cold, with frost	Dec 17
Within the last few years, and during the latter part of the life of the Right Hon. Wm Vist. Melbourne, the parish has considerably improved as regards the state of its Agriculture. Better and more beneficial systems of cropping have been pursued – better kinds of seeds introduced – draining effected, good buildings for farm-steads erected - useless timber cleared away – gates kept in repair, and a more systematic arrangements [sic] adopted in the general management of the details of farming. The surface also has a much neater and more cultivated appearance owing the [...] large and overgrown hedges, being cut down and converted into small trimmed fences (more especially round arable fields) and this neighbourhood now promises to vie with the best cultivated districts of Norfolk and Lincoln -	Dec 18

1848/1849

Dec 22   Very hard frost -
Very cold -

Dec 25   No singers came round
no berried holly to be had

Dec 26   Thaw. Rain.

1849

Jan 2   Very hard frost -

Jan 5   Wheat 46 shillings per
quarter -

Jan 5   Snow four inches deep -

Jan 5   Lord Melbournes
escutcheon now hangs
on Melbourne Hall.

Jan 7   Thaw

Jan 21   Soft mild weather

Feb 12   Mild weather - Hedges
and trees budding -

Feb 12   Corn duty free –
Wheat 50/- pr. qr.

Feb 17   Extraordinary mild
weather like summer.

Feb 22   Hedges bursting into
leaf -

Feb 22   A fall of timber, on the
Newton land, by Lord
Melbourne -

• Park Farm. This new farmstead on Lodge Hill in Melbourne Park, built 1834-40, was one of the most costly projects undertaken by the Melbourne Estate in the 19th century. Photographed in 1988.

Feb 26   Inquest held at the New Inn Melbourne on the body of Francis Smith, Miller who was accidentally killed in the Melbourne Pool Mill, by getting his body entangled amongst the Machinery.

Mar 15   Mr Mundy of Markeaton came to Melbourne he being a candidate for the representation of South Derbyshire in the room of Mr Mundy of Shipley just deceased

Mar 16   George Dawson of Birmingham gave a lecture in the National School Room "on the tendencies of the present age."

• *A dramatic scene at Melbourne Mill, probably taken during the severe floods of 1932.*

Beautiful mild weather.	Mar 16
Seed time commenced -	Mar 18
Snow on the ground – Cold weather	April 18

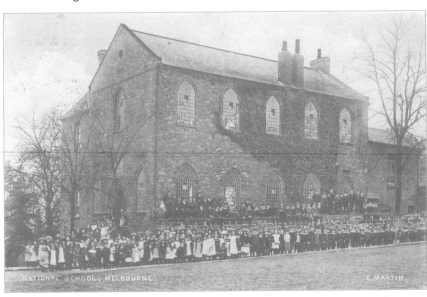

• *The National School photographed by Edward Martin (d1921), with a surprisingly large number of children. The school was built of second-hand bricks in 1821-22 and the wing on the left was added in 1876.*

1850

July 28   Hay harvest finished - The weather hindering but not spoiling -

July 30   Grand fete in Melbourne Gardens in aid of the Mechanics Institute. About 4000 people there - Receipts about £120"0"0 -

• *A view looking westwards across the Hall gardens, showing the early 18th century fountains and statuary.*

July 31   Old Chadbourne, Lord Hastings gamekeeper fell from a Tree in Donington Park and was killed.

Aug 3   An old man named Newbold 72 years of age hung himself from the ceiling of a house in the Blanchcroft.

Aug 5   Rev Mr Cox preached his first sermon.

Aug 6   Corn harvest commenced - Oats cut.

Very mild winter. Sickness and death prevalent - | Jan 1

Wheat 42s/- Barley best 24/- Oats 20/- | Jan 7

Old Mr Thos Robinson formerly of the Shaw died at Melbourne aged 80. He had four wives. He was buried in the churchyard on Jan 21 - | Jan 14

• *Shaw House, Robinson's Hill, home of the Robinson family from the 1790s until 1873. The conservatory was added by a subsequent tenant.*

The young Lord Hastings died at Dublin aged 19 – In two years he would have inherited Donnington [sic] and the other family estates – He held a commission in the army and went over to Ireland to join his regiment when he was taken ill and died - His remains were brought by rail to the Ashby-de-la-Zouch Station and thence to Donnington Hall where they lay a few days. Lord Hastings younger brother the next heir being only 9 years of age, the property will remain 11 years longer in the hands of Trustees and no doubt accumulate to a large sum. | Jan

Lord Hastings buried at Castle Donnington [sic] Church in the same vault with his father - | Jan 24

This winter extraordinary mild - | Jan 28

Seed-time commenced - | Mar 20

1851

May 1   Rev. H. Cox, Curate of Melbourne, left the place to take possession of the living of Duston, Northamptonshire. [94]

May 3   Snow fell -

July 25   Very showery hay-harvest

July 28   Eclipse of the sun

July 29   Tremendous rain – Thunder - I never saw so great a weight of wet fall in so short a time.

Aug 22   The members of the "British Archaeological Association" who this year held their Annual Congress in Derby, paid visit to Melbourne. They were received near the Church by the Vicar and several influential inhabitants and proceeded to the National School room where two papers were delivered, one by the Rev J Deans "on the Church" [95] and the other by Mr J. J. Briggs "on the antiquities of Melbourne" - Having examined the Church and visited the gardens they proceeded to Repton.

- *Church Close as Briggs knew it. This early view was probably taken in 1874.*

Sep 12   Corn harvest finished. Upon the whole a favourable one.

---

94 Duston was part of the Melbourne Estate, which probably explains how Rev. Cox obtained the new post.

95 A newspaper cutting, with the text of Deans' paper delievered on this occasion, was pasted by Briggs into his own copy of his 1852 "History of Melbourne" (Derby Local Studies Library ms4606). In it, Deans puts forward the suggestion that the church might have marked the spot where Queen Osthrid was murdered in the 7th century, as recounted in his History of Melbourne Church (1843). However, Deans no longer believed that the church was Anglo Saxon, and believed it to be an early Anglo-Norman building erected soon after the Norman Conquest. He mentions the need for substantial repairs.

For 17 or 18 years the state of the church in this place has been bad – the poor have not been visited and the schools in a neglected condition owing to the inattention of the resident minister. A number of resident laymen wishing to better the state of things, some time ago formed themselves into a committee, raised in the parish an annual subscription of about £120, caused a curate to [96] provided - put the schools on a better footing - opened a service in a little chapel at Kings Newton [97] &c &c.

Sep 18

Some land near the Baptist Chapel sold for £500 an acre -

Sep 29

Stone fruit very scarce. Damazins [sic] £1.0.0 the strike.

Sep 30

• Church House, Main Street, King's Newton, so named after its short career as a chapel of ease to Melbourne Parish Church. This stylish house was built by the Beresford family and was described as "new-built" in 1708 (Cantrell deeds, Derbyshire Record Office D73).

96 sic. not "to be". Presumably this curate was Rev. H. Cox.
97 This was at the house still known as "Church House", Main Street, King's Newton. The property was let by Joseph Thomas Cantrell, the owner, to Messrs. Deans (Vicar) and F.F.Fox for ten pounds a year from 11th October 1850. The relationship between Cantrell and Fox became strained and the agreement was cancelled on April 1st, 1852. Perhaps it was replaced by a new one, or the chapel continued on a less formal basis, as White's Directory of Derbyshire 1857 says that services were still held weekly at King's Newton. (DRO D73 (Cantrell) 31/2/1-88).

1851

Oct 1   Numbers of persons went from Melbourne to the "Great Exhibition" in London of the Industry of all nations.

• *Inside Crystal Palace, from a Victorian stereoscope slide.*

Oct 10   There is in Derby a set of poachers about 30 in number who almost live upon the game from this neighbourhood. They visit the Trent and other streams, or the covers of Calke or Foremark almost every night and carry off the game in spite of the keepers - They will eventually put an end to game preserving hereabouts.

Oct 17   Potatoes somewhat diseased this year - Those which were planted deep - early - and without manure and of a red kind are found little hurt.

Oct 22   Court Leet & Baron held. It was altered this year from Saturday to Wednesday. Those who did not appear to answer their names were fined 2d. The Constable of Chellaston did not appear – fined 10s/-. Headborough of Normanton appeared.

Oct 23   The "Curates Aid & School Committee", held their concluding meeting this day at the National School room. It was agreed to wind up their accounts and to address a letter to the Bishop of Litchfield [sic] stating the cause which had brought their labours to a close -

Wombwells collection of wild beasts came to the town and staid [sic] two nights. Oct 24

A remarkably fine Autumn. Oct 24

Mr Haimes has lately built a new Factory [98]. Oct 24

• *Haimes's factory competes with the houses in the foreground for dominance of this view, taken from the church tower around 1893.*

A Brewery established in Melbourne [99] Oct 25

• *John Hair's Brewery, Church Street, Melbourne.*

98 It is probable that Briggs is referring to an extension of Castle Mills (which was certainly a multi-phased building), rather than to a factory on a new site. Alternatively, the new factory could be building that still survives as nos. 33-37 (odd), Castle Street.

99 This was Hair's Brewery, established at the top of Church Street in pre-existing buildings that were formerly the property of the Mills family, woolcombers etc. The brewery closed in 1954 but the buildings survive.

1851

- *The closing night at the "Barm Tub", a small licenced premises attached to Hair's Brewery. Only a small number of privileged regulars were welcome. It closed, along with the brewery, in 1954.*

Oct 25   Wheat 35s/- Barley 26s/- per qr.

Oct 27   Mr Orton who purchased Mrs Archers (late Nicklinsons) property has altered the house in Newton standing upon it [100] - He has raised the roof – made pointed gables - put in windows and made it Elizabethan in character. It has cost about £250 – the plans were by Stevens of Derby

- *Chantry House, Main Street, King's Newton, showing the "Tudorised" skyline added by Mr. Orton and his architect Henry Stevems in 1851. Photographed by Edward Martin (died 1921).*

---

100 i.e. Chantry House, Main Street, King's Newton.

1851

The "Melbourne Vegitable [sic] show" was held at the New Inn. The roots were divided into two classes. Those grown on the farm, in an <u>ordinary way</u> of cultivation were called "Field produce"; Those grown in a garden and <u>forced</u> were called "Garden produce" - The field produce was not large, but extremely well grown and symetrical [sic] and of fine quality - The garden produce in some departments was large, although the Mangold Wurtzel was inferior in size to that grown in the two previous years - In 1849 & 1850 Mr Briggs grew at Kings Newton in each year a mangold bulb weighing with the top 36 lbs without it 26lbs: The following were the weights of some of the Field produce this year, when closely topped and tailed.

Mr Robinson	6 Skirvings Sweedes [sic]	weighing	70 lbs
Mr Banton	6 Tankard Sweedes	Do	48 lbs
Mr Briggs	6 Green Tops	Do	44 lbs
Mr Banton	6 Red Tops	Do	55 lbs
Rev W. Cantrell	6 Globe mangold	Do	70 lbs
Rev W. Cantrell	6 Long red Do	Do	100 lbs
Mr Robinson	1 Ox cabbage	Do	25 lbs
Mr Cope	4 Do Do	Do	160 lbs
Rev W. Cantrell	6 Sweedes after dills	Do	42 lbs
Mr Gutteridge	6 Do after dills	Do	32 lbs

The largest field grown mangold was shewn by Rev W Cantrell weighing 20lbs.

Garden produce

Mr Robinson	10 Onions	weighing	10 lbs
Mr Salisbury	16 Carrots red	Do	10 lbs
Mr Robinson	6 Sweede Turnips	Do	93 lbs
Mr Robinson	6 Globe mangold	Do	82 lbs
Mr Robinson	6 Long red do	Do	107 lbs
Do Do	1 Ox cabbage	Do	66 lbs
Mr Briggs	1 Red pickling cabbage	Do	16_ lbs
Mr Warren	12 Potatoes (red farmers)	Do	16 lbs
Mr E. Salisbury	6 Cauliflowers	Do	22 lbs
Do Do	66 weeks turnips 2nd crop	Do	24 lbs

The largest Sweede turnip was shewn by Mr Robinson which weighed 17 lbs.

Some potatoes shewn by Mr Warren were of extraordinary size and excellent quality. He planted 10 potatoes whole (the largest he could procure) 1 yard apart each way – When dug up the produce weighed 116 lb or at the rate of 17 strikes to the acre. The largest potatoe [sic] was 2 lbs 6 ounces - Not much manure was used - They were never touched with the hoe, but fresh earth was thrown round them as required - Some fine cabbages were shewn, which were produced by the application of lime and salt. Sweede turnips sown by the 2nd week in April attained the largest weight – those sown later were of the best quality.

1851

• An early view of the Melbourne Hotel, prior to 1884.

Oct 31 There has been a ferry at Weston Cliff since the reign of King John, about 650 years. A rope is streched [sic] from bank to bank, by which a boat is pulled over, probably much in the same manner as in his time - Until within these last few years horses were taken over as well as pedestrians but the boat becoming unsafe, a smaller one was substituted which is not sufficiently large to take cattle over so that no horse men cross now in it.

Nov 1 The large tythe barn, where all the tythe corn was housed previously to the enclosure is still standing on Mr Briggs farm. It is half- timbered paned and thatched - [101]

Nov 1 Field gardening is all the rage. If a piece of land falls vacant it is readily taken at £3"0 0 to £6"0 0 an acre to grow vegitables [sic] for the Derby market.

• Hoeing on the market garden of Messrs. Hatton Bros. and Snape, long after Briggs' time. Oswald Hatton is at the left hand end, with identical twins Jack and George next to him.

---

[101] This must be the barn formerly known as Rivett's Barn, which stood where 27, Trent Lane and the adjacent bungalow now stand. In 1808 it was described as "A Barn of three bays and a threshing place, a Hen-house, Hay-house, Straw House and Cartlodge adjoining – part Stone part Brick Walls part Boarded and thatch'd, and in indifferent repair" (MHMR Estate Survey, 1808).

1851/1852

• *A Ransome portable engine and thrashing machine at work, c1870.*

First snow fell this season. The leaves are yet on many trees.	Nov 4
A Steam Thrashing Machine has been introduced into this parish to thrash out corn and promises to become generally used.	Nov 10

1852

Messrs. Haimes and Hancocks warehouse robbed of £50 worth of pearl white hosiery silk.	Nov 5
Melbourne Vegetable show held at the New Inn – Sweede [sic] turnips 22 lbs – Mangold 23lbs – Ox Cabbage 64 lbs.	Nov 6
Court Leet held at the Swan – altered from the Saturday before the Wakes – Mrs Archer surrendered some property -	Nov 11

1852/1853

Nov 13   The highest flood on the Trent which has occurred since the great flood of 1795 when Swarkeston [sic] bridge was washed down - No damage of any amount occured [sic] here but in the neighbourhood much loss was sustained. Mr. Hepworth of Donington had 15 fat sheep drowned. Mr. Kilburne of Hemington 10, Mrs. Fritchley of Hemington 29 ewes in lamb: Mr. John Smith of Sawley 82 sheep. A person who was gardener to James Sutton Esqre of Shardlowe [sic] Hall was drowned whilst endeavouring to rescue some cattle - Mr Eaton of Cavendish Bridge had about £100 damage done by the flood getting into his brewery. Two walls were washed down at Shardlowe [sic].

- *A snow scene at Swarkestone Bridge, 1965.*

1853

May 19   The most extraordinary weather that ever occurred in the month of May. During the last part of last week and the beginning of the present there have been cold, cutting, easterly winds, dark and gloomy skies with alternate showers of rain, hail sleet and heavy snow falls. These altogether have constituted the fabled union of January and May. On the afternoon of the 9th snow fell as heavily as ever I saw it at Christmas for about an hour covering the grass and expanding foliage of trees like a sheet. The next morning snow lay on the ground in sheltered places a foot thick —

At Chapel-en-le-Frith in the Peak it snowed incessantly for 15 hours and a rougher day was never seen in January. The roads over the hills had to be cut. Where the [102] was level it was half a yard deep and where drifted three or four yards in depth.

---

102 sic. Presumably Briggs meant to write "the snow".

At Glossop the snow fell without intermission for 20 hours - Near Woodhead on the Moors it fell a yard thick at Matlock Bonsall, Winster and the neighbourhood six inches. There was a similar storm on May 10th 1817. -

Mr Orton and myself discovered in the "Smithergreen" near King's Newton a remarkable fine bed of Clay. It has been made into bricks of most superior quality and burns red and bright - Some clay which was sent for trial into the Potteries made some very beautiful ornamental earthenware of dark red colour. The bed varies (as was tested by boring) from 3 to 16 feet in thickness[103] .

May 1

• *Richard Bennett's bill for roofing and ridge tiles for Ticknall Baptist Chapel, 1885. The bill heading lists King's Newton as one of his works, but the brickyard there had disappeared by 1899, when the Ordnance Survey of the area was revised.*

103 See also DLS Glover's History of Derbyshire (1831 & 1833) with original notes and observations by J. J. Briggs 1869 (and later). At page 82, where Glover lists the places where bricks and tiles are made, Briggs writes: "Within the last 20 years, an extensive brick yard has been opened at King's Newton in the parish of Melbourne where a great number of bricks have been made. It has now a "siding" on the "Derby and Nuneaton" Railway and is now in active operation. About 20 men receive constant employment there. The bricks used in the reconstruction of the Tunnel on the Midland Railway near Chapel-en-le-Frith (after the accident which happened to it) were drawn from King's Newton. Some years ago, whilst this yard was in posession of Mr Orton, he procured very good pot clay there and opened a Pottery Works in Newton village, but although he contrived to make some elegant vases and ornamental ware the project did not answer. Eventually the works and clay field were sold, and the making of bricks again resorted to. 1873."
In F. White's Derbyshire Directory of 1857, Henry Orton is listed as "maltster & manfr. of superior front, floor, paving, & common bricks, quarries, drainage pipes, &c., &c.; also flower pots, plain & ornamental; edging tiles, vases, seed pans, sea-kale pots, & every description of ware suitable for the garden, hot-house, or conservatory, plain & ornamental chimney pots, lead pots, & pans, glazed coarse ware, pickle jars, bottles, &c., and picture frames in different colours cut in gold & novel designs".

1853

• *An undated photograph of the King's Newton brickyard, taken by R. H. Bleasdale of Derby. To help readers in orientating the view, Trent Lane runs across the horizon. "Stone Fronts" (extreme left, now demolished) and Elms Farm (right of centre) can be discerned with difficulty on the original, which is badly faded.*

June 1   "Table moving" all the rage. I was present at an experimental trial made before twelve persons in Melbourne on May 30th. A small mahogany table was procured and mounted on the top of another table, a larger one. Four persons including myself began the trial - We placed our hands on the top of the little table, linking them together by the thumbs and fingers to form a chain through which the magnetic influence might pass.

   In about 10 minutes the table shook and made a loud crackling noise several times. In about 7 minutes after that, (being 17) from the commencement of the trial [104], the upper table began gradually to move in a circular direction round the top of the lower one. After moving round two or three times, the speed increased and the table began to undulate and become more unmanageable in its motion until at last it defied our best endeavours to keep it on the lower table and it jumped on to the floor of the room.

June 1   Again partook in two experiments in "table moving". Three persons including myself tried to move a very small mahogany table according to the usual manner - They were persons that I could thoroughly depend upon. We sat 20 minutes without the table having the least motion - We again sat 25 minutes with the same result. I think that there must have been some trickery by persons connected to the first experiment, as I believe if we had sat for 10 hours on the last occasion and under the most advantageous circumstances the table would have remained perfectly quiet. My impression is that much as the papers have sanctioned this "table moving" it is quite a delusion.

---

104 sic. The brackets should really be closed only at this point.

- *Short Hill, Wilson. A postcard by Edward Martin of Melbourne (died 1921).*

Mr Nicklinson of Wilson, has lately been pulling down a half-timbered, old-fashioned house, situated there. Between the plaster in one of the walls the workmen discovered a bag of coins. The bag being rotton [sic] and decayed fell to pieces, but the coins were preserved. They were chiefly coins from a foreign mint one a small gold coin about the size of an English shilling had on the obverse the head of a King with hair flowing over the shoulders bound with a wreath of laurel. The inscription ran thus LUD. XIIII. DG. FR. ET. NaV. REX. On the reverse was a shield (surmounted by a crown). The shield was charged with three flour-de-lis

June 1

[sic] - The inscription was as follows. CONR. LAUFTERS : RECH: PFENING. Another kind of coin found was of silver about the size of an English half-crown but the specimen which I procured was so much disfigured and jagged at the edges that I could only just make out the following - Ob. Profile of a king crowned, having just above his shoulders the figure XII. The only portions of the surrounding inscription visible were the letters D.G. MAGTRI. Reverse; a shield quartered; each quartering different but defaced - Inscription only letters visible ICE. REGNO CHA

- *"Viscount Palmerston laying the foundation-stone of the Melbourne Athenaeum" from The Illustrated London News.*

1853

[An extensive newscutting from the Derby Reporter describing Lord Palmerston's visit to lay the foundation stone of the Melbourne Athenaeum on Saturday 27th August 1853. The following is a very brief precis:

The weather on the day was poor so a lot of potential attenders were put off. The town was decorated with a series of triumphal arches, designed by Messrs. Haimes, Hemsley, Orton and others. At 11 O'clock there was an address from the working men to Lord Palmerston at the Hall, who gave an address back to them in return. At 12 o'clock a procession formed at the Hall to accompany Lord Palmerston to the Athenaeum site. Flags were absent in the procession, because it was too windy.

The ceremony was opened by the Rev. Joseph Deans, vicar. Commenting on the provision of the Infants School he noted that the trade of the town required that women should frequently leave their homes, and the Infants School would help prevent the children being left to insufficient care. The savings bank would encourage the artisans to save and spend less on drink, while the Institute would provide a place to meet for recreation and mutual instruction.

Lord Palmerston spread the mortar for the foundation stone in a masterly manner. After the stone was lowered, he addressed the spectators. He commented that the new building catered for all periods in life – education, instruction of man in his maturer years, and provision of savings for advanced and declining age. He talked of progress and improvement of the country as a whole, including technological advances. He hoped that Melbourne would look to provide a school for girls as well as boys in the future.

Afterwards, there was a collation (by ticket only) at the National School, provided by Mr. Huggins of the Royal Hotel. After the meal, toasts were proposed, and Lord Palmerston spoke again. When the collation finished, the Hall gardens were opened. "Some wandered amidst the groves and fountains listening to the distant music, some threaded the dance, while others played at merry games or speculated in a voyage on the lake".

Lord and Lady Palmerston were in the grounds for the greater part of the time. On seeing Lord Palmerston walking up an avenue, some of the party cried out "Three cheers for Lord Palmerston". "His Lordship did not merely acknowledge the compliment in the usual manner, but most good humouredly took off his hat and calling out, "Three cheers for yourselves," cheered most heartily for the people."]

The preceding account is taken from the "Derby Reporter" as being the most correct and full of any that appeared. The "Times" was very ["severe"?] and humerous [sic] in its leading article : "Lloyds Weekly Newsper [sic]" Edited by Douglas ["Jerrold"?] was witty and clever : "The Illustrated London News" terse and correct. The scene as presented in the latter is extremely good especially the portrait of Lord Palmerston.

The foundation stone of the "Melbourne Athenaeum" [105] laid to day by Lord Palmerston. This building will combine accommodation for a Mechanics Institution - Infant School and Savings Banks. The Stone was laid by his Lordship at 12 o'clock and he handled the trowel in a masterly manner. If his vocation had been that of a mason instead of a diplomatist I have no doubt that he would have been the first mason in England - On the occasion were present Lady Palmerston, Lord Cowper, Honble Wm Cowper Honble Mrs Lamb, Lord and Lady Harrington, Lord Ferrers, Lord Petersham, Lady Anna Pole - Mr Kinglake, author of "Eothen" Joseph Thos Cantrell Esqre and many of the neighbouring gentry –

Aug 27

After the stone was laid Lord Palmerston made an admirable speech showing a wide range of learning, and a fund of good common sense expressed in a peculiarly happy garb of language - The town was embowered in evergreens and triumphal arches spanned the streets - There was also a procession, flags, banners, music dancing in the gardens and on the islands – About 200 dined together at the National School Room to meet Lord Palmerston - Most admirable speeches were delivered by his Lordship Hon Wm Cowper, Lord Cowper, Mr Cantrell and other [sic], and the affair passed off most agreeably -

The Trowel was of silver chased and was presented to his lordship on a crimson velvet cushion massively embroidered with myrtle leaves –

The Athenaeum when completed will cost about £800 -

- Is it, or isn't it? This photograph is thought to show Lord Palmerston standing by the "Birdcage" in Melbourne Hall gardens. There is indeed a resemblance to other portraits and photographs of him, but we cannot rule out the possibility that this is someone else, one of the Victorian tenants of the Hall, perhaps?

- The Athenaeum today.

---

105 This building, on Potter Street, still survives. It was renamed Wesley Hall when the Methodist Church bought it in 1945. However, it still bears the name "Athenaeum" carved in large stone letters on the front, and is known today by both names. The architect was H. I. Stevens of Derby.

1853

Oct 19   The ill-fated ship called the "Dalhousie" was lost in the Channel about 17 miles from Beechy [sic] Head - She was bound for Australia - She had ridden out bravely some previous gales and went down as before stated without any apparent cause. All the souls on board perished except one Joseph Reed a seaman who clung to a piece of wreck and after battling with the surges for 10 hours was picked up nearly dead by the "Mitchel Grove" whose crew restored him to life.

Six persons who had been living in the parish of Melbourne all perished — one of these was Miss Radford daughter of a Devonshire clergyman a young lady about 26 years of age of high accomplishments and prepossessing appearance - She lived for some time in the family of Joseph Thos Cantrell Esqre whose only daughter she educated - Miss Radford when the vessel sank was not seen on board and is supposed to have been drowned in her cabin.

Mr Underwood who with his wife and three children also perished lived some time in this parish. He had been in a London mercantile house and saved some property with which he was proceeding by the "Dalhousie" to settle in Australia. He was man [106] much respected for his urbanity of manner & kindness of heart - He and his wife and two children were swept off the vessel by a heavy sea and drowned together - His other daughter was washed out of her cabin by the waves but by means recovered by the crew and lashed by Reed to a spar as her only chance for life - She was seen floating for a short time afterwards and then drifted by the waves from sight.

Nov 3   Remarkably late harvest - Some wheat in this parish and neighbourhood is not yet harvested. The long continued wet weather has spoiled thousands of quarters - Wheat yields 1 qr less per acre this year than usual.

Nov 5   The Town of Melbourne lighted with Gass [sic] Lighted up on this for the first time - the upper end of Potters [sic] Street illuminated with a star of gass. About 650 burners taken. Mr Atkins of Oxford is the gass engineer who put up the works [107].

Nov   Vegetable Show held at the New Inn. 6 Sweede [sic] Turnips weighed 137 lbs. 1 Cabbage 68 lbs. Pickling Cabbage 22 lbs.

Dec 25   The Holly this year is very beautiful, berried to a most extraordinary degree.

Dec 27   Heavy fall of snow — the first this season of any consequence - Severe frost.

Dec 28   Melbourne Pool iced over. Some boys ventured upon it one got in and was drowned.

---

106 sic. Presumably Briggs meant to write "a man"

107 The Melbourne Gasworks were situated on Castle Lane, at the entrance to what is now the Melbourne Industrial Estate. The modest Victorian detached house belonging to the gasworks survived until recent years.

1854

The German custom of having Christmas Trees introduced into the parish [108] .   Jan 3

Snow covers the ground. - Last night intensely cold - the water in bed-rooms   Jan 3
frozen over thick as a half-crown piece - the dung in stables and cowsheds frozen
- Trent and brook frozen over. To day the feathered tribes were driven to extremities.
Rooks cut a miserable figure. Small birds seem to have gone southwards with few
exceptions. All the Sparrows in the parish seem to have congregated together and
repair to the neighbouring brickyard where sitting close to the kiln fires they
warm themselves.

Robins keep coming into the house - 5 or 6 may be seen flying about at one time.
About noon, whilst we were at Dinner one came thro' the kitchen and entered into
the parlour, where within a yard of the table, he perched upon a bunch of holly
with which the room was decorated - once he descended upon the table to pick
up the crumbs –

Snow falling – A blustering East wind drifting it into large heaps many of them 4   Jan 4
and 5 feet in depth. I noticed one in a field near the Trent 10 feet high and 20
yards around, which looked like a little snow mountain. It was conical in shape
terminating in a sharp point at the top - and the wind had smoothed the surface
as even as that of a sugar loaf. Persons passed and repassed upon the ice at Weston
Cliff. The road between Staunton and Melbourne blocked up with snow.

Mr Haimes has ecrected [sic] a Steam Engine in Melbourne [109] – the first   Jan 4
introduced there. Melbourne trade good.

Last night another fall of snow. The mail between Derby and Melbourne 5 hours   Jan 5
after time owing to the road being stopped in various parts by drifted snow. The
mail carrier instead of bringing his cart as usual was obliged to come from Derby
to Swarkeston [sic] on horseback with the letter bags slung about him and where
the road was impassable to turn into the adjoining fields and thread his way as
well he could. Horsleys van which plies between Melbourne and Derby daily managed to get to the latter place yesterday but could not get back. The roads are
being cut through near Staunton and Melbourne. Cunery Lane [110] is impassable.

---

108 Queen Victoria and Prince Albert, with their children, were shown standing by a Christmas tree in the Illustrated
London News in 1846. The Queen and her consort were popular, so the public followed their lead enthusiastically.
The Hanoverian Kings of England, George I – IV and William IV, had introduced the Christmas tree many years
before, but they were less popular and less public figures than Victoria and Albert, so the Christmas tree failed to
become fashionable before the 1840s.

109 This must have been at Haimes's Castle Mills. It is worth noting that a painting of Melbourne Hall dated 1853, which
also shows the lower end of the village, does not show a factory chimney at Castle Mills. This painting, by Hilton
Pratt, was (2002) at the Homestead, Spondon. The factory chimney at Castle Mills is prominent in late Victorian
photographs.

110 Cunery Lane is now part of Derby Road. It ran from approximately the bottom of Dunnicliff Lane to the junction of
Derby Road and Newton Lane. A cunery or conery was a rabbit warren.

1854

• *Melbourne Post Office decorated for the coronation of King Edward VII in 1902. It was replaced by the present building soon afterwards, in 1907.*

Jan 7   It appears from accounts in the Derby papers that on the night of Jan 1. the thermometer fell to 18°, on the 2nd to 23°, and on the 3rd to 4° being 28° below freezing point. The river Derwent frozen over for the first time in 40 years, the last time being in 1814. The Streets of Derby deserted by man and beast and presented a dessolate [sic] appearance. Men carted the snow on the sides of the streets. Railways blocked up – few or any trains running on most lines. The New Years Ball was postponed – the country families could not get to Derby on account of the snow drifts.

March 11   First Division of the Baltic Fleet under Sir Charles Napier left Portsmouth for Wingoe [i.e. Vingä] Sound.

March 28   England in conjunction with France declared war against Russia.

April 2   Great anxiety respecting the progress of the war evinced by all classes.

April 26   A day of Humiliation and Fasting appointed by Her Majesty on account of the war. Service in Melbourne church and special prayers read. Sermon by the Vicar upon the subject of the war from the Text "And David encouraged himself in his God." A collection was made for the wives and families of the soldiers engaged in struggle amounting to £7 " 9 " 3. Service was well attended and the day strictly kept.

April 27   We have not now had any rain of consequence for many months - Remarkably beautiful seedtime.

News arrived about a week ago that Admiral Dundas had bombarded Odessa in the Black Sea with success. This account is now confirmed. An English boat having been sent to Odessa to carry away the English and French Consuls it was fired upon by the forts although the boat hoisted a flag of truce. This circumstance caused the Admirals of the combined fleets to open the ["vale"?, i.e. volley, perhaps] - Odessa was bombarded by a division of steam frigates , which destroyed the Imperial Mole and batteries, twelves [sic] war-ships in the port, blew up two powder magazines, but saved the neutral vessels in the quarantine harbour as also the private property belonging to the inhabitants.

May 15

The affair was very gallantly done — our loss was one man, the French lost 4 and 68 wounded - Our steamer the Tribune behaved exceedingly well but was riddled with 12 of the enemys shot, the French steamer, Vauban was fired by the enemy's hot shot but the fire was got under. The Russians had it is supposed about 1000 killed - Our fleet also took 12 vessels laden with munitions of war.

News has arrived Admiral Sir Charles Napier has been killed and 3000 of the seamen of the Allied fleet, but that Cronstadt was taken. This requires confirmation - (Not true [added])

May 15

Very great interest excited about the war - It is very popular with persons in all ranks of life.

May 15

For many weeks news of the war has arrived perhaps one day and has been contradicted the next - so that persons now pay no attention whatever to Telegraphic reports Amongst those events which really have taken place up [111] the present time are the following.

July 18

Odessa bombarded by Ad^l Dundas as before described.

Demonstration of the Black Sea Fleet before Sebastopol.

Forts on Circassian coast destroyed by Sir Edward Lyons.

Schamyl obtained a victory in Circassia over the Russians: the latter losing about 3000 men and 1000 prisoners taken.

Her Majesty's ship Tiger got ashore near Odessa: hot shot was fired upon her from the forts and consequently being incapable of defending (herself owing to her position) her crew were all captured by the Russians: the vessel set on fire and the guns mounted upon the batteries of Odessa and her flag sent to St Petersburgh [sic]. Captain Giffard resisted most gallantly as well as his crew until further attempts were hopeless & was just on the point of blowing up the ship when he was captured. The Russians behaved well to all the prisoners supplying them with all kinds of provisions & medicine. Mrs Giffard is allowed to find a home at Hampton Court Palace and allowed (at the request of the Queen) a pension of £200 a year.

---

111 sic. Presumably Briggs meant to write "up to".

1854

Silistria has not been taken without the assistance of the Allied Troops: 12,000 Russians having fallen before its walls. In the last assault about 3000 fell and 37 officers killed or wounded. Paskiewich [*Paskevich*], Luders [*Lüders*], Gortschacoff [*Gorchakov*] and other superior officers were wounded. The Russian soldiers were so dispirited by their fruitless attempts to take it, that it is said when ordered for the last time to storm it they were forced to it by cavalry and led on by the leading generals but that they perceived they were merely led as oxen to the shambles and and [*sic*] in the battle fired upon their own officers The Russians have now retired from the banks of the Danube, having lost 50,000 or 70,000 men, spent an enormous sum of money, and shewn themselves very inferior soldiers; indeed they have not gained a single advantage since they crossed the Pruth.

70,000 English & French Troops are now near Silistria and Shumla.

Sir Charles Napier in the Baltic has not been idle. He has been bombarding several forts and military works with perfect success. He then lay before Hesingfors [*i.e. Helsingfors, now Helsinki*] where the enemy has 16 Sail of the Line; but could not tempt them to come out.

He sent Capts Yelverton and Nemisis Hall to of the Arogant [*sic*] and Hecla to pitch into Eckness at which place they did some dashing thing taking the enemy's ships from under the noses of their own cannon.

Sir Charles has now about 60 Sail under him, independantly [*sic*] of smaller vessels. about 30,000 men and more than 3000 guns. A Division is now before Cronstadt so that something may soon be expected.

July 19   Very wet hay-harvest. Very little grass mown at present and scarcely any ricked. Wheat is promising and green crops are excellent.

Aug 21   Mr William Haimes died at Melbourne. In conjunction with his brother Mr Thos Haimes he established in Melbourne a manufactory for the manufacture of silk shawls and gloves which has been very successful, and given employment to a great number of operatives [112].

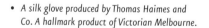

- *A silk glove produced by Thomas Haimes and Co. A hallmark product of Victorian Melbourne.*

---

112 Haimes also brought the "New Jerusalem Church" to Melbourne, and built an extension to his home at Pennfield House, Penn Lane, to accommodate a small chapel seating 125. It was formally dedicated on December 31st, 1826. Haimes later bought the site for a new chapel on Derby Road, and gave a sum of money towards building it. It was eventually opened in May, 1864. The building is now converted into flats (New Jerusalem Magazine and Intellectual Repository).

Hay harvest finished. Corn harvest is begun in the neighbourhood.	Aug 21

Corn Harvest nearly finished. The crops are most beautiful and abundant and probably the yield will be the greatest ever known. The weather too has been most favourable. — Sep 6

News arrived of the British and French having landed in the Crimea without opposition. — Sep 15

News arrived of the Allied Troops having carried an entrenched camp on the heights of Alma near Sebastopol at the point of the bayonet. The struggle was desperate. On our side about 1600 were killed and wounded amongst whom were 25 officers killed and 72 wounded. The Russians laid down their arms and fled within the walls of Sebastopol. — Sep 24

The Allied Armies commenced the bombardment of Sebastopol with about 117 guns and 50 thousand men. — Oct 17

News was received that the Russians had attacked the position of the Allies, captured 11 guns and nearly annihilated the English Light Cavalry. There was some truth in the report. The guns were served by Turkish recruits who upon the appearance of the Russians abandoned them, scarcely firing a shot. A regiment of cavalry somewhere about 700, were on the field and the commanding officer mistaking the words "act on the defensive" for "act on the offensive" made one of the most brilliant charges ever witnessed amongst the Russian battalions but being too weak were awefully [sic] cut up. [113] They left about 500 horses dead upon the [114] had about 171 killed and 266 wounded amongst [115] were 4 or 5 officers. — Nov 13

"Cannon to the right of them,
Cannon to the left of them,
Cannon in front of them
Volley'd and thunder'd;
Storm'd at with shot and shell,
Boldly they rode and well,
Into the jaws of Death,
Into the mouth of Hell
Rode the six hundred."
From "The Charge of the Light Brigade" by Alfred, Lord Tennyson (1809-92)

News came that the Russians attacked the position of the Allies near Inkerman with an army of 70,000 under Prince Menchicoff [Menshikov], two sons of the Emperor of Russia being on the field. After a whole days fighting the Russians were beaten with a loss of 9000 men. This was fought principally by the English who had scarcely a fifth the number of the enemy. — Nov 14

---

113 This was the infamous "Charge of the Light Brigade" on 25th October, 1854, at the Battle of Balaclava. Note the length of time taken for the news to reach Briggs in Derbyshire!
114 sic. There is clearly a word accidentally missed out here.
115 sic. There is clearly a word accidentally missed out here.

1854

Whilst this battle was being fought the garrison of Sebastopol made a sortie upon the French besieging lines and were repulsed with the loss of 1000 men. Thus was obtained by the Allies a victory scarcely less brilliant that that of the Alma. When the Roll was called over after the battle of Inkerman the Russians had 15,000 men killed, wounded and missing.

Nov 14   The weather has been most extraordinarily dry and fine; so much so that wheat sowing has been deferred until now on acct of the plough being unable to penetrate the soil. We have been about 3 months without rain of any consequence.

Nov 24   A Fund of £300 was raised to provide employment for the mechanics in Melbourne a great number of whom are now thrown out of employment by the stoppage of the manufactories. They are to be employed in altering the Woodhouse Hill.

• *Woodhouse Hill in an undated photograph. The gradient of hills often seems understated in photographs, but the easing of the hill here in 1855 was a welcome improvement which cyclists can still appreciate today.*

Trade in Melbourne still bad. About 30 mechanics now employed in lowering Woodhouse Hill and widening the bridge over the brook. Mr. John Earl is superintending them [116].

Jan 30

Bitterly cold and snowey [sic] weather. Trent quite frozen over sufficiently hard to bear persons. Thermometer stands at 10° below freezing point. Vast flocks of larks made their appearance: numbers of wild fowl passed southwards. Several rare birds shot. flocks of Golden Plover appeared. A Snow Bunting: a couple of Tufted Ducks: a wild goose: a grebe: a Common Gull: a Herring Gull &c killed.

Feb 11

[Newspaper article, entitled "THE LATE FROST. THE BIRDS – BREAKING UP OF THE ICE ON THE TRENT – THE FLOOD." Provenance and date unrecorded. The author writes about the sighting of wild birds including 54 Hoopers or Wild Swans. He also comments that workmen wheeled barrows of plaster from Weston Cliff to Kings Mills, over the ice on the frozen river. The article concludes by describing the thaw and subsequent flooding. The author is not named on the article, but the style and content leave little doubt that the author was J. J. Briggs.]

Snow on the ground 3 inches deep. frost.

Mar 18

Day of Humiliation on acct of the war.

Mar 21

Snow one inch deep. When the great frost broke up, vast sheets of ice were left on the surface of the ground in a field opposite Weston Cliff. They were left there on Feb 28th and were only just melted on March 23rd having been three weeks and two days undergoing the process of thawing.

Mar 23

Great water famine. Wells that never have been short of water within the memory of man are now nearly dry. Persons are obliged in many instances obliged [sic] to drive their cattle a long distance to drink.

Mar 26

Cold, backward spring. Hedges as black and bare as in December. They have not made the least effort to bud : this is the case with forest trees. The song birds (even the earliest) are still silent. Snowdrops and ["Hepaticas"?] just in flower.

April 4

Barley-sowing just commencing.

April 5

An amusing incident occurred at Melbourne a few days ago. A vessel called the "Caesar," forming part of the squadron now about to sail for the Baltic, advertized [sic] in the "Times" newspaper for a band to accompany the crew. The Melbourne Band smitten for the moment with a martial spirit answered the advertizement. Down sent the Chaplin [sic] of the vessel (Rev. - Smithard) a Derbyshire man, to engage them. The terms were rations, clothing, and 80 pounds a man for two years. Many members of the band "turned tail" however, (owing to the solicitations of wives and sweethearts), and much to the innocent amusement of their neighbours, the liberal offer was declined.

April 5

---

116 Earl would be well-placed to do so, as he was a railway contractor.

1855

MELBOURNE TOWN PRIZE BRASS BAND.

• *The Melbourne band, in a postcard by Edward Martin (died 1921). A brass band was re-established in Melbourne in the 1990s, with great and continuing success.*

April 13   Gooseberry trees leafing. Violets and cowslips in flower.

April 23   Hedge-buds beginning to swell. Frosty nights – ice this morning as thick as a crown piece.

April 23   Barley sowing ended. Beautiful seed time. After the severe weather in the winter of 1853-4 the seed time was good and the crops yielded well. It will probably be found the case this year that after a long severe winter we shall [117] a bountiful harvest.

May 1   Cold Winds with hailstorms. Grass has yet [118] begun to spring. Migratory birds unusually late this season. The House Martyn [sic] which arrives in average seasons about the 19th of April reached us on the 21st. Rays Wagtail usually reaches us about Ap 9 did not do so until the 17th. Sand Martyn arives [sic] about the 9th this year 20th. Willow Warbler the 11th this year 17th. The Cuckoo was remarkably late. She is usually heard from the 16th to the 20th this year she was not heard until the 30th.

The trees are only just beginning to shew symptoms of returning life. The buds are swelling. The Hedges, which in 1849 (which was extremely mild) were bursting into leaf on February 22nd and even budding on Feb 12th are only just now tinged with green. The Laburnums which in average years are in flower have not now budded. Last year the Lilacs were in leaf here on the 5th of April : now they have not even budded on May 1st.

---

117 sic. Briggs presumably meant to write "shall have".
118 sic. Briggs presumably meant to write "not yet".

Hedges just in leaf.	May 10

Extremely cold. Last night hundreds of Swallows were found dead, very poor, and evidently starved out. At Newton field [119] 30 were picked up by one person. Numbers were picked up, having the feathers of their plumage cut and mutilated and had evidently been killed by a severe hailstorm, accompanied by a high wind which occurred on May 30th. Some Swallows were so tame that they allowed themselves to be taken up by the hand. Some which had met with death apparently in an instant lay floating upon the waters of the Trent.
 — May 31

A few pairs of Swallows still remain. The House Martins, Sand Martins and Swifts did not suffer.
 — June 3

The scarcity of native song-birds, such as the Blackbird and Song-Thrush this year has been noticed by others as well as myself. Even in Donington Park where the air in ordinary seasons seemed one melodious and continued warbling scarcely a note is heard.
 — June 4

Ash-tree leafing. Walnut tree in partial leaf. Elm expanded, Oak budding.
 — June 4

Remarkably hot and sultry. Towards evening fell the rain in torrents, accompanied by thunder and flashes of lightening [sic] incessantly. At every fash [sic] the earth seemed envelloped [sic] in a pale blue light. The weather strikingly contrasted with that which occurred a week ago when the Swallows died by thousands, hail fell and the air was as cold as in the depth of winter.
 — June 6

The Hawthorn in full blossom and very beautiful.
 — June 12

The Laburnums in full blossom.

Gooseberry and currant trees very full of fruit

Very few apricots.

Apple and pear trees promise an abundance of fruit. Field beans begin this year to blossom close to the root and promise an abundance of bloom.

About this period heavy showers of rain fell accompanied by thunder and lightening [sic] and causing vegetation to make rapid progress.
 — June 15

Cold North wind. Throughout the whole of this spring the weather has been extremely variable severe cold alternating with oppressive heat, and causing colds sciatica, and rheumatism to be very prevalent. On June 6, boys were bathing in the Trent and was [sic, a word or two missing?] as agreeable as during the hottest summer ; to day most people have had recourse to their warm winter clothing.
 — June 17

---

119 King's Newton Fields is a farmstead, now divided into several dwellings, originally built by George Sims in 1820 (DRO Newbold diary).

1855

Yesterday (June 16th) a singular circumstance occurred. A flock of sheep were grazing in a field close to Melbourne, when the electric fluid struck one of them and set its wool on fire and one half of the skin was singed quite bare. Probably the whole would have been so but the fire was extinguished by a person who superintends the Gass [sic] Work. The effect produced upon the ground upon which the sheep stood was remarkable.

The electric fluid having struck the animal was then apparently conducted down each of its legs into the earth and where each of its feet stood penetrated into the ground to the depth of 20 inches making four small round holes.

At a short distance from the spot where the sheep was killed the lightening [sic] struck the earth, ran just beneath the turf for some distance and again came out. A man in the employ of George Briscoe Esqre of Melbourne [120] who was mowing tares not far distant had the whiskers on one side of his face burnt off and as he was falling to the ground was caught in the arms by another man.

June 20	Early Lammas wheat came into ear.
June 28	The season has proved tolerably favourable for the hatching of partridges numerous pairs bringing off their broods between the 15th and 25th. We have known several large broods to be hatched. Out of one nest containing the unusual number of 22 eggs 19 were hatched and out of another containing 19 eggs not one was abortive. The cold weather had a predjudicial [sic] influence upon the eggs of pheasants and in a great many nests 4 or 5 eggs have been found "addled".
Sep 10	Corn harvest nearly finished.
Sep 10	News arrived of the fall of the Malakoff Tower, Redan and all the south side of Sebastopol. Flag floating on the Church and the bells ringing. This long-looked for event has caused great joy.
Sep 13	Lord and Lady Palmerston visited Melbourne. The Inhabitants received them with great joy.
Sep 14	The Inhabitants formed a procession and proceeded to the Hall to present an address to his Lordship which was read by myself.
Nov 22	Mrs Cantrell of Kings Newton (mother of Joseph Thomas Cantrell Esqre. Judge of the Derby County Court) died at Kings Newton. Aged 86.
Nov 29	Mrs Cantrell was buried in Melbourne Church [121].
Dec 6	Frost set in.
Dec 9	First snow fell.
Dec 10	An amusing correspondence has been going on for some weeks in the "Derby Reporter" about the state of Chellaston roads which has caused a good deal of

---

120 Mr. Briscoe was the tenant of Melbourne Hall.

121 The Cantrells are buried in the north transept of the parish church. Burials in the parish church were prohibited from 1857, so Mrs. Cantrell's would have been one of the last. (DRO 655A/PV1 Vestry Minute Book 1851-70).

conversation. Chellaston Roads have been cut up very much with the traffic in plaster and various writers under the signatures of "Concrete" Surveyor " Philo " T. P." and other writers have been drawing public attention to the state them [122]and in no measured language. As their letters may some years hence appear curious I have preserved a few of them.

[Two newspaper cuttings on the state of Chellaston roads from the Derby Reporter. The first, by "Concrete", is undated. It refers to the hope that an Act of Parliament would be obtained to turnpike the Chellaston roads, and accuses the Chellaston people of neglecting their duty to maintain the roads in the meantime, until the turnpiking of the road relieved them of their duty.

- *Derby Road, Chellaston in a postcard by Edward Martin (died 1921). A couple of these buildings still remain, but the same view today is vastly changed and urbanised.*

The second, again by "Concrete", is dated 16th November, 1855, and laments the state of that "wretched, miserable , filthy line of communication which ought to be a road that worms its sinuosities between Chellaston-hill and Shelton wharf." *He comments that the Chellastonians persisted with making the road concave in profile, even though it had been shown that convex surfaces were much better for roads. An Act of Parliament for turnpiking the road had now been obtained. The writer believed that the public favoured it because it was the only way of getting a decent road through Chellaston, and not because they believed it to be the proper way of solving the problem. "Concrete" feared that the road would now be abandoned by the Chellastonians over the coming winter, before being taken over by the Turnpike Trust in the Spring.]*

[Two newspaper cuttings. The first is the conclusion of the article of 16/11/1855. The other, by T. P. of Chellaston, Dec 1855, says that the allegations by "Concrete" are exaggerated: "I grant our roads are like some human characters – not so good as they might be .... but.... Has the public a right to expect a good road when it does not pay for its repairs? Let those who don't like them, leave them." *]*

---

122 sic. Presumably Briggs meant to write "of them".

1855

[Newspaper cutting, being a letter from "Concrete" to the editor of the <u>Derby Reporter</u>, published in issue dated 14th December, 1855, in response to the comments of "T.P." "Concrete" asks whether "T. P." stands for "Thomas Pigtrough", in which case his name would be "beautifully suggestive of that peculiar hollow shape, which distinguishes the road which he has undertaken to defend". "Concrete" says that the public indeed does have a right to expect good roads, because Chellaston is no different from any other parish which maintains roads for public traffic at its own expense and manages to keep them in order. The damage to Chellaston's roads is caused principally by Chellaston's own plaster traffic, yet Chellaston neglects to repair them. In other parishes, roads are repaired even though the damage is caused principally by through traffic.]

Dec 19   Very severe frost. The Trent frozen over in one night. Vast numbers of wild fowl appeared: flocks of Hoopers, Tufted ducks, Goosanders, Water Rail, Golden Plover, and Hooded Crows.

The Trent froze over in a different manner this year from the usual one - In ordinary seasons masses of ice form – some people say at the bottom of the river – then rise to the surface and floating down the river lodge in the still parts and congeal together: thus forming an uneven – rough – irregular coat of ice. But this year the surface was frozen over in the same way as an ordinary pool and the ice was smooth uniform and even.

Dec 20   Great Water famine. Holy Well quite dry. Very few wells in Newton have water. Water for steeping barley to malt is being fetched from the brook. The Wells at the upper end of Melbourne are quite dry and the inhabitants come down to "Hatton's Well" [123] for a supply.

- *The pump and trough over Hatton's Well can be seen in the middle of this photograph, probably taken in the 1880s.*

---

123 Hatton's Well was in front of No. 65, Church Street, opposite the Parish Church, and was an open well surrounded by a low stone wall. It was covered in after George Kinsey, for many years the parish constable, fell in and drowned while on his way home. A pump was provided to draw the water from the well, but it became obsolete after mains water was supplied in Melbourne, and has long gone (A.S.Jacques <u>Melbourne</u>, 1933, page 96).

Christmas Day. Last night the band and two choirs of singers came around – sang "Christians Awake" and other hymns. Holly is most beautifully berried this year, and seems to have kindled an improved taste for dressing houses and the church. Instead of private houses being decorated as usual with a few branches of holly or ivy stuck in the windows: wreathes [sic] of evergreens crosses stars and other ornaments are made and hung upon the walls which have a very pleasing appearance.

The Church too is dressed differently from the usual manner. No evergreens are stuck about the pews but the pulpit, and gallery are garlanded most tastefully with evergreens. The large arch under the tower is beaded broadly with evergreens above which are the letters I.H.S. in ivy.

Testimonial presented to Mr C. S. Barker consisting of a Silver Tea Service. Value 23 pounds. From the members of the Melbourne Agricultural Socty. Presented by myself.

Dec 25

Dec 27

1856

Jan 11   The river Trent frozen over. The second time this winter.

Jan 16   A series of Lectures were delivered this winter at the Athenaeum by the following persons on the following subjects.

By the Rev W. Spooner	On "Matter".
Dr Spencer Hall	On "Heroism in humble life".
The S. C. Sargeant	On "Reading".
Mr J J Briggs	On "Illustrious Englishwomen".
The Rev. W. F. Wilkinson	On "The Plurality of Worlds.[124]

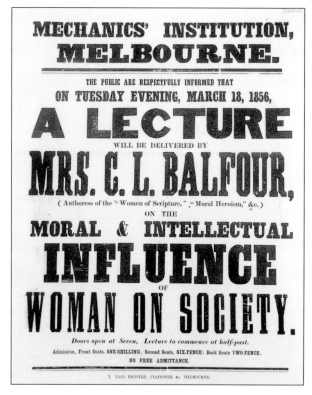

- *"This seems to be a lecturing age"* [see diary entry for 2nd January, 1858].

Feb 16   Remarkably mild genial weather. Gooseberry trees beginning to bud. Several individuals of the Peacock Butterfly were seen flitting about.

March 31   News arrived in Melbourne that Peace with Russia <u>was concluded</u>. The Paris conferences had terminated to the satisfaction of the English people. The bells of Melbourne Church have been ringing merrily and a flag floating on the Church tower - Dancing at the New Inn.

---

124 sic. Inverted commas not closed.

During last winter a row of Lime Trees have been planted on the side of the highway in King's Newton between the Hall and the Chauntrie House.

A very heavy storm of rain and hail. Thunder and Lightening [sic]. The storm passed over for Donington at which place the electric fluid struck the spire of the Church, causing some damage to the weather vane. It then ran down the Conductor into the body of the church and damaged the gas pipes and other things. It also broke about a dozen squares in the windows of the New School Room.

Thanksgiving day for the conclusion of the war with Russia. Sermons preached at Melbourne and King's Newton. About £11 " o " o collected.

This spring a row of lime trees has been planted on the left side of the road at the upper end of King's Newton. A document shewing upon what terms they were planted was drawn up between F. F. Fox Esqre Lady Palmerston's agent and the principal ratepayers of Newton. Lady Palmerston found the trees and pailings [sic] to guard them and Mr Orton of King's Newton was keep [125] the pailings in repair until the trees grew up.

Great rejoicings in King's Newton on account of the conclusion of Peace with Russia. If all the work had been paid for which was performed by the working classes and farmers gratis it would have cost £100 " o " o. No village in Derbyshire celebrated the Peace with so much spirit. The following is the account from "Derby Reporter". The persons who subscribed and the amount of their subscriptions was as follows:

Jos. Thos. Cantrell Esqre	£4 " o " o	Mr Thos Worral	5 " o
Robt. Green Esqre The Hall	4 " o " o	Mr Scott	5 " o
Mr Briggs Senr.	2 " o " o	Mr Wm Buck	5 " o
Mr Briggs Jun	2 " o " o	Mr Robt Smith	5 " o
Mr Haimes	1 " o " o	Mr Wm Earp	5 " o
Mr Orton	2 " o " o	Mr P Gregory	3 " 6
Mr Taylor	1 " o " o	Mr Vernon	5 " o
Mr Sims	2 " o " o	Mrs Newbold	10 " o
Mrs Fowler	10 " o	Mr Jos[h] Earp	10 " o
Mr Newbold	2 " o " o	Mr Knowles	5 " o
Mr Taft	10 " o	Mr Chas Knowles	5 " o
Miss Ince	5 " o		
Miss Ratcliff	2 " 6	Total Amount	£23 " 11 " o [actually £24.11.0]

---

125 sic. Presumably Briggs meant to write "was to keep".

1856

Almost every person in the village gave a day or twos work and worked day and night at making flags, rosettes for garlands, and devices. Mr John Briggs and Mr Newbold procured the subscriptions and very [126] active in making the arrangements for the Fete. About 90 women had Tea and 110 men had dinner. The Provision for them was as follows:

	£	s	d
64 Gallons of Ale	5 "	18 "	$10^1/_2$
The Melbourne Band	1 "	10 "	0
Expenses incurred in decorating the village	1 "	0 "	0
14 St. Plum Cake, bread and rolls	3 "	6 "	10
4lbs of Tea 20lbs of Lump Sugar 14lbs raisons [sic] 10lbs of Sugar nutmegs mustard 8lbs of butter 4 lemons 3lbs of Tobacco pipes - 2/- eggs	3 "	14 "	3
6 Quarts of Old Rum	1 "	7 "	0
195lbs of meat (beef and mutton)	4 "	6 "	6
Nuts for the children		18 "	6
Gown pieces to run for		10 "	6
Total Amount	**£24" 2 " 0**		

The parties who carried out the arrangements were divided into the following Committees.

Finance Committee
Mr Taylor (Chairman)
Mr Briggs
Mr Newbold

Dinner Committee
Mr Haimes
Mr Robt Smith
Mr Newbold
Mr Taylor
Mr Wm Buck

Decoration Committee
Mr Orton
Mr Briggs
Mr Wm Earp
Mr Thos Worrall
Mr Geo Earl

Tea Committee
Mrs Taylor
Mrs Fowler
Miss Taylor

[Newspaper cutting, June 6th 1856 describing the peace celebrations in King's Newton. A special effort to celebrate the Peace was made there because a large part of King's Newton belonged to Lady Palmerston and "the peace was hastened considerably by the decision and energy of her distinguished lord" i.e. Lord Palmerston.

126 sic. Presumably Briggs meant to write "were very active".

The various decorations through the village are described: "Near the Sir Francis Burdett Inn, a showy garland and seven flags, made by Mr. and Mrs. Buck; near the Pack Horse Inn a dressing of evergreens and flags, by Miss Ince; at Mrs. Gregory's, in the Hollow, a garland; at Mrs. Worrall's a garland; at Mr. Thomas Worrall's a garland, blond flag, and four others; from Mr. Geo. Earl's house to the Hall, a garland, large white flag, and several others; at Mr. Orton's a beautiful arch, the upper part of which was decorated with medalions [*sic*] of blue and gold, encircled with flowers and evergreens; cottages occupied by Wm. Collier, Saml. Thompson, Morrison, Farebrother and others, dressed with evergreens; from Mr. Vernon's to Mr. Holt's, a garland and flags; the "Cross Tree," a beautiful lime, was dressed with numerous flags, the steps being covered with red, white and blue flowers – from the tree three garlands, flags and banners; on Mr. Haimes's house was an elegant design, the letters V. N. chastely executed in green, crown of flowers and floral arch; near Mrs. Harper's a double garland, with large flags; near Mrs. Hall's house a flag of white lace, made by herself, and garland; houses dressed with evergreens; between Mr. Briggs' and Joseph Thompson's a showy garland, with flags neatly executed by the wives of the cottagers, and very elegant; near Thomas Beresford's, garland and flag; near John Farebrother's, garland and flag;

near Thomas Dexter's, garland and flags." *After tea and dinner on the premises of Mr. Briggs there were pastimes including races for gowns and calico, leap-frog and dancing, also on the premises of Mr. Briggs. "The Melbourne Band contributed much to heighten the pleasure of the day by playing in their best style"]*

[Newspaper cutting, no date or provenance, rectifying omissions and errors "in the last number of our journal" concerning the King's Newton celebrations and a tea for the ladies on the following day, held in the large ornamented shed where the festivities had taken place on the previous day]

THE CROSS TREE
KINGS NEWTON,
PEACE REJOICINGS, 1856.

1856

June 10   No public "rejoicing" in Melbourne. Many of the working classes much disappointed. Two black flags hoisted: one in Potters [sic] St, the other in Back Street. On one was represented the bones of an animal and skeleton of the head with the inscriptions "Poor Melbourne" and "Here are the bones but the spirit is fled to Newton."

June 15   The Rev Gervase Wasse Curate of Melbourne published his own bands [sic] of matrimony in Melbourne Church his intended bride being present. He said "I publish the bands of marriage between the Rev Gervase Wasse and Anne Deans both of this parish: if any of you &c &c." This announcement caused a slight titter to run through the congregation.

June 16   A note written last month (see May 16th) states that some lime trees had been planted in Kings Newton. Mr Josh. Cantrell objects to their remaining considering that they are an encroach [127] upon the Highway by Lord Melbourne [128]. The origin of their being planted was on this wise. Some of the inhabitants of King's Newton had expressed a wish to have some planted and communicated that wish to Lord Melbournes agent Mr Fox. He agreed to plant and fence them until they grew up then remove the fence : the Overseers of Highways were to have power to trim and prevent them from growing to an inconvenient size but that Lord Melbourne should have the priviledge [sic] of cutting them down and carrying them away.

This reservation on the part of Lord Melbourne was made more particularly in order that should his Lordship choose to build near them he might have the power of removing them should they prove inconvenient. "At a meeting of the ratepayers of the hamlet held on Jan 31st 1853 at the Pack Horse Inn we were authorized to state that if Ld Melbourne is willing to plant a few lime or other ornamental trees in the main street of King's Newton paralel [sic] with the line of road and in front of the property belonging to Ld Melbourne we the Overseers of Highways of the said hamlet engage that neither we nor our successors shall in any way obstruct Ld Melbourne or his successors or agents or servants if at any time hereafter Ld Melbourne shall be desirous or think fit to cut down and carry away the trees in question."

> John Joseph Briggs ⎫ Surveyors
> Henry Orton   ⎬

Ratepayers present at the Meeting
> Thomas Worral
> Robt Smith
> Joseph Earp
> James Newbold

July 20   Very abundant hay-harvest which was secured in excellent condition by almost all farmers.

---

127 sic. Presumably Briggs meant to write either "they are an encroachment" or "they encroach".
128 sic. There was no Lord Melbourne by this time, but the following part of this diary entry shows that the proposal to plant the trees had its origins during the lifetime of the third and last Lord Melbourne (d1853), before the estate was inherited by Lady Palmerston.

1856

July 26

Considerable excitement prevailed hereabouts on account of the performance of a very remarkable pedestrian feat. Alfred Helson a native of Melbourne and formerly in the employ of Robt Pegg of Castle Donington Chimney Sweep, undertook to walk seventy miles a day for six days. He commenced his march on Monday July 20th and concluded it with ease at 8' O clock on Saturday evening the 26th : thus walking a distance of 420 miles in six days. The 70 miles were usually walked in about 14 hours, but on one of the days they were completed in 12. Whilst on travel he took very little food except beef tea, or a small bit of mutton half cooked, with a little stimulant occasionally. Whilst on travel Helston appeared to be going at the rate of some two or three miles an hour, but in reality he was walking probably six.

Aug 1

Extraordinary hot weather. The Cattle in the fields which usually cannot be approached by some yards lie down oppressed with heat and allow you to stroke them. A horse dropt [sic] down dead on Mr Bostocks farm and two more could not get out of the field. A market gardener had some persons plucking peas for the market but the intense heat of the sun spoilt the peas as soon as they were plucked and he was obliged to desist. In the sun, the thermometer stood at 112 : in the shade 82.

Aug 2

Thermometer in the sun stood at 116. Heat intensely oppressive. The reappearance of the Great Comet of 1556 is expected about this period and the extreme sultriness of the weather seems to warrant the belief that the celestial visitor is at hand.

Aug 22

The oppressive weather at the beginning of this month has been followed by terrific rolls of thunder and tremendous showers of rain. For about a week rain has scarcely ever ceased to fall causing serious damage to the barley crop. Wherever barley was mown it begun to sprout and in the "laid" places of standing corn both barley and wheat it grew to a considerable length. I saw ears of wheat standing perfectly upright putting forth the green blade. A good deal of corn is down hereabouts much damaged.

Sep 2

Mr John Earl introduced into the parish a beautiful Steam thrashing machine. The corn is put in the straw at one part of the machine and comes out perfectly thrashed winnowed and bagged ready for market at the other.

Sep 2

About 8 'O clock p.m. a most aweful [sic] storm visited the parish. It seemed to break over King's Newton and for three hours the rain and hail fell in a continuous torrent. The terrific rolls of thunder shook the earth in a manner which I never before witnessed and at intervals the earth and air were lighted up with blue-coloured flame. Corn which was in stack uncovered was drenched through and had the next morning to be pulled in pieces and again dried.

1856/1857

The horses in our stable, to use the waggoner's expression "danced about like parched peas". A horse depastured in Mr Haimes field, wild with fright, rushed at a thick, mortared stone wall near Mr Cantrell's shrubbery and broke down about four yards of it. He cut the flesh off his breast and injured himself much.

In the Haymeadow field near the Trent the lightening [sic] made a large hole in the ground about two feet wide.

Undue Interference of Peers at Elections.

THE SOUTH DERBYSHIRE ELECTION.

Copied from the "Morning Post" of April 17th, 1857.

To the Earl of Harrington.

MY LORD,—You have addressed a letter dated 4th of April, 1857, to the editors of the *Times* and *Morning Post* respecting a "letter or squib" received by Mr. Briggs, of Melbourne. I was one of the three gentlemen to whom Mr. Briggs submitted that letter, and I was the one who recollected its contents, consequently I cannot allow your communication of the above date to pass unnoticed—not with the object of imputing to your lordship either want of candour or discretion, but to show that you have written a letter calculated to mislead the public.

You cannot be permitted to shelter yourself behind the crinoline of the lady who stands at the head of the poll at Elvaston Castle; neither can your sins of omission be extenuated under the plea that you "have no will but by her high permission."* Bear in mind, my lord, that the deeper the humiliation to which you submit from that quarter, the more society will persist in holding you responsible for the acts of the sharer of your coronet. Although your power may be usurped by a determined will and an unscrupulous conscience (see the letter or squib), society condemns it, and common sense despises it. The "letter or squib" shows the power which rules at Elvaston, and also the principles by which that power is actuated. Therefore, my Lord, the quibble of initials, or no initials, is of little consequence.

You say this "letter or squib" "bears on the face of it proofs that it was not written by you." I fear, my Lord, you would have added that you were altogether ignorant of it, had you not written to Mr. Briggs to thank him for having kept possession of it.

You observe further that the "letter or squib" was "private"—again proving your knowledge of its existence; and although its animus against Mr. Colvile is terrible, you say "you never harboured a thought against him".

You proceed to say the contents of the letter were "surreptitiously obtained." In reply to this rash charge, permit me to observe that, although I recollected its contents, I did not reveal them until I was requested to do so by Mr. Briggs. Your lordship must admit he could not do otherwise, as he was requested in the "letter or squib" "to tell the Melbourne folks not to be humbugged by these fellows."

It must be evident to you, my Lord Harrington, that the vindication of your honour rests on the publication of the *entire correspondence held by Mr. Briggs* upon this subject. Don't fear my position; respect your own. You have appealed to public opinion; give the public the only means to judge. Authorise and request Mr. Briggs at once to forward to the Editors of the *Times* and *Morning Post* your letter, or Lady Harrington's letter, a copy of which Mr. Colvile sent to you; also your letter, or Lady Harrington's letter, blaming Mr. Briggs for making the contents of that letter known; and also your letter, or Lady Harrington's letter, thanking Mr. Briggs for having kept possession of the "letter or squib" above alluded to.

My lord, you cannot hesitate; this is not a warfare of pellet-guns against your "Dear Parson Pop," or your harmless vagaries on the Maine law in the Temperance Hall; *it is matter involving character, position, and honour,* and you cannot shrink from the issue. You must either sanction the publication of the correspondence, or submit to the verdict of public opinion without it.—I am your lordship's most obedient servant,

Melbourne, near Derby: April 14.   **W. HEMSLEY.**

* See Burns at greater length.

☞ The Editor of the "*Derby Reporter*" was compelled to omit the above in the last publication, his reason for which he does not assign.

Mr Thos. Scott had three cart-horses died [sic] between the 11th and 13th. They were apparently in good health on the 10th. The interior showed no signs of disease and the animals are supposed to have been accidentally poisoned: by whom it cannot be ascertained.

Jan 11

Contested election for South Derbyshire. Candidates on the Conservative side Mr Clowes son of Colonel Clowes and Lord Stanhope son of the Earl of Chesterfield. On the Liberal side Charles Colvile Esqre of Lullington and Mr. T. Evans Esqre of Allestree Hall. Mr Evans this day addressed the Electors of Melbourne in the Market Place and was received with loud applause. In the evening he gave a Lecture in the Athenaeum Room on "Socrates". Room crowded to excess.

Mar 17

Mr Clowes and Lord Stanhope met the Electors and addressed them in the Market Place. They came attended by about 100 horsemen. Several ladies were in carriages. They were very quietly but rather coldly received.

Mar 23

The following quaint fly sheet appeared some time ago. To those who understand the allusions to persons and things it is very amusing. It is from a paper called "Historical Contributions about the Melbournites [129], by "A Spectacle Man"

Mar 23

• *Blanch Croft, c1975.*

[The following is a full transcription of the piece just mentioned. It tells the story of Mr. Wood, a schoolmaster turned Baptist minister who built a house on "Mount Pleasant" and had an ill-fated relationship with a lady of Blanch Croft, who has yet to be identified:]

129 sic. Inverted commas not closed

1857

1. And in those days there was plenty of employment for him that would work, and many rose up early and sat up late and ate the bread of carefulness.

2. And many waxed rich, and became strong in the pocket, and they said one to another, It sunshines now, but rainy days will come.

3. But some of them were greatly unwise for they carried their wages to the beggar manufactury [130] [sic] and spent them in rioting and drunkenness, while their wives and brats were starving at home.

4. And divers among them said, Go to, wherefore should we dwell in other peoples houses? and they gathered together many thousands of bricks and of morter [sic] a great heap. So they set up for Landlords.

5. And they went forth into the north, by the delectable hills, and lighted upon a certain estate, called Tomlin's acres [131] , it is a delsghtsome [sic, clearly a printing error for "delightsome"] land, for the orient blush of Aurora tinged the ridges thereof, and dew of heaven descended thereon.

6. And they said, here will we dwell, so they covenanted with the owner thereof for two hundred talents ; and the land is called Mount Pleasant unto this day.

7. And they divided the land into lots, and made highways [132], and they digged wells therein and builded many houses, and they became Freeholders and dwelt in their own houses and grew their own cabbages.

8. And a certain pedagogue covenanted with men of brick and wood and straw, to build him a mansion on the mount.

9. And after a time they arose and built the mansion, and it was goodly to look on, with surrounding landscape with its silvery winding Trent was very pleasant to behold but the stone wall of the garden was not built, neither is there any gate in the front thereof.

10. And the pedagogue was pleased with his mansion and he rubbed his hands and said thus unto hinsel!, [sic, clearly a printing error for "himself"] 'it is not good that man should be alone, I will arise and seek me one of the daughters of Eve to be my wife' And he arose and went his way.

11. Now there was in the city a certain widow, and she was rich, and fair to look upon, moreover, she was virtuous & gave much to the poor.

12. And she was of the sect called Dippers, and a great friend to the cause [133], for whenever there was a dabble, so it was she would be there with her 'drops of brandy' to prime them for the splash [134].

---

130 i.e. the public houses.
131 i.e. the "Mount Pleasant" estate of the Tomlinson family.
132 The Mount Pleasant Estate was divided into building plots, and the streets built to serve them are today Commerce Street, Union Street and Hope Street.
133 "the cause" is in italics in the article. Italics have not been used in this transcription, to avoid confusion with editorial comments.
134 This is clearly a reference to the Baptists and the practice of baptism by total immersion.

13. Now the widow dwelt in the croft which is called Blanch, and she mourned many a time and oft that her three former husbands had gone the way of all flesh.

14. And she laded her asses and sent many presents to the pedagogue, even to his mansion, and his cupboard was filled with loaves and fishes, spices and precious things. And the man's name was Lignum [135].

15. And it came to pass after a time and a half that the pedagogue was baptised in love for the kindness of the widow quite overwhelmed him, and he wot not what he should do.

16. And he went unto the widows house and they commun'd together and whisperd [sic] sugary things, and their hearts waxed hot within them, and they cudcled [sic, printing error for "cuddled"?] each other,

17. Now the widow had three sons, Filo the Juror, and Jamie the Bard and Willie the Aesculapian, and when they heard of this catter [sic. printing error for "matter" or "chatter", perhaps?] they looked down their noses.

18. But Jamie had within him a quick spirit, and on a certain day he went unto the man Lignum, and was very courteous unto him and warned him that if he married the widow he would blo [sic] his brains out

19. Now Lignum thought that an hard saying, nevertheless he went again to the widow. But after a time their love became overgrown with moss, [136] and the greenness thereof was very great.

20. And the stone wall of the garden is not built, the gate is not hung, and the widow is not wed unto this day, wherefore they say this man began to build and was not able to finish. And they called the name of the mansion Warning Castle.

Printed by Quid pro Quo, at his Boiler, four doors from the Ides of November [137]. ["196U5"?]

• *Pingle cottages prior to their demolition in 1969: "...the orient blush of Aurora tinged the ridges thereof, and dew of heaven descended thereon..." [see diary entry for 23rd March, 1857].*

---

135 Lignum (Latin) = Wood. J. H. Wood was a schoolmaster in Melbourne and preached occasionally at the Baptist Chapel. He left Melbourne in 1856 to become minister of the General Baptist Church at Sutterton (Rev. T. J. Budge, Melbourne Baptists (1951) page 35). This flysheet was presumably written only when Mr. Wood was no longer in the community! The house built by Wood was probably Pingle House, which stood between George Street and Commerce Street and was demolished in the 1960s. The identity of the rich widow and her sons has yet to be discovered!

136 "moss" is in italics in the article. Italics have not been used in this transcription, to avoid confusion with editorial comments.

137 The quaint biblical style of this flysheet is similar to another one (see A. S. Jacques Melbourne (1933) pages 83-86) which exposed the abuse of the Grays and Greens charities. It is very likely that the author of both was Thomas Pass of Potter Street, an eccentric bookseller, printer, stationer and patent medicine vendor, who also produced an almanac. The present chemist's on Potter Street occupies the same site today.

1857

- *Pingle House was probably the house built by J. H. Wood and alluded to in the story in the diary entry for 23rd March, 1857. It was demolished in 1967 and its site is now occupied by nos. 8 and 10 George Street and 2, 4 and 6, Commerce Street.*

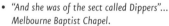

- *"And she was of the sect called Dippers"... Melbourne Baptist Chapel.*

April 21   Mrs Fox the wife of Henry Fox Esqre (long agent to the Melbourne family) was buried in the churchyard of Melbourne. Aged 73. Pall bearers Mr Hasard, Richd Tasker Esqre Mr J. J. Briggs Mr. John Earp.

- *A Victorian view of Chantry House, Church Street, Melbourne, once the home of Henry Fox, agent to the Melbourne Estate.*

Elizabeth Thompson, the wife of Joseph Thompson labourer of King's Newton died suddenly of disease of the heart. She had been at work in the hayfield and came home towards 12' O clock. About 2' O clock she was sitting sewing a chair [138] when she suddenly dropt [sic] down and died. Not five minutes before she had been saying how well she had been all Summer.	July 22

Corn Harvest commenced. Wheat cut.   July 27

Barley cut   Aug 3

Thunder, lightening [sic] and incessant rain for 16 hours. The rain fell in torrents. The brook rose 10 feet in 6 hours. A considerable flood on the brook. Much wheat and barley is now cut and having been exposed to heavy rain for nearly a week is sprouting and is much damaged. Wheat sprouts as it stands uncut in the fields.   Aug 13

A beautifully fine day. A remarkably high flood on the Trent. Several fields of corn near the Trent are overflowed knee-deep. Altho' it is Sunday Mr Newbolds men are loading wheat out of the flood. It is considered that wheat and barley have not sprouted to such an extent for about half a century.   Aug 16

Day of Humiliation appointed by Her Majesty in order to implore the blessing and assistance of the Almighty on our arms for the restoration of tranquillity in India.   Oct 7

- Note. This photograph relates to the entry for 15th March, 1858, about the tumulus at Breedon found by men at the limeworks.

[A slip of printed paper is inserted at this point, provenance and date unrecorded. It reads as follows: "In this reign we find it recorded that "Prior de Repyndon habuit quasdam terras in Melton, Pakynton, Tokenhall, et Repingdon, que fuerunt acquisite de diversis personis" (152). We also learn that "Simo de Melburne & alii dederunt cuidam capellano 20 messuagia, 10 tofta, 50 acras terre, 14 acras prati, 40 acras pasture, &c., in Melbourne, Newton, & Repingdon, divina in ecclesia beate Marie de Melbourne celebratura," &c. (153).]

---

138 sic. Perhaps Briggs meant to write "sitting sewing in a chair".

1858

Jan 1   The author of this work printed for private circulation 50 copies of a local work called the "Trent and other Poems" embellished with wood cuts of the Holy Well Kings Newton and an oak tree in Donington Park.

• An oak tree in Donington Park, from Briggs' "Trent and Other Poems".

Old Oak Tree in Donington Park.

Jan 2   During this winter numerous Lectures have been given in the Melbourne Athenaeum Room. This seems to be a lecturing age.

Jan 2   A movement commenced for restoring the interior of Melbourne Church.

March 15   Annular Eclipse of the Sun. The day was cloudy and overcast and the only difference perceptible to the eye was that over the east a dense gloom was cast.

March 15   A week or ten days ago some men were bearing for limestone at Bredon [sic] when they came to what was evidently a a [repeated word, sic] Barrow or tumulus. Upon digging into it a kist or cist-vaen was cut into the rock in which were the bones of a human beings [sic], charcoal, several querns or hand mills for grinding corn and a rude bone weapon made apparently from the horn of a red-deer. It was of this shape and size. long [139] (vide page [sic, no page number included, but obviously refers to the sketch in the entry for 6th May, 1858]). Also a boar's tusk and a beautiful pebble.

Querns have been found on previous occasions when bearing upon the rock. Sometimes they are found with an iron rivet. The stone of which they are made was probably procured from a hill near Melbourne about 2 miles off called "Charnhill" or Quernhill [off Calke Road]. This stone is extremely hard and durable.

---

139 This word seems to be the remainder of a phrase otherwise deleted

With reference to this discovery Mr Bateman of Yolgrave [sic] the distinguished Antiquary says : " The account of the discovery at Bredon is interesting. The following are the thoughts that occur to me on reading your letter and which I have no doubt have presented themselves to your own consideration. The weapon of bone is interesting. The horn of a cow would be too vascular to use as a weapon or implement. I have uniformly found the red-deers antlers employed for these purposes where horn of any description is used. An inspection of the texture would at once decide the question. I have one or two similar instruments of stags-horn but I cannot say what they have been adapted to with sufficient certainty to satisfy myself.

Portions of Querns have been occasionally found in Barrows without having any definite connection with the interments. I possess one perfect Quern which was said to have been found with a skeleton by the man from whom I obtained it and I found two millstones making one complete Quern placed with two skeletons of the Saxon period in graves at Winster. Altogether I apprehend that Querns found in a barrow with human remains would indicate a rather late period perhaps the Romano-British. I have been led to form this opinion from the nature of the pottery found in connection with Querns both in this locality and in other parts of England.

The iron pin found with Querns at Bredon is rarely to be observed, the peg was no doubt most commonly of wood, though in the Querns introduced by the Roman Legionaries with the pin of the nether stone and the rhind of the upper were often of iron : the stones themselves were frequently of lava from Andernach on the Rhine then largely exported for the purpose whilst the British stones are mostly of the stone found in the neighbourhood."

It would appear from the remains found at Bredon that the Barrow was early British the monument of some British Chieftain who probably had often hunted over the neighbouring forest of Charnwood. His implement of woodcraft – his bone dagger – was buried with him as an emblem of his occupation. This was always the case with the Ancient Briton. Whatever was the pursuit of the deceased, he had implements of his calling buried with him. Thus a hunter had frequently a red-deers horn, a flint arrow head placed near him and his dog at his feet. It was supposed that they would be wanted to [140] when the owner pursued the same calling in another world.

The Querns found at Bredon were evidently Romano-British. The iron pins seem to indicate that. Besides which the hill was occupied and fortified by the Romans : portions of the vallum still remain   Three querns were found. One was very perfect; it had evidently been originally divided into three pieces bound together by a ring round it this ring being fastened to the quern by pins of iron. Human bones (not calcined) were found and charcoal. [141]

---

140 sic. It seems that Briggs was originally going to write "wanted to pursue the same calling in another world", and then changed it to "wanted when the owner pursued the same calling in another world", without deleting the word "to".

141 A text very similar to this diary entry was contributed by Briggs to the British Archaeological Association, and published in Volume 15 of their Journal (1859), pages 337-338.

1858

April 6   About six months ago a County Police Force was established. The Superintendent of this Division had [sic] his residence at Melbourne.

April 6   It having been resolved to close the old churchyard belonging to the Church and situated in Melbourne a New Cemetry [sic] is to [142] made. The ground has been already chosen near the Cow Pasture on the eastern side of the Upper Road leading from King's Newton to Melbourne. The ground has been purchased from Lady Palmerston at £220 per acre.

April 7   For many months very little rain has fallen and many well [sic] are nearly exhausted. The arable land, owing to the dry weather, is in beautiful order for sowing barley.

May 6   A man who was digging in the "Castle Ochard", [sic] near the Churchyard and on the spot where Melbourne Castle formerly stood, turned up a rude stone vessel of the date of about 1400. Upon sending a drawing of it to Mr Bateman the Antiquary he writes me word that it has probably been a kind of Stoup or vessel for holding Holy Water used in a private chapel: He found one like it in 1837 at Rowsley where tradition says there was formerly a chapel. This vessel was found very near the spot where in old prints of Melbourne Castle a chapel or a church is represented to have stood and I have no doubt formerly belonged to it. The vessel was nearly circular at the top, but having two little projections from the rim by way of ornament. It had two solid handles without ornament.

It was about a yard in circumference, at the centre, and something like the following rude drawing. [143]

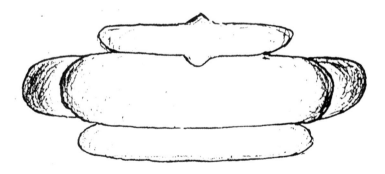

142 sic. Presumably Briggs meant to write "is to be made".

143 Briggs contributed a note of this discovery to the British Archaeological Association. It was published in Volume 15 of their Journal (1859), page 339, where Briggs says: "...It is very antique in shape, without sculpture, massive, evidently cut out of one solid block; circular at the top, having two little projections from the rim by way of ornament. It is about a foot in diameter, and it has two remarkably massive and solid handles."

Drawings of objects found in the Romano-
British Tumulus at Bredon [sic] March 1858

No. 1. Boar's tusk, natural size.

2. Rude bone implement or hunting-dagger made from the antlers of
a red-deer : natural size.

3. A stone pebble, natural size : pink in colour and pretty-looking
supposed to have been a token of affection buried with some
person in the Tumulus.

4. A Quern Complete. The Quern of which this is a sketch stands
about 18 inches high and is probably 36 in circumference.

A. represents a bead of stone running around the edge of the
Upper Millstone

B. Inside where the corn was put.

C. Upper Millstone.

D. Represents the spot into which a wooden handle was inserted to
turn the Upper Mill stone upon the lower.

E. Division between the Upper and Nether stone between which the
corn was ground.

F. The Nether Millstone.

This sketch is very interesting from the fact that is [144] by Sir Gardner Wilkinson
the great authority on Egyptian Antiquities who presented to me [145] as a
memorial of his visit to me at King's Newton.

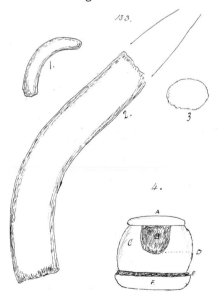

1858

June 13   Remarkable thunder storm. The cracks, rolls and peals of thunder were terrific. The electric fluid struck a house in Melbourne, splintered the rafters and destroyed the tiles. It also killed a horse at Ingleby. The sails of Chellaston Windmill were struck and the fragments carried a considerable distance. Near King's Newton an ash tree was struck and on both sides of the bole the lightening [sic] ran down slitting off a narrow strip of bark to the wood for perhaps 7 or 8 feet.

June 23   To day was held an important meeting at the Athenaeum, Melbourne having for its object the Restoration of the Interior of the Church. It was agreed to endeavour to raise by subscription the sum of £1500.

The town of Melbourne was canvassed for subscribers by Mr King, Mr Hasard, Mr Wm Hemsley and Mr J.J. Briggs. Individuals of all creeds subscribed very liberally. The following are the names of the Committee.

Joseph Thomas Cantrell Esqre (Judge of the Derby County Court)
The Rev William Cantrell
Philip Hubbersty Esqre
Mr H.W.Fox.
Mr F.F.Fox.
Mr Thomas Haimes.
Mr William Hemsley
Mr King
Mr J.J. Briggs
Richard T. Tasker Esqre
Mr Dunnicliff (Nottingham)

[Newspaper article about Melbourne Church, no date or provenance. Text as follows:

THE CHURCH - We are much gratified to observe that this noble fabric is about to receive that attention which it so richly deserves. It appears that a vigorous effort is now being made to restore in some measure this ancient fabric. The committee purpose [sic] commencing with the interior, and making such alterations as will not interfere with any further restoration of other parts of the building at a future period. Of course, the extent of the alteration will depend much upon the amount of subscriptions received but it is confidently hoped that the present undertaking will enable them to restore the interior, as well as re-floor and re-pew it, remove the whitewash from the walls, repair certain parts of the pillars, &c., which have been mutilated and effect alterations in conformity with the original character of the edifice. The object is certainly a laudable one, and we trust will receive the encouragement which it merits. Few parishes labour under greater difficulties for the prosecution of such a work than that of Melbourne. The Church itself is very large - a Norman Temple, in fact, 144 feet long - the town of Melbourne is small. To restore even the interior of the fabric will require a larger amount of money than has been sufficient in many cases to build a new church. An appeal, then, is made not only to this county but to the country - for Melbourne Church is a national monument - and we hope that that appeal will be responded to.

We congratulate the committee on the success already received which is considerable. It appears that the parish of Melbourne has been successfully canvassed, and that individuals probably of every religious creed have handsomely contributed towards the object, as the subscription list published in our columns to-day abundantly testifies.]

[Newspaper article, no date or provenance, describing the establishment of the fund and committee for the restoration of Melbourne Church. Text as follows:

RESTORATION OF
MELBOURNE CHURCH, DERBYSHIRE

MELBOURNE CHURCH is believed to have been erected before the Conquest, and is a fine specimen of Anglo-Norman Architecture. Its main characteristic features are so preserved, that there is, probably, no example of the Village Church of that early period now existing in the kingdom, at all to be compared with it. It has, however, suffered so much from long neglect, that it has become absolutely necessary to take some steps for its preservation, and a Committee of Gentlemen have undertaken to make an earnest effort for this purpose. Complete Restoration, however, would require a very large outlay; - larger than any sum which they can hope to raise at the present time; but, as a first step, and to make the entire Restoration eventually more possible, they propose to begin with the interior (by which much additional accommodation will be gained), and they desire to raise a sum to commence with, of not less than £1,500.

Subscriptions in aid of this object are earnestly requested, and will be received by the Treasurer, ROBERT GREEN, Esq., King's Newton Hall, Swarkestone; by any member of the COMMITTEE; or by the DERBY and ASHBY BANKS.

COMMITTEE

Rev J DEANS, Vicar.
ROBERT GREEN, Esq., Treasurer.
Rev. GERVASE WASSE, Curate, Secretary.
Mr. HASARD, ⎫
Mr. KING,   ⎬ Churchwardens.
J.T.CANTRELL, Esq., King's Newton.
Mr. J.J.BRIGGS, King's Newton.
Mr. H.W. FOX, Melbourne.
Mr. F.F.FOX, Melbourne.
Mr. HAIMES, Melbourne.
Mr. WM. HEMSLEY, Derby-road, Melbourne.
Mr. TASKER, Melbourne.
Mr. JOHN D. DUNNICLIFF, Nottingham.

1858

	£	s		£	s
Viscountess Palmerston	100	0	Mr. Wm. Briggs	5	0
Robert Green Esq.	100	0	Mr. James Dolman	5	0
J.T.Cantrell Esq	100	0	Mr. Bernard Dolman	5	0
The Duke of Devonshire	25	0	Mr. Orton	5	0
The Marquis of Hasings [sic]	25	0	Mr. Henry Barrs	5	0
The Lady Forester	25	0	Mrs. Thomas Earp	5	0
Sir John Harpur Crewe	25	0	Mr. Rimington	5	0
Philip Hubbersty, Esq.	25	0	The Misses Gutteridge	5	0
Rev. W.H.Cantrell	25	0	A Friend	3	0
Messrs. H.W., and F.F.Fox	25	0	Mr. Banton	3	0
Rev. Joseph Deans	20	0	Rev. F.A.Weekes	3	0
Rev. Gervase Wasse	20	0	Mr. Earp, Woolstapler	2	10
Mr. J.J.Briggs	20	0	Rev. J.M.Webb	2	0
Mr. Wm. Hemsley, Derby-road	20	0	Mr. Arthur Dolman	2	0
Mr. J.D.Dunnicliff, Nottingham	20	0	Rev. R.H.Cox, Duston	2	0
Mr. John Warren, Cincinnati	20	0	R.G.Creswell, Esq., Ravenstone	2	0
The Earl Ferrers	10	0	Mrs. Barber, Lamb Close	2	0
The Hon.W.Cowper	10	0	Mr. Rowland Ordish	2	0
The Bishop of Lichfield	10	0	Mr. John Earp, High-street	2	0
T.W.Evans, Esq., M.P.	10	0	Mr. Alfred Dolman	2	0
Mr. Hasard	10	0	Mr. John Buck	2	0
Mr. King	10	0	Mr. George Horsley	2	0
Mr. Haimes	10	0	Mr. Ensor, White Swan	2	0
Mr. Tasker	10	0	Miss Tomlinson	2	0
Mrs.Arkwright and			A Friend, by Mr. King	2	0
Friends, Spondon	9	0	Mrs. T .King, Newcastle	2	0
The Earl Howe	5	0	Mr. John Dunnicliff	1	10
Viscount Hardinge	5	0	Mr. Stephen Adcock	1	10
The Hon. Mrs. Lamb	5	0	Mr. T.Hollingworth	1	10
Archdeacon Hill	5	0	Mr.Bullock	1	10
W. Fell, Esq., Lichfield	5	0	Mr. John Bostock,		
E.A.Holden, Esq.	5	0	Breedon Lodge	1	1
Rev. J.K.Newbold, Sheffield	5	0	Mr. G. Weller, Derby	1	1
Mrs. Pedley	5	0	Mr. Fenton	1	1
Mr. Thomas Briggs, Alvaston	5	0	Mr. John Bowles	1	1
Jos. Harris, Esq., Leicester	5	0	A Friend, by Mr. Green	1	1
The Rev. T.W.Whitaker	5	0	Rev. E.W.Foley	1	0
Mr. Wm. Hemsley, sen.	5	0	Mr.Richard Sale, Barrow	1	0
Mr. Thos. Hemsley	5	0	Miss Bailey	1	0

1858

SUBSCRIPTIONS

	£	s		£	s
Mrs. Massey	1	0	Mr. Pitt	1	0
Miss Haimes	1	0	Mr. Thompson, tailor	1	0
Miss Amelia Haimes	1	0	Mr. Toon	1	0
Mr. John Ratcliff, Wilson	1	0	Mr. Dallman	1	0
Mr. Jos. Hollingworth	1	0	Mr. Bogle	1	0
Mr. Warren, Woodhouses	1	0	Mr. Hair	1	0
Miss Draper, Stanton	1	0	Mr. James Earp	1	0
Mrs. Ensor, White Swan	1	0	Mr. Robert Lomas, Manchester	1	0
Messrs. Hyde	1	0	Francis Shaw, Esq.	1	0
Mr. Campion	1	0	Mr. John Hemsley	1	0
Mr. S. Warren	1	0	Mr. Garratt	1	0
Mr. John Earl	1	0	Mr. John Shaw, Normanton	1	0
Mr. George Ward	1	0	Mr. H. Webster Earp	1	0
Miss Carr, Back-street	1	0	Mr. George Ensor	1	0
Mr. Jos. Brookes	1	0	Mrs. Rossel	1	0
Mr. Whyman	1	0	Mr. Briggs, Hemington	1	0
Mrs. Haimes, Pen-lane	1	0	Mr. Tilley, Paris	1	0
Mr. Brown	1	0	Mr. Engledow	1	0
The Misses Robinson	1	0	Fete in Melbourne Gardens,		
The Misses Ashmore	1	0	Aug. 23rd, 1858	53	11
Mr. Keetley	1	0	Small Subscriptions		
			amounting to	17	5

A BAZAAR will be held in MELBOURNE GARDENS, by permission of Col. GOOCH, sometime during the Summer of 1859, of which due notice will be given, in aid of the FUND for the RESTORATION of the PARISH CHURCH.

The following Ladies have kindly consented to become

PATRONESSES

Viscountess PALMERSTON
The Countess FERRERS
The Countess COWPER
Lady CREWE
The Lady FORESTER
The Hon. Mrs. LAMB
Mrs. GOOCH
Mrs. HOLDEN]

[Newspaper article, no date or provenance, about the weather so far in 1858 and the effects on crops in South Derbyshire. Written "By a South Derbyshire Farmer", quite possibly J. J. Briggs.]

1858

• *This printed view shows Donati's Comet as viewed from Mr. Slater's Observatory at no. 136, Euston Road, London. Briggs has cut it from a newspaper but no date or provenance is given.*

Aug 8   One of the dryest [sic] summers ever known within the memory of man. The fields are now as bare as in the middle of December. People are foddering their cattle with oat straw and hay. Turnips and mangel wurzel are hoisting the yellow flag of distress. Many trees, especially limes, are assuming the sere and yellow leaf. Water is so scarce that cattle in some cases have to be driven for miles. The weather is magnificent for harvest. In some cases wheat is reaped and carried the same day : and barley is cut one day and carried the next.

Sept 12   A most lovely day: extremely hot and sultry. Evening clear and cloudless. About 9' 0 clock the Comet was visible to the naked eye and continued so for some hours. Its situation was a little below Ursa Major.

It appeared like a bright star to which was attached a tail of fire about a yard long: the tail pointing upwards, something like the sketch.

[Simple sketch of the comet, the first of several whose purpose appears to be to show the changing alignment of the tail in relation to the nucleus.]

Numbers of people were watching it for some time. It is called the "Comet of Donati".

Sept 25   Remarkably lovely night. Heavens clear and cloudless. Moon about the full [sic]. Donati's Comet very bright: much more clearly visible that a week or ten days ago. To the naked eye the tail seems about 10 feet : the neucleus [sic] being paler than an ordinary sized planet. Still the Comet is a remarkable object shining as it does the only one for a great space in a clear blue sky. The tail points upwards in a direct line for the Pole-Star. It is usually seen now to the greatest advantage about 8, 0 clock. It has an appearance something like the following:

[Another very simple sketch of the comet.]

Donati's Comet presented a magnificent appearance from its proximity to the star Arcturus. Within a short distance of the Comets neucleus [sic] Arcturus was seen and shone through the Comet's tail with peculiar brilliancy. It sparkled like a jewell [sic], and much out shone the neucleus, as it seemed to do every other star in the Heavens. Its appearance I have endeavoured rudely to depict.

Oct 5

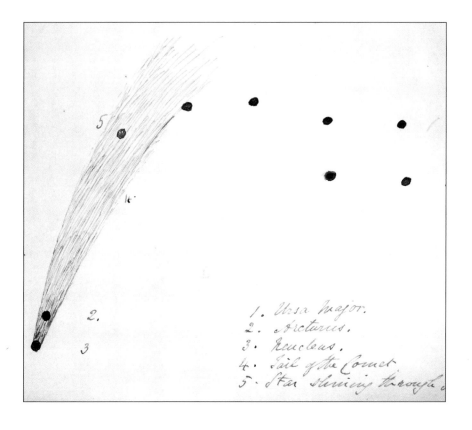

1. Ursa Major.
2. Arcturus.
3. Neucleus.
4. Tail of the Comet.
5. Star shining through it.

[Fourth rough sketch of the comet.]

1858

Oct 8   The Comet still very beautiful and seen in a cloudless sky. The <u>position of the tail was more perpendicular</u> as represented in the sketch. A thin line of light striking thro' <u>Ursa Major</u> to the horizon was seen at 8 'o' clock p-m. The heavens were most magnificent: powdered with stars.

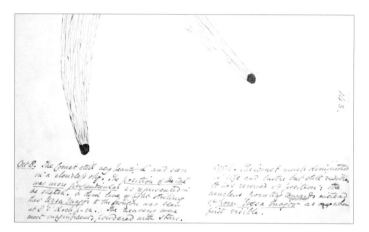

Oct 11   The Comet much diminished in size and lustre but still visible. It has reversed its position : the neucleus [sic] pointing <u>towards</u> instead of <u>from</u> Ursa Major as when first visible.

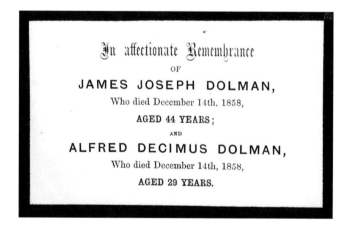

In affectionate Remembrance

OF

JAMES JOSEPH DOLMAN,

Who died December 14th, 1858,

AGED 44 YEARS;

AND

ALFRED DECIMUS DOLMAN,

Who died December 14th, 1858,

AGED 29 YEARS.

Nov 19   The Subscriptions for the Restoration of the Interior of Melbourne Church now amount to about £1000.

To day Mr. Scott the eminent London Architect, who built Doncaster Cathedral, restored Litchfield [sic] Cathedral, Chesterfield Church and numerous other edifices came down to Melbourne Church and was met by the Restoration Committee. He is to give a Report upon it. He was much struck with its remarkable appearance. Mr. Scott is decidedly the first Architect of the present day.

• *Sir G. G. Scott's memorial brass at Westminster Abbey.*

Mr Scott's Report received. He estimates the Restoration of the Interior and re-pewing and re-flooring at £1500.

Dec 10

This morning about 5, O Clock died Mr Alfred Dolman of Melbourne and about 9, O' Clock in the evening of the same day died his brother Mr James Dolman Surgeon. Both corpses now lie in the same house.

Dec 14

The two brothers Dolman buried to day in one grave, in Melbourne Churchyard.

Dec 18

Last summer partridges were more plentiful hereabouts - and indeed everywhere else - than almost ever was known. They sold at one time as low as 6d the brace. All kinds of fruit were most abundant and ripened to perfection owing to the beautiful dry character of the weather.

Dec 18

Professor Bowles of Langley Priory Co Leics assuming the name of Shakespear.

Dec 19

[Press cutting, no date or provenance, quoting an advertisement in The Times dated 15th Nov, 1858, describing the Queen's grant of a licence for Charles Bowles and his issue to be known as Shakespear, and bear the arms of Shakespear, in accordance with the last will of his maternal uncle John Shakespear. The licence is conditional upon the arms being exemplified and recorded in the Herald's Office.]

1859

Jan 2   Copy of a curious tile found on Sinfin Moor some years ago supposed to have belonged originally to Repton Priory and presented by the author of this volume to the "Archaeological Association" and engraved by Llewellynn Jewitt Esqre for their Journal.

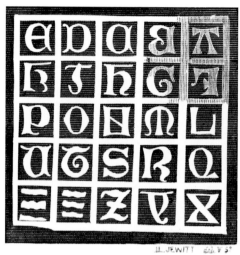

March 26   A most remarkably mild season. We have had but one short frost and snow [sic]. The pastures are as forward as at the beginning of May. Violets, primroses and the early spring-flowers are over. Snowdrops ceased blooming by the middle of February. The Thrush was singing as sweetly in January as it does in May. I saw on the 24th of March Robins fully fledged and ready to leave the nest. The hedges are now in full leaf. The Sycamore, Lime, Willow & Chesnut [sic] are in leaf. Gooseberry trees are in full leaf & blossom. Apricots bloomed early in February and the fruit is now as large as marbles. Although the season was so forward the Chiff Chaff our earliest summer migrant arrived as late as March 26th. I have known it in late seasons arrive by the 28th.

March 28   The New Cemetry [sic] is beginning to assume a beautiful appearance. Mr Wilson of Alfreton is the Architect. Mr Cooper of Ashby the Builder. A good deal of disatisfaction [sic] is manifested by the larger holders of farms on whom the rates for its maintenance fall heavily. They think it might have been built for a much less sum and that it is of too good and ornamental a character. Posterity will think differently. In 20 years the debt upon it will probably be swept off and our descendants will then have a handsome building bequeathed to them by their forefathers without the inconvenience of paying for it. The cost is estimated at £2050, which is to be borrowed on Government security.

Within the last few years many useful works have been completed in Melbourne. An Athanaeum [sic] has been built : Gass [sic] has been introduced into the town : the schools have been put upon a healthy footing : the Cemetry [sic] has been built : the Church is in course of Restoration. We have endeavoured in our day and generation to leave the world better than we found it and I hope those who come after us will strive to accomplish the same object.

• *The date plaque on the Baptist schoolrooms.*

To shew the forward character of the season it may be noted that several of the boys in King's Newton have taken from 30 to 40 eggs of the Hedge Sparrow, Thrush, Missel [sic] Thrush &c Some boys went to Stanton Hill a week or ten days ago and took more than 40.

Mar 29

<u>Sunday.</u> This morning whilst the Rev. Joseph Deans the Vicar was reading prayers the pipe of one of the stoves in the Church gave a startling crack and down came from the roof a shower of sparks. At the point where the pipe went through the roof the timber apparently had caught fire and in a short time the roof would have been in a blaze. Measures were immediately taken to get out the fire: the Churchwardens calling some of the congregation to their aid. A ladder was procured and reared inside the church, where [or "when"?] a man ascended it and put out the sparks, the Vicar all the time continuing to read the service probably to prevent alarm spreading amongst it. In about an hour all was quiet as before.

April 3

• *This is the only known photograph, and indeed the only known illustration of any kind, of the interior of the church prior to its restoration in 1859-60. Note the three-decker pulpit, box pews, coat pegs, whitewashed walls, mutilated stonework and the little stove.*

1859

[A printed flysheet is inserted, being an advertisement for "The Trent and other Poems" by John Joseph Briggs F.R.S.L., being an enlargement of the first edition. The book is dedicated to the Right Hon. The Lady Edith Maud Abney Hastings, and profits are to go to the fund for the restoration of Melbourne Church. The leaflet also includes a page of press reviews and a specimen page featuring the poem "Silence". See entry for April 6th, 1859.]

April 6   The author of this volume is preparing for publication a work entitled "The Trent and other Poems" embellished with a beautiful lithographed title page and engravings on wood of the Holy Well, at King's Newton, an old oak growing in Donington Park, a view of Weston Cliff, view of Kings Newton Hall and view of the Boat House at Donington Park. It will be printed on tinted paper, with marginal line round each page. 450 copies will be printed : price 5/-. The profits of the book will be given to Fund [146] for the Restoration of Melbourne Church. The accompanying is the prospectus of the work. The following are specimens of the cuts.

• *Front cover of "The Trent and other Poems", from a copy held at Matlock Local Studies Library.*

The "Holy Well."
[Woodcut of the Holy Well.]

Oak tree in Donington Park.
[Woodcut of tree.]

April 4   The accompanying is a view of the proposed alteration in the interior of the Church with a revised List of Contributions towards the object: together with the opinion and remarks of Mr George Gilbert Scott the Architect. (No.1)

[Plan of the church, probably from Deans' History of Melbourne Church (1843), labelled by Briggs "Original Ground Plan of the Church".]

[• A leaflet is inserted labelled "No. 1" by Briggs, printed for the purpose of getting subscriptions for the restoration of the church. On the front is a fanciful reconstruction of the interior, showing a vault over the nave. Inside there are extracts from Scott's report, the names of the Committee members, and an updated list of subscribers to the fund. The two quotations from Scott's report are as follows:]

Restoration of the Parish Church of St. Michael, Melbourne, DERBYSHIRE.

THIS fine old Church has been standing for a period of about eight hundred years. The style of Architecture is the Anglo-Norman, and there is probably no other Parish Church now existing, in which the main features of that style are so well preserved. It has, however, suffered so much from long neglect, that it has become necessary to take steps for its preservation.

---

   146 sic. Presumably Briggs meant to write "to the Fund".

"Your Church, as you are well aware, is one of uncommon interest. It appears to have been erected, shortly after the Norman Conquest, on a plan remarkable for its massive symmetry; and though its western façade has never probably been completed, its eastern tri-apsidal termination almost obliterated, its high-pitched roofs lowered, and several others [sic] of its features mutilated, it still retains, particularly within, very much of its original nobleness of character; and if restored, though but in a partial degree, would exhibit them to greater advantage"

"I fear that these repairs must be extensive, as not only has the stonework been most recklessly mutilated, but the Church appears at some early period to have suffered from fire, and the surface of the stonework, in the lower parts, is consequently much injured. I would, however, recommend much moderation in its treatment, introducing no more new stone than is absolutely required; and, in cleaning off the white-wash, taking the utmost care not to disturb, in any degree, the original surface of the stone."[147]]

Copy of the monumental slab of Henry and Elizabeth Hardinge in Melbourne Church now nearly obliterated.

The "Sweedish [sic] Singers" who have had the honor [sic] of appearing before her Majesty came to Melbourne and gave a Grand Concert in the Athenaeum Rooms.

April 5

In the year 1832 occurred a trial at Derby between King's Newton and Melbourne about the Roads. It was found upon examination that from time immemorial each village had repaired its own roads. There was never any demarkation [sic] between the land belonging to each: that varied according to circumstances as will be hereafter shewn. The boundaries of the Newton roads were found to be well defined and were as follow [sic].

April 5

---

147 A copy of Scott's report can be seen at the Derbyshire Record Office ref. D655 A/P1 54.

1859

On the West and North West : The Derby Road terminates at Stanton Gutter : a bridge which crosses the road on a level being the boundery [sic]. The Breach Lane belongs to K. Newton as far as the brook in the hollow.

As you come from Melbourne the Newton portion of the Derby Road commences a little before you come to Cunnery Lane and ends as we have stated at Stanton Gutter.

With respect to the top road to Melbourne only about 100 yards extending from the Pack-horse belongs to Newton.

The West field Lane is not a public road but should be repaired by the occupiers of lands lying upon that road as far as a gate near a pool just beyond Newton Field farm-house.

The lower road to Melbourne is repaired by Kings Newton, as far as the guide post at the three roads: one of which leads to Donington.

The Donington Road is repaired by Newton as far as the Forty-foot Lane and also down that Lane as far as the Bridge which crosses the brook This bridge is repaired by Newton, Melbourne and Wilson jointly (see former note page 14 [i.e. entry dated 4/8/45])

The manner in which a Rate is levied for the maintenance of the roads both at Newton and Melbourne is curious. The "Case" well defines it. In many hamlets if an occupier ceases to occupy lands and houses the lands still continue to pay to the liberty in which they are situated. It is not so with respect to those of Newton and Melbourne : they annually fluctuate. The <u>place</u> where the occupier <u>resides</u> has a right to receive the rates of his occupancy although he may chance to reside in one liberty and his lands lie in another.

1. If a farmer or merchant <u>resides</u> at Kings Newton and his farm or his premises are <u>situated at Melbourne</u> the township of <u>King's Newton receives the rates</u> due upon the occupancy : and <u>vice versa</u>.

2. If however the said farmer or merchant <u>goes to reside at Melbourne, that place then receives his rate</u> and Newton has <u>no claim</u> to it.

3. When lands are occupied by individuals who reside in <u>neither</u> King's Newton nor Melbourne but, say, Stanton, Wilson, Tickenhall [sic] or elsewhere : then the lands pay to <u>that place</u> either Newton or Melbourne <u>in which the last occupant resided</u> : If the previous occupant has resided at Newton, the land pay [sic] to Newton : if at Melbourne to Melbourne.

4. Suppose these lands to be given up by the individual who resides at Stanton Wilson &c and to be taken by a person resident in Melbourne : the lands pay to Melbourne : although the Stanton occupant may have paid to Newton in consequence of the tenant immediately preceding him having resided at Newton and <u>vice versa</u>.

5.   In some cases, in order to secure the payment of the rates to the place in which their lands are situated, the landlord has let his lands <u>subject to his paying the rates upon it</u> and then handed over the rate to the overseers of the hamlet in which his lands are situated. Such a proceeding is <u>illegal</u>. The tenant and he alone has to pay the rate to that place in which he resides and then make his own arrangement with the landlord.

6.   It is very common for an occupier to live in King's Newton and hold lands on the borders of Melbourne or even property within it and <u>vice versa</u> for a resident in Melbourne to hold lands in the heart of the liberty of King's Newton. I have known a manufacturer living at Newton to pay rates for his Mills in Melbourne and for [sic] a farmer in Melbourne to pay for his lands situated by the side of the Trent.

As the Rate will vary annually great difficulty will always be experienced in making out a Rate : owing to the minute subdivision of land in many cases. As land gets into more numerous hands – as I apprehend it it [sic, repeated word] will – this difficulty will greatly increase.

A few days ago a man was digging in the garden lately occupied by James Dolman Esqre Surgeon and turned up several coins two of which I saw. One was of the reign of Elizabeth and the other James 1st.

April 6

On the <u>1st of April</u> the following letter appeared in the "Derby Reporter". Taking into consideration the day on which it appeared the writer probably intended it as a squib.

April 7

[Cutting of the letter to the editor of the Derby Reporter, from "P.C.", suggesting a railway line from Wychnor (Staffs) to Sawley Junction. It would bear "near to Ashby Baths, whereby the public would have more ready access to the valuable medicinal waters which may be there enjoyed at a very moderate expense – family tickets for 20 hot baths being issued at one guinea, the baths to be taken within one year from date of ticket".]

During the last ten years there has been a great rage in this parish for converting agricultural land into garden ground. Upon Lady Palmerston's estate a good deal of old turf has been broken up and let from £4 to £12 an acre.

April 7

Very forward season. Barley sowing completed. Grass ankle deep in pieces [sic] which have not been spring eaten.

April 7

• *Matthews the gamekeeper [see next page] lived with his wife and children at the far end of this terrace of three late 18th century cottages at Woodhouses. Photographed in 1986.*

1859

April 8   A circumstance of an affecting character recently occurred at the Woodhouses near Melbourne. Mr. Mathews, Gamekeeper on the Melbourne estate, who lived there had five children, several years old. About a week ago one of them was seized with a kind of putrid fever and was dead in a short time and owing to decomposition beginning to take place was obliged to be buried in a few hours. In this manner the whole five died and were buried all within a week or ten days: the eldest child living the longest.

         The little hamlet of Woodhouses has usually been considered a healthy place. The weather at the period was about 90 degrees and it is supposed by some persons that acting upon a quantity of putrid meat which he had collected for his dogs and upon a dunghill situated near the house, it had generated in the immediate locality an unhealthy state of the atmosphere and caused the death of the family. Mr Mathews being a person much respected his loss has occasioned much sympathy [148].

April 9   One of Mr. Mathews' children was buried on the 6th another on the 7th another on the 8th and two on the 9th (to day.) [149]

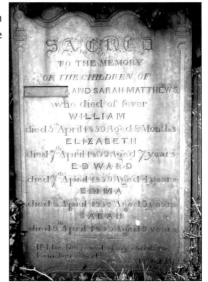

• *The tombstone of the Matthews children in the old graveyard, Castle Street, Melbourne.*

April 10   A funeral Sermon preached upon these children in Melbourne Church by the Rev. Gervase Wasse, Curate. His text was " [150] Luke Chapter 13th verse 4th "Or those eighteen on whom the tower of Siloam fell, and slew them think ye that they were sinners above all men that dwelt in Jerusalem"?.

         The preacher drew attention to the aweful [sic] character of the visitation - their sudden death - their remains having been brought almost at once into that house - the crowd attending to see them desposited [sic] in their last resting places and lastly the distressing position in which the bereaved parents were placed but he

---

148 The cottage occupied by the Matthews family still survives at Woodhouses, adjacent to the present lorry yard. After the tragedy, an adjoining stable was pulled down and the house was extended over its site.
149 The gravestone of the Matthews children can still be seen in the old burial ground on Castle Street, close to the street.
150 These inverted commas are not closed.

1859

argued that we were not to infer from the sudden calamity which had befallen them that they were greater sinners than ourselves - that rather we should examine into our own hearts and see whether we did not deserve a similar fate &c. &c.

[Cutting from the Derby Reporter, no date, consisting of a letter to the editor from "Antiquarius" about church restoration. Text as follows: April 10

SIR,

This seems to be the age of Church Restoration, and very laudable are the endeavours which are being made in almost every locality to give to these interesting fabrics their original character and beauty. With this movement I cordially agree, and wish these restorers of old churches all the success which their exertions seem to merit. But, Sir, may I offer one suggestion. In most old churches there are hidden behind whitewash or stucco, or concealed beneath the boarding of pews or in similar spots, many antiquarian remains not perhaps particularly interesting to the restorers themselves, but very much so to antiquarians generally, and very frequently illustrative of local or family history. Thus on the walls will occasionally be found rude paintings of the earlier centuries, perhaps illustrative of some remarkable event connected with the fabric or locality, or they [sic] may be monumental inscriptions, &c. Beneath the flooring of the pews, too, may be sculptured crosses, or curiously figured tiles or other relics very interesting to the antiquary. When restoring some churches those remains have been rather summarily dealt with, and now all trace of them is lost. I see by yours, and the papers of other towns, that many churches are now to be restored, as Melbourne, Mickleover, Kegworth, Loughbro', &c., and the object of this letter is to ask those committees who have the management of such works, to be careful to preserve the antiquarian remains which may be brought to light. If omitted to be preserved at that period, they will be eventually lost. If paintings, drawings, or inscriptions, are met with, fac-similes of them might be taken by some competent person, and preserved in the Church : if crosses, brasses, tiles, sculpture, flag stones, sepul-

chral slabs, &c., they might also be preserved, a little nook being reserved for them in some retired part of the fabric. Independently of giving interest to the antiquary, and being illustrative of local history, they would give to the church itself additional interest.   ANTIQUARIUS.]

• Crude undated sketch of a painting, now destroyed, discovered in Melbourne Parish Church in the Autumn of 1842. Its discovery is described in an article by Rev. Joseph Deans [see diary entry for 5th October, 1859]. This sketch was inserted by Briggs into his own Grangerised copy of his second edition History of Melbourne, now at Derby Local Studies Library.

1859

• *The wallpaintings in the church did not survive the restoration, with one notable exception. Fortunately, the outstanding Norman sculpture has survived in excellent condition.*

April 10   This winter has amply fulfilled the truth of the adage "A green Christmas, a full churchyard." A milder winter perhaps never occurred and one never more productive of sickness and death. The average number of deaths for last [151] 13 years has been about 48 per year i.e. in the parish of Melbourne. From September 29th 1857 to April 6th 1858 there occurred only <u>16 deaths</u> : between September 29th 1858, and April 6th 1859, <u>47 deaths</u> : or 23 more in the winter portion of the half year.

Taking a district comprising Melbourne, Bredon [sic], Derby Hills, Stanton, Swarkeston [sic] , Barrow, Sinfin, Arleston, Weston-upon-Trent, the number of deaths which occurred from Sep 29th 1857 to April 6th 1858 <u>was 36</u> : between Sep 29 1858 and April 6th 1859 <u>was 72</u>.

April 15   The following Letter shewing a contemplated line of Railway to pass near Melbourne appeared in the Derby Reporter of to day.

[*Cutting from the Derby Reporter, no date, consisting of a letter to the editor about the Derby, Ashby-de-la-Zouch and Atherstone, Burton-upon-Trent, Loughborough and Lincoln Railways. The scheme proposed by "P.C." will never be carried out in the writer's opinion, "as there is a plan of greater magnitude before the Midland Company."*]

[*Newspaper cutting, no date or provenance, entitled* "DESTRUCTION OF KING'S NEWTON HALL, BY FIRE".

It had been occupied for the last five or six years by Robert Green Esq. and family. The family had gone to Hastings a few days ago, leaving the hall in charge of the cook and coachman. About 2 o' clock on Sunday morning, the cook was woken from her sleep by a difficulty in breathing and realised that the room beneath her was on fire. The cook's cries woke the coachman, and she rushed down the burning staircase wrapped in a blanket. The cook and coachman saw that the entire west end of the building was in flames, fanned by a forceful wind from the west.

---

151 sic. Presumably Briggs meant to write "for the last"

The coachman went to summon the Melbourne engines and fire brigade, while the cook alerted the principal inhabitants of the village, which was by now lit up with the spreading fire. No hope of saving the interior of the building was entertained, and efforts were made to stop the fire spreading to adjacent trees and buildings. The Derby fire engine was said to have arrived within an hour and a quarter of the coachman leaving Newton. "The roof at last fell in with an awful crash, magnificent fixtures, sporting trophies, furniture, stone and timber all were buried in the mass, and the old stone walls were left standing almost alone."

• *King's Newton Hall, seen here soon after the fire which gutted it in 1859. Photographs taken over the following fifty years record its further deterioration and gradual shrouding by a flourishing mantle of ivy.*

The villagers made heroic efforts to save some of the furniture and fixtures. "The molten lead ran in heavy streams and fell from the roof and sides of the building with great weight below : but neither this nor the other many dangers prevented extraordinary efforts being made for the preservation of property".

A telegram was sent to Mr. Green on Sunday and he reached King's Newton on Monday afternoon. The ruins were in charge of a member of the county constabulary. "The bare walls, half covered with black and scorched ivy, were still hot..". *The servants were generally freed from blame, and the cause of the fire was unknown. The timber was old and dry, and some of the rooms were oak panelled and recently varnished, so the spread of the fire was not surprising.]*

Sunday. This was a day long to be remembered by the inhabitants of King's Newton. A fire occurred at the Hall and completely gutted it. About two O'clock this morning the Cook awoke, with a feeling of suffocation and found to her consternation that the house was on fire. She immediately called the butler and then the nearest neighbours. The Melbourne fire Engine was quickly on the spot and although most efficiently worked failed to check the progress of the flames.   April 17

1859

The fire seemed to originate in the dining room and issuing thence ran up the oaken staircase to the window which lighted it at the West front. It then soon reached the roof and soon destroyed the whole of the west wing. Then the part over the Entrance Hall took fire and fell with a crash and lastly the eastern wing took fire and was destroyed.

The Derby Engine arrived in a marvellously short space of time and immediately began to play upon the building with marked effect. But it was too late to save any portion of the interior. In a few hours it got the fire under altho' the timbers and ruins smoked for 10 or 11 hours. The villagers were very active and saved as much property as possible, occasionally at the peril of their lives such as all the wine, ale, books, feather beds, some tables, book cases, and a little plate. The fire had melted some of the silver into a lump. The lead also ran down the walls in narrow molten streams. The Fire Brigade from Derby were able to recover a box containing legal documents and papers and a silver Tankard which had been presented to Mr. Vaulentine [sic] Green. The Hall was occupied by Robert Green Esqre wife and two daughters who at the time of the fire were absent at the sea and thus probably their lives were spared.

April 18   Mr Green arrived from Hastings where he had been staying and went over the ruins of the hall. The furniture was insured. The bulk of the plate was at his bankers.

April 19   The fire has created a great sensation in the neighbourhood : thousands of persons have been to visit it. Several sketches have been made of it since the fire by artists. The only one ever taken of it previous to the fire was one sketched by Llewellynn Jewitt Esqre for one of the illustrations of my work "The Trent and other Poems".

April 20   Men busily employed in getting out the rubbish from the ruins. They have found the time-piece - a silver skewer, molten lead and other trifles. The champagne bottles were fused by the intense heat and were found in lumps like white coral : beautiful in appearance. At the time of the fire the poor cat driven out by the flames sought shelter beneath my roof. Her instinct might have taught her that as "A Naturalist" she ought to place herself under my protection.

During the fire the people of Melbourne slept soundly : not half a dozen were there. Our villagers shewed heroic couage [sic]. These were the "Victorious Cross" men on the occasion and I do not see why their humble names should not be gratefully as honorably [sic] recorded. Probably had it not been for their exertions the whole village would have been destroyed.

Johnny Collyer : carried water and materially assisted from first to last.

Robert Dunnicliff

Samuel Collyer : rescued a deal of property.

Joseph Barton ⎤ Brought furniture down the blazing stairs.
George Barton ⎦

Joseph Thompson. Rescued many articles from the entrance hall and elsewhere whilst the roof was blazing overhead.

John Collyer Junr

James Hulse work [sic] the Melbourne Fire Engine pipe and materially prevented the flames catching the outbuildings.

Tom Elliot: One of those who saved the parchment deeds, carpets &c.

Wm Earp Junr ⎤ Saved the hams, bacon &c
Thos Earp ⎦

Cook: Promply [sic] gave the alarm not even stopping to dress or save any of her own property.

Coachman (Ordish) Fetched the Engines.

Jos Worrall: Helped to save the deeds carpets &c.

Thomas Wright.

Mr Bullock, Melbourne: worked at the Engine.

Mr Whyman Melbourne: ["br"?]anchman occasionally.

Robert Smith.

Robin Yeomans saved the books &c.

William Ince.

Mrs Smith ⎤
Mrs Jos Worrall ⎟
Mrs Jos Berresford ⎟ Worked well all the time carrying wine, china and endeavouring to secure all the property possible.
Mrs Thos Berresford ⎟
Mrs Mac Kay ⎟
Mrs Thos Worrall ⎦

The following were very useful in carrying water and articles &c:

The Melbourne & Derby Police.	Fredk Middleton.	Sam Garratt.	Jos Hatton.
Jno Thompson Junr	John Middleton.	John Barker.	- Hattons wife.
James Earp.	William Collyer.	Job Elliot	Robt Newbold.
George Earp.	Thos Harpur Senr	George Taylor.	Saml Holt.
Jno Thompson Senr	Thos Harpur Junr	Jos Littleford.	Saurin Briers.
Thos Thompson.	Thos Smith.	James Parks.	Thos Briers.
Richard Pearson.	Jos Earp.	Mr Briggs's three servants.	Wm Banton.
Henry Taylor.	Mac Kay	James Thompson	Thos Beresford.
	Emma Kirkman		Jos Berresford
			Wm Salisbury

KING'S NEWTON HALL

King's Newton Hall was the home of the Hardinge (formerly known as Hardy) family from the mid 16th century until 1729. It was once supposed that it replaced an earlier Hall in a field called Hall Close on Trent Lane, now bisected by the railway, but there is no evidence for, or necessity of, any connection between the two sites.

The early deeds to King's Newton Hall are lost, but the Melbourne Hall muniments record that Nicholas Hardy (d1582) bought the Hall as a freehold property from John Newton, along with arable, meadow and pasture land[i] . The Newtons were an old mediaeval family of King's Newton and it was apparently this family, rather than the village, which was the direct source of the name of Newton Hall. It belongs to a small group of houses in the parish named after their occupying families, such as Bewley Hall (where the Dower House now stands) and Blackwall Hall (demolished). Historically it is therefore more correct to refer to it as Newton Hall than King's Newton Hall. However, it is the largest house in the village, so it is easy to see why people came to assume that it took its name directly from the village and not from the family, and added the "King's" accordingly.

The house as it stood immediately prior to the fire in 1859 was of early 17th century character, but we don't know whether it was built all at once or had evolved from an earlier building. When Henry Hardie died in 1613, his belongings included £20 worth of stone in the yard and at Melbourne Castle. Perhaps his younger brother Nicholas (d1631) used the stone to remodel or rebuild the hall in its final form.

In 1649/50, Nicholas's son Robert Hardinge (1621-1679) made a series of land exchanges in order to enlarge the grounds and create a small park behind the house [ii]. Further acquisitions for the same purpose continued until at least 1660[iii] . It was possibly this work that resulted in the clearance of buildings along the main street between the Hall and Holywell Lane. Remains of long-demolished structures can still be seen there, fossilised in the park wall, while the old ridge and furrow ploughlands brought into the park were fossilised under pasture for some 350 years, before being ploughed flat and reseeded a few years ago. The stone superstructure of the adjacent holy well was built by Robert Hardinge in the 1660s to ornament the edge of his new park. It was destroyed by vandalism in 1948 and was rebuilt by the Melbourne Civic Society in 1984. By 1674, when Robert Hardinge was knighted by Charles II, his house and grounds were a match for his new status.

---

i   MHMR 8/4/10 and 9/2/3,4.
ii MHMR 15/1/2 – 6; (DRO 73/24/10 and MHMR 8/7/15 are counterparts of two of these deeds).
iii MHMR 7/11/6; 9/7/1 – 6;.

If the Hardinges of King's Newton had survived, the park might have grown larger and more formal, and the house might in due course have been remodelled or rebuilt as a more fashionable 18th century mansion. But this was not to be. When John Harding (1685-1729) died childless, the development of the Hall and park was permanently arrested.

The Hall was let to Mrs. Mundy and the whole estate was sold to the Melbourne Estate in 1735 . The Hall remained tenanted until its destruction in 1859[iv].

After the fire, the Hall lay in ruins for half a century and parts of it fell down from time to time. But when the Hall was purchased and rebuilt by Cecil Paget in 1910, large parts of the old walls and chimneystacks were still sound enough to be incorporated into the new building. Some of what we see today, therefore, is the genuine article, including the four main gables facing north and south, and parts of the chimneystacks. It is a happy fusion of the early 17th century original with an "Arts and Crafts" twist provided by the early 20th century rebuilding.

P.Heath

- This poster is preserved at Derby Local Studies Library DA 374.2 (52573)

1859

April 23   Both the house and furniture insured the former for £1500: the latter for £600. The value of the property destroyed was probably ove [sic] £6000. It is said that the house will not be re-built: but even if it is its ancient glory will have passed away. The walls may be rebuilt but not the historical associations connected with them [152]. In company with Mr Green I have this morning examined the ruins minutely: to all appearance the fire began on the left side of the dining room fire-place and ascended to the room above by the old newly-varnished oak wainscoating [sic].

April 23   <u>Afternoon</u>. Nearly a week has elapsed but the ruins are still hot. The silver plate that was in the house at the time of the fire is melted into a black mass. The wine bottles were found: many of them were still corked but the wine had dried up into a black-looking material like burnt paper.

April 23   The engraving below was drawn and carved in wood by Llewellynn Jewitt Esqre F.S.A. It is a North West view of King's Newton Hall and has a somewhat melancholy interest attached to it by having been taken about a fortnight before the hall was consumed by fire. It was drawn for my " Trent and other Poems."

King's Newton Hall as it appeared the 3rd of April 1859.

---

152 The Hall was eventually rebuilt by Sir Cecil Paget, but not until 1910. Parts of the ruins had fallen down during the half-century since the fire, but Sir Cecil kept whatever he could including the four principal gable ends and parts of the chimneystacks.

The election all the talk. The members are for the Southern Division, Mundy (Conservative) Evans and Vernon (Whigs.) In the Borough of Derby, Bass, Beale and James all Whigs. Party spirit is running very high in Derby; the contest creates a good deal of interest here. The following squibs have appeared in Derby and been much praised on account of the fidelity of their likenesses of the individuals caricatured.

April 23

Mr. Bass is a Brewer of the Burton "Bitter Beer".
Mr. Beale is a Director of Railways.
Mr. James a Barrister.

[A satirical printed sheet called "Soliloquy of Michael [Bass], Prince of Denmark (after Shakespeare's play), by H.H. Bemrose". It begins:

M.P., or not M. P. ; that is the question –
Whether 'tis nobler, at the Poll to suffer
The slings and arrows of outrageous fortune ;
Or to take arms against a sea of troubles,
And, by retiring, end them?.....]

[(1) appears hand written at the side of the name in the title, (2) appears in the margin at the side of a line later in the passage, reading: 'And throws its greasy cap for Melbourne and for Sam'.]

(1) Mr. Michael Bass

1859

(2) Mr. Samuel Robinson, of the Shaw house, who takes an active part on the Liberal side at Elections. He frequently introduces candidates to the Electors when they come to Melbourne and has been rather ironically ' [sic, word missing] the judicious controller of "the popular element."

Bass Solo!
The man who won't coalesce must go upon his own Bottom.

April 26   At page 132 of this Journal a description is given of some Romano-British remains which were found at Bredon [i.e. the description and drawing given under the entry for 6th May, 1858]. Upon enquiry I find that other objects of antiquarian interest have been found upon and near the rock at Bredon [sic]. The querns appear to be of various designs. One which I have seen this morning in possession of Bernard Dolman Esqr of Melbourne and found at Bredon had no beading or finish round the rim, but was beautifully made of a hard, coarse stone and it differs from any quern which I ever saw in having <u>two</u> holes for handles in the upper stone. The pin was evedently [sic] of iron.

About a mile from Bredon near a place called the Highwood some years ago a Celt was found with other things. I have only been able to see the Celt of which I give a rude drawing the size of the original. It is broken so that I cannot tell what shape the handle assumed. Apparently it is of brass or bronze. The symetrical [sic] shape and it [sic] metalic [sic] composition would lead one to suppose that it was very late date[153] even approaching to the Roman period.[154]

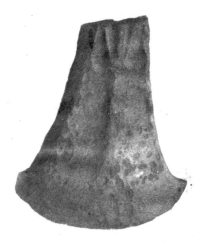

---

153 sic. There is clearly a word or two omitted here.
154 A text very similar to this diary entry was submitted by Briggs to the British Archaeological Association, and published in Volume 15 of their Journal (1859), page 338.

Mr. Mundy the Conservative Candidate visited and addressed the Electors of Melbourne in the Market Place at seven o'clock. Proposed by Robert Green Esqr. Very well received.

April 26

- *In Victorian times, Melbourne Market Place was the usual venue for the gathering of crowds. Increasing road traffic meant that Castle Square later became the more usual focus for such gatherings instead.*

Messrs. Evans and Vernon the Liberal Candidates addressed the Electors in the Athaneum Room. There seems to be a more conservative feeling in this neighbourhood and indeed throughout the country than there was years ago. The agitation for Reform produces no effect; even the working classes seem indifferent to it.

April 27

Great regret felt at receiving the news that France and Russia had formed an alliance to prosecute the war in Italy. It is feared that war over the whole of Europe is inevitable.

April 28

An address presented to Mr. Green. The following account is from the "Derby Mercury".

April 30

RUINS OF KING'S NEWTON HALL, NEAR MELBOURNE, DERBYSHIRE, DESTROYED BY FIRE ON THE 17TH INST.—SEE PAGE 147.

[*Cutting from Derby Mercury entitled 'Presentation of an address to Robert Green Esqr.'*]

1859

April 30   The accompanying admirable sketch of the ruins of King's Newton Hall appeared in the "Illustrated London News" of this date.

May 2   It is rumoured that Mr. Cantrell (judge of the Derby County Court) intends to pull down his house at the Cross (Newton) and build another. It is a very old house that has been modernised at various times but still retains in the interior evidences of great antiquity. The most singular feature in it is the ceiling over the staircase, painted something like one at Hampton Court. The subject is an allegorical one: the moon and stars are figured in gold on a coloured ground and probably represent night the season of sleep. In one of the old rooms in the house died Lady Huntingdon [155].

• *The remains of the painted ceiling over the stairwell in King's Newton House.*

May 7   The Poll for representatives of the Southern Division of Derbyshire took place. Evans and Vernon on the whig interest. Mundy of Markeaton on the conservative. Political feeling running very high. The contest was most severe. Vernon and Mundy ran "neck and neck" and when the Sheriff proclaimed the victor Mundy was found the elected Candidate by a majority of only – <u>one vote</u>.

May 11   Mr.Green held his sale at King's Newton Hall for his stock, implements and the books furniture and other articles which were rescued from the fire. The sale was well attended and the articles sold at high prices.

---

155 This is the house now known as King's Newton House. Mr. Cantrell did not pull it down and it survives to this day. The painted ceiling over the staircase was re-exposed several years ago by Nicola Fowler who now lives there with her husband and family. It had been whited out since the early 20th century, after an attempt at touching in and over-painting had been deemed unsuccessful (information from Mrs. Edna Ashfield). Sadly, much of its original detail seems to have been cleaned off at some stage, including the coloured ground. Perhaps some of the colours used were water soluble.

• It was a sad departure for Mr. Green, who left King's Newton "in consequence of the Hall having been burnt down", as the sale poster states.

View of the Holy Well at King's Newton taken from a different point to that at page 152.

Several Nightingales have this year visited this neighbourhood: a rather uncommon occurrence. One has taken up his abode at Weston Cliff: another at a small copse near Stanton Hills and a third at the Bond Elm near Melbourne. They sing very plaintively but sweetly for many hours towards midnight and have [156] habit of making very effective pauses in their song which seem to heighten the charming character of their songs. The pair at Weston Cliff have a nest.

May 20

---

156 sic. Presumably Briggs meant to write "have a habit".

1859

There was a nest at Donington Park last year and it is supposed the young which were reared have visited the same locality in which they were born. The bird at Weston Cliff may be heard on a clear still evening nearly a mile off.

May 20 The Cemetry [sic] Chapels now finished and have a very pretty appearance. They are erected on the boundary of the consecrated and unconsecrated ground: are arranged in the form of a cross and united by a large handsome covered archway admitting hearses and mourning coaches passing through and surmounted by a beautiful bell turret, upwards of 80 feet to the top of the ornamental gilt weather-vane. Each chapel will accommodate from 40 to 50 persons.

The Chapels are erected of stone, the floors laid with black and red tiles and the roofs covered with blue and green coloured slates diamond pattern and ornamental ridge tile cresting. The roof open framing having arched principals filled with Gothic tracery and springing from carved stone corbels: the rafters are wrought and chamfered and the ceilings covered with wrought and beaded boarding. The design was from numerous others which were sent for competition. It is the decorated style of architecture [157].

- The cemetery lodge had been unsympathetically altered, but it complemented the chapels which are now a Grade II listed building and its demolition is to be regretted.

157 The cemetery chapels still stand today and are a Grade II listed building. The cemetery lodge, of matching style and built at the same time, has sadly been demolished.

Grand Bazaar Fete in Melbourne Gardens in aid of the "Church Restoration Fund [sic, inverted commas not closed]. The following is an account of it.

July 29
&
July 30

[Newspaper article, no date or provenance, entitled "GRAND BAZAAR FETE AT MELBOURNE GARDENS". The success of the day had seemed doubtful. The death of Lord Ferrers prevented Lady Ferrers from taking her stall, and the destruction of Kings Newton Hall had not only destroyed a large amount of valuable material, but had resulted in its occupants the Green family leaving the place. They had been great supporters of the restoration cause. Moreover, the weather had been dull, dark and rainy.

As it happened, the two days of the fete were bright and favourable, and the event was a splendid success. The tent, positioned near the "Four Seasons" proved too small, as the bad weather had led to a prediction of a small turnout. About 800 children were allowed into the Gardens at 1 o' clock, assembling around the Bird-cage pool to sing the "Old Hundredth" psalm. Then they were allowed to view the tent and the goods on sale before leaving the gardens, each receiving a bun. About 1,500 tickets were sold on the first day, and there were about 3,000 visitors on the second day. Bands played on both days and boats were plying on the pool.

"For the gratification of those who wished to see a specimen of camp life, there was set up in one part of the grounds, the tent occupied by Colonel Daniel, of Donington Park, in the Crimea, which contained the writing-stand, bed, and other articles with which it was then furnished for the gallant Colonel's use as commanding officer of the Coldstream Guards. It formed an attractive feature and gave a practical idea of the hardships voluntarily endured by the aristocracy in the defence of their country".]

[A printed leaflet entitled "MELBOURNE BAZAAR FETE, June 29th and 30th. 1859 [158]" is inserted at this point. It contains several poems advertising the goods on sale at several stalls, e.g. Lady Crewe's Stall, The Vicarage Stall and Mrs. Gooch's Stall.

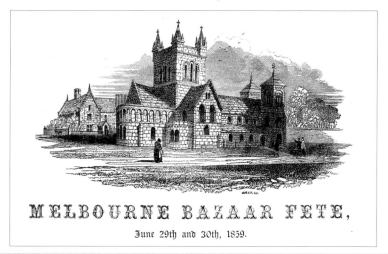

MELBOURNE BAZAAR FETE,

June 29th and 30th, 1859.

---

158 Briggs writes that the fete took place on July 29th and 30th. The printed leaflet gives the date as June 29th and 30th, as does a flysheet (DLS DA921 Mss 28491) for the event. It is presumably Briggs' diary that is in error.

1859

A poem entitled "A Word about every Thing" includes the following lines:

"Come, then, and let your money flow,
'Tis for the Church's good, you know,
Those massive pillars to repair,
That arch to open out with care,
The floor to pave with varied marble,
The seats to make most comfortable,
The chancel – that abomination !
To build it on its old foundation;
To deeds like these our souls aspire ;
The money only we require"]

- "Lady Crewe's Stall", from the Melbourne bazaar fete leaflet, 1859.

Lady Crewe's Stall.

LET all who want good bargains, as I think all comers do, Sir,
Bring open purse and open eyes to the Stall of Lady Crewe, Sir,
Of every sort, of every size, you'll find a mighty crop, Ma'am,
And their price decidedly much less than 'twould be in a shop, Ma'am—

Canaries? yes, so ope your ears, they've voice enough to din them ;
At least if they're not singing now, I'm sure they've got it in them,
And Rabbits, too : no end of pets : observe their loving eye, Sir :
Or if you like to use them so, they're fitted for a pie, Sir :
You don't know how to carry them? see, baskets made of pins, Sir,
They'll stop the Rabbits running out, by always running in, Sir.

You love the Arts? love Poetry? look here, to Nature turn, Ma'am,
Ruins and moonlight, very cheap : 'twill never ruin you, Ma'am,
A bracket made of beads—superb ! a drawing room adorner ;
Buy it, or take the bracket's place, and that is in the corner.

This is " Miss Wadding ;" this to see, is worth a ten mile walk, Sir,
A perfect prodigy in girls—you never hear her talk, Sir.
But though you never hear her talk, yet be it not forgotten,
She *could* spin a tremendous yarn, because she's made of cotton.

Come fat, come thin, come large, come small, come lame, come
nimble trippers,
And see our large assortment of illuminated slippers ;
Come buy, and you'll confess, when from corns for relief you thirsted,
Your feet were vastly better'd, though your slippers might be worsted.

But stay ; to tell you all we've got, a volume it would ask, Sir :
To tell you what we haven't got, would be a lighter task, Sir :
So come and see, and come and buy, you'll find, I promise you, Sir,
All you can possibly desire, at the Stall of LADY CREWE, Sir.

Aug 2   Bazaar Pic-Nic in Newton Hall Gardens - in aid of the Melbourne Church Restoration Fund of which the following is an account. [*No such account is included!*] £90 were realized [*sic*].

Aug 8   The rewards for assisting at the fire at Kings Hall [159] were distributed at the stables in the Hall yard. Seven of the most daring men received 7/6 each: 28 others 5/- 22 others 2/6 each. Altogether about £20 were distributed at the joint-expence (sic) of the Insurance Companies Robt Green Esqre. and Lady Palmerston.

Aug 8   Several contracts have been sent in for the Restoration of Melbourne Church. Mr Hall of Nottingham sent one amounting to nearly £1800 which was accepted by the Committee.

Sep 2   The Restoration of the Church commenced, and was marked by an untoward accident. One of the workmen, whilst examining the roof, fell from it to the ground and was taken up apparently lifeless [160].

---

159 sic. Briggs clearly meant to write "King's Newton Hall".

160 This must be the incident referred to in a letter to J. J. Briggs from his father, dated 9th September, 1859 (Derbyshire Record Office D4627/1/24): "...Mr. Hall of Nottingham is come over to do the Church he was at the top of the Leads doing something when the Ladder gave way and he fell down upon a heap of Bricks and Broke his Back Mr Tassar and Wass saw it done he now lies at the White Lion without a hope of Recovery Mr Tassar thought he could not live many days..." Briggs seems to suggest that the man was not Mr. Hall, who was the builder in charge, but one of his work men. "Mr. Tassar" must be Mr. Tasker, the Melbourne surgeon.

1859

The arches of the interior are now opened: the pews are pulled down and the floor taken up and the church presents a forlorn and dessolate [sic] appearance. Near the

west end a flagstone was found upon which was carved a fine Cross [161]. This flag had evidently covered a person of distinction. Curiosity led one individual to dig beneath the stone and he came to the remains of a skeleton: the bones were charred and black: the teeth and skull were well preserved the former being beautifully sound and white although the person to whom they belonged had been buried perhaps 400 years.

- *A drawing of the interior of the church during restoration, by a member of the Ilam Anastatic Drawing Society.*

Underneath the pews skulls and human bones were found in abundance: hundreds of persons had evidently been buried in the church. In a little brick vault in the middle aisle was a coffin about 2 feet from the surface. The individual had been buried about 60 years. Upon raising the lid of the coffin it was found that the flesh had fled from the bones but that the hair nearly as fresh as in life was retained upon the scalp. The body had been wrapt in the leaves of the bay tree : although dry the leaves retained their shape. All these remains and bones which have been found will be carefully gathered and interred the former in their original position in the church, the latter in the churchyard.

The man who fell from the Church, having lingered some time, was taken to Nottingham and having died there was buried this day.

Melbourne Church now presents a ruinous aspect filled as it is with scaffolds, planks, broken beams, rafters, mutilated boards and having the floor taken up and lying in heaps. The walls of the church, especially the nave and chancel seem to have been covered with rude paintings and monumental inscriptions. On one of the pillars in the nave near the west end was evedently [sic] an inscription to the Berresfords [sic] written on the ["bare"?] pillar. This was written over another which had been covered with whitewash.

Sep 17

Oct 4

Oct 5

161This is clearly the mediaeval stone slab, bearing a cross in relief, that is now in the vestry in the south transept. The Melbourne Parish Magazine of August, 1862 (DLS) says of it: "This Cross was found under the second arch from the West, on the North side of the Nave: the middle part of the stone was much worn by the long trampling of feet, and unfortunately was broken after being taken up; but the parts were joined together, and it is now set up against the wall in the south Transept." See also the diary entry for 2nd March 1860.

1859

On another pillar was represented a figure entering the cell of a monk the monk receiving him with open arms. Another fragment of painting on the same pillar shewed the figure of a female naked to the waist hanging by a cord: near to her was represented a man ["rudely"?] spitting in her face and about to beat her with a rod. The female's face had a sweet expression and was nicely executed. These drawings were executed in a kind of red paint in outline.

In the Chancel were found underneath the plaster, several inscriptions chiefly texts of Scripture in old English characters of a date probably near 1600. On the north side of the altar was written "Whether ye eate or drynke or whatever ye doe – doe all to ye glorie of God". On the south "He that eateth and drynketh unworthilie, eateth and drynketh damnation to himself, not consideringe ye Lord's bodie". Over the Chancel door "Take my yok upon ye for my yok is easie and my burden light". These texts were bordered with ornamental work painted blue and red.

The most remarkable painting found was one evedently [sic] of very early date and containing on a scroll a curious inscription. The following is a copy of the inscription.

IC EẾĞĴE LIADẶRBOL

It is the opinion of two eminent scholars Professor Bosworth "author of the Anglo Saxon Dictionary" and the Rev. Samuel Fox of Morley that this inscription is Latin, the word [sic] being considerably abbreviated. By supplying the letters dashed under they make the inscription to read thus:

HIC EST RELICTUS A DIABOL

"Here he is left by the Devil": or more liberally "Here the Devil leaveth him", having allusion to the Temptation of our Lord.

• *The surviving wall painting in the parish church, discovered in 1859. Its subject remains a matter of debate.*

[Printed insert from Volume I of <u>The Reliquary</u>, entitled " ON SOME WALL PAINTINGS DISCOVERED IN MELBOURNE CHURCH", by Rev. Joseph Deans, Vicar of Melbourne, with an additional note by "LL. J." i.e. Llewellynn Jewitt. It describes the discovery of two wall paintings in the church in 1842, painted one on top of the other, and also the discovery of the "devil" painting which still [2004] exists, found on the opposite pillar in 1859. Focusing on the "devil" painting, the article suggests interpretations both of the scene represented and the legend on the scroll. Jewitt expresses regret that careful drawings of the whole of the paintings discovered in the nave and chancel were not made "before they were covered up or destroyed".]

Several parties of Surveyors have been very actively engaged in surveying two lines of Railway from Derby to Nuneaton in Warwickshire. One line was projected to run into Melbourne near the new Cemetry [sic]: the other to have a station at the New Bridge for Melbourne.

Oct 20

1860

Jan 12　This night at 9' O clock p.m. the Hardinge vault in Melbourne Church was opened by the Committee for the Restoration of the Church. The scene was a gloomy and singular one. The little groups half light - half shade - standing about the tombs - the workmen pecking at the entrance – the few lights serving to make darkness visible and half revealing scattered planks, broken arches, mutilated pillars and the solemnity of the hour made the scene one not ordinarily met with and one which we shall not witness again. Night was chosen for the opening of the vault on account of the inspection being more private.

The vault contrary to expectation was remarkably small and rude and contained only three coffins. Two were placed on the floor of the vault and one on the top of them. With the coffins were two lead plates containing the following inscriptions:

Jno Hardinge Esqre died Jan 19 – 1728 in the fifty fourth year of his age. Miss Alice Hardinge died May 18th – 1758.

Over the vault are long Latin inscriptions [162] to Sir Robt Hardinge the Royalist: His wife Anne - Henrie Hardinge and others. Their coffins are not there. If ever they were buried they must have been buried in woollen as was the custom and buried without a vault: their dust having now mingled [163] the common dust.

Jan 25　The workmen have been obliged to take up the Hardinge slabs [164]. Underneath that of Sir Robert Hardinge Knt. was a skeleton (doubtless that of Sir Robert) without coffin the bones were hard and firm and the skull perfect, the teeth being sound and very white. The bones were carefully interred in another part of the Hardinge Transept.

• The Hardinge slabs in the south transept of the parish church, photographed by Edward Martin [died 1921].

---

162 This must refer to the inscriptions on the alabaster slabs, which are now upright against the wall.
163 sic. Presumably Briggs meant to write "mingled with".
164 The three alabaster slabs now stand against the east wall of the transept.

1860

At eleven O'clock today, died Mr William Briggs, of Bleak House, near Melbourne whch he purchased about 4 years ago, It was built by Mr Handcock. Mr Briggs was buried at Elvaston. Before he came to reside at Melbourne he lived at a farm at Thulston near Derby, under the Earl of Harrington. The Briggs's had long been landed occupiers at Thulston [165].

Feb 14

• *Bleak House, Robinson's Hill, was built on land allotted to Thomas Dugmore when Melbourne Common was enclosed [see diary entry for 1820]. The house is in an Italianate style and resembles the work of Henry Stevens of Derby.*

A terrific hurricane. The wind un-roofed ricks thatched buildings and houses and effected a vast amount of damage in this neighbourhood. Six trees were blown down in the park belonging to King's Newton Hall and numerous others in the neighbourhood. At Derby it blew a cwt of lead off a house and about [blank] feet off the top of St Alkmunds Church.

{ Feb 27
Feb 28

---

[165] John Joseph Briggs' own ancestors had also come from Thulston, so it seems likely that William Briggs and J. J. Briggs were related, and that Briggs would have known about the connection, even though he does not say so.

1860

Feb 29   A frightful death occurred in Melbourne. A boy employed by Mr Barrs of Derby Hills was bringing a horse down to Melbourne to be shod. It was a high mettled hunter. The boy to hold him more securely had wrapt [sic] the reins round his wrist. The horse took fright at something and off [166] dragging the boy over the fields, through hedge and ditch and kicking furiously. The poor lad's skull was kicked open and his body frightfully mangled. He died immediately.

- *Derby Hills House, designed by Benjamin Wilson for the Melbourne Estate, and built for their tenant Mr. Barrs in 1861. It had highly ornamented bargeboards and large finials, typical of the time.*

166 sic. Verb missing

1860

On the 27th last, the Church Restoration Committee agreed to enter into a contract with Mr Hall to restore the western end and build the towers.

Feb 29

As the workmen dig into the interior of the Church, underneath the floor, skulls, bones and bone-dust are mingled together in a decaying mass. The skulls are by hundreds. The stench arising from them and from the decaying bodies in vaults is almost unbearable and produces a peculiar sensation in the throat like hot pepper.

Mar 2

- *An unusual view of the parish church, probably in the 1880s, taken from what was once the farmyard of "Bewley Hall". The west door is seen through a gap in the farm buildings. The west end of the church was the only part that was significantly restored rather than repaired.*

1860

The workmen are now in the Chancel and it is found absolutely necessary to remove some of the coffins. It appears that many of the Cokes of Melbourne were buried there but there [167] no monuments to them, nor ever have been. To day the workmen came upon the their [sic] vault. The first coffin found was that of George Lewis Coke Esqre – a leaden one – of very peculiar shape, very pointed at the feet, and of foreign make and remarkably narrow. It was in a good state of preservation. It was placed there about 109 years ago.

This gentleman died beyond the seas whilst on travel and was brought to England. With him when he died was his valet, an individual of the name of Jaques – or one similar who probably accompanied his remains to England. This person was much esteemed by Mr George Lewis Coke and at his request assumed the names of Lewis after his master and the third name of Pasteur from the calling, which he afterwards pursued i.e. that of a shepherd: pastor being the Latin for shepherd. He settled at Bredon [sic] and kept numbers of sheep on the hills [168].

• *George Lewis Coke of Melbourne Hall (1715-1750) while on the "Grand Tour". A portrait by Pompeo Botoni, with the Coliseum in the background.*

---

167 sic. Verb missing. Briggs presumably meant to write "there are".
168 F. Taylor, in his History of Breedon-on-the-Hill: Church & Village (1906) notes that 33 houses in the parish had formerly owned the right to run three sheep and their lambs on the hill, which was a common. By the early 20th century most people had abandoned their rights to graze sheep there, so the hill has since become overgrown with scrub.

The next coffin found in the Coke vaults was that of Thomas Coke the Vicechamberlain to Queen Anne. It was externally of wood covered with purple velvet and ornamented at the edges with very large brass nails. Upon being opened all the velvet dropt [sic] off and left the nails bare. It bore upon the inscription plate a coat of arms and this inscription "The Right Honble Thomas Coke Esqre Vicechamberlain to his Majty and one of his Majtys [sic. *Quote ends here, apparently incomplete, with the inverted commas left unclosed. Briggs left space for the remainder of the inscription, but never filled it in.]* This coffin had been placed there about 133 years ago. On each side of the Vicechamberlain was a vault: that on the south side <u>empty</u>: in that on the north a child in a coffin of peculiar shape with the head lying westward: thus

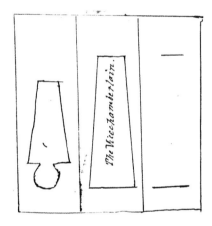

[Two short printed articles on Melbourne Church, both from Volume I of "The Reliquary". One is a note by "J.E." of Barrow, dated Feb 25th, 1861, suggesting that the scroll on the painting in the church was intended to say "HIC EST FELIA DEABOLI". The other, illustrated with a small engraving by Llewellynn Jewitt, concerns a monumental slab 6'6" x 2'1" with a floriated cross on it, discovered during the recent alterations at Melbourne.]

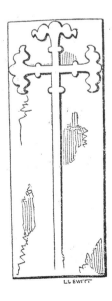

- *The floriated cross found in the parish church, engraved by Llewellynn Jewitt and published in Volume I of "The Reliquary". This copy of Jewitt's engraving is taken from the Melbourne Parish Magazine of August, 1862.*

1860

The most curious and interesting coffin found in the Church was a very ancient one: it was found in the middle aisle nearly under the lantern tower. It was of lead: the body it contained being that of a female. The lid of the coffin had mouldered away and exposed what once was the body: the skull was perfect, but the flesh had fallen away but the hair was as perfect – although it was false hair – as the day the body was put in the coffin. It flowed in long curls over the shoulder and I have no doubt when the corpse <u>was placed there nearly 258 years ago</u> I have little doubt [*sic, repeated use of "doubt"*] that it had been dressed as in life and the cheeks painted. There is little doubt, but that it was that of Isabelle Dawson the wife of William Dawson, and mother of Bryan Dawson, Herald Painter, of King's Newton: She died in 1602.

• *The early 17th century Dawson monument now in the south aisle of the church. Before the restoration of 1859-60, this monument was fixed to a pillar in the north arcade of the nave.*

Mar 5   The remains of the Rev. John Middleton which were found in the Chancel were taken away and interred carefully in the churchyard at 4, 0, clock, in the morning.

Mar 6   The remains of the Cokes were taken out of the chancel and carefully interred under the superintendence of Mr F. F. Fox, Lady Palmerston's Agent, in a new vault, in the churchyard at 4 ,0 clock in the morning.

Any other remains and bones which were unavoidably turned up were similarly interred.

Mar 24   An Organ for the Church ordered from Beavington of London: cost £320.

Mar 28   The sale of my work "The Trent and other Poems" published to aid the "Church Restoration Fund" has produced £50 which has been handed over to it.

One of the longest winters known. It has lasted about seven months. The fields are yet bare and the cattle are being foddered, Hay from £7 to £10 a ton. Some farmers are spending from £20 to £40 a week upon hay for their stock. There is scarcely a bit of hay to be had in this neighbourhood. The hedges are but just budding.

Mr Llewellynn Jewitt F.S.A. and myself examined the neighbourhood in order to find out whether any Roman Roads intersected it. After a minute examination we are [169] opinion that a road left Derventio (now Little Chester near Derby) ran by Osmaston, to the west of Chellaston, crossed the Trent by a ford near Swarkeston [sic] Church, (of the existence of whch I never knew until to day) (and not at the point where the present bridge stands) ran along a raised embankment over the Swarkeston meadows crossed the middle of Stanton over Melbourne Common and by St Brides (formerly a hostelry belonging to Calke Abbey [170] and now a farm occupied by Mr Asher). Here traces of it are very distinct, which are visible nearly to Calke.

On this road (as Sir Gardner Wilkinson observes in a communication to me) the size and form of the stones and their "general appearance might perhaps lead us to give them a Roman origin, particularly those large ones which have been found in great numbers in the fields about "St Brides" – The Road near St Brides appears originally to have been fashioned with care of stones (not found in the immediate locality) and raised rather slightly above the adjoining ground. This road continued its course by Derby Hills, where it is very distinct by Calke to Ashby.

One objection exists against this road being Roman – the Romans usually made their roads <u>straight</u> this is somewhat <u>irregular</u>: still it has a remarkably ancient look: bears the stamp of antiquity. The late Sir George Crewe Bart. who resided in the immediate locality considered this road to be Roman and that it crossed Calke Park. There is a tradition too that some years since when some alterations were made at Calke the remains of a Roman Bath were found.

Another road of Roman origin I believe ran from Verometum (now Willoughby on the Foss in Leicestershire) to Ad Trivonum (now Berry Farm, Braunston near Burton-on-Trent. [171] Starting from Verometum this road has been traced by Mr Potter the author of "Charnwood Forest" westward and in the direction of Ad Trivonum as far as Wymeswold Lane and again slightly at Zouch Mills, by Long Whatton & towards Bredon [sic]. This remarkable hill was evidently fortified by the Romans and visible traces of their encampment still remain. Here also Romano-British remains have been found: The road after leaving the camp of Bredon [sic] is lost for some distance until it is again visible on Melbourne Common and is now known as "Sir Henry (Harpur's) Lane[172] : continuing its course it intersects at right angles the road before described from Deventio [sic] to the station near Coventry. The two roads meet near Calke . The Verometum road then continued its course (although now cultivation

---

169 sic. Presumably Briggs meant to write "are of opinion" or "are of the opinion".
170 This must be a guess on Briggs' part, as no evidence has been found to substantiate it.
171 sic. Brackets not closed.
172 (Inverted commas not closed) Sir Henry's Lane was not laid out until the parish of Melbourne was enclosed in 1787-91. An earlier track in a similar spot cannot be ruled out, but Briggs appears to be "clutching at straws" to back up his claim for a Roman road from Breedon to Branston near Burton.

1860

has erased it) to Ad Trivonum near Burton on Trent.

To day the portion of the Cemetry [sic] belonging to the Established Church was consecrated by the Bishop of Litchfield [sic]. A large number congregated to witness the ceremony. At half past two O'clock the Bishop arrived at the Lodge, situated at the entrance of the grounds, where he was received by a number of the neighbouring clergy. Service was performed in the Cemetry Chapel by the Rev. Joseph Deans after which the Bishop and clergy peramulated [sic] the grounds and the deed of consecration was signed. After the ceremony was over the Wesleyans school children arrived on the ground attended by their teachers and sung the old 100th psalm upon the portion of the cemetery devoted to Nonconformists. This little act was intended to constitute an opening to their ground.

June 3   The first body interred in the Cemetry: that of John Taft who died at King's Newton.

Aug   Mrs Newbold widow of the late Mr John Newbold was buried in the old church yard: permission having been obtained from the Secretary of State for the purpose.

Aug 12   Very late - cold - wet summer. Thousands of acres of hay spoiled. At this time last year many persons had finished harvest – now it is still quite green. It will be about six weeks later than usual.

Aug 13   "The Reliquary" a new quarterly journal published by the Messrs Bemrose of Derby contains an account of King's Newton and the hall – the Hardinge family &c also sketches of the figures on the headstone of Newton Cross – a sketch of the ruins of Newton Hall – also a curious cross found in Melbourne Church.

          [Printed insert from "The Reliquary", Volume I, entitled "MEMORIALS OF KING'S NEWTON VILLAGE AND ITS OLD HALL" by J. J. Briggs. The article talks of the fire at the Hall; authors who lived in the village both in the past and at the present time; discovery of the mediaeval cross head in a well; the Hardinge family and the Hall. Illustrations include views of the Hall before and after the fire, the Holy Well and the four faces of the cross head.]

          [Newspaper article, no provenance or date, about objections to High Church practices at St. George's in the East, London, resulting in the departure of the Rev. S. Hansard – cf Briggs' diary entry for Oct 24, 1860.]

Sep 1   Very wet summer: The wettest since the summer of 1816. Hay – harvest not finished: the hay being black and worthless. It has already been about nearly 10 weeks. Corn just beginning to be cut: it is about seven weeks later than last year. With the exception of about one week at the end of June, rain has fallen nearly every day since the middle of April. Fruit is unusually backward and very small. Potatoes are affected with the disease. Mangold wurzel very backward about one sixth of the usual size at this period of the year.

In accordance with the wishes of the Vicar and Curate a meeting of the Committee for the Restoration of the Church took place at the Athenaeum Room, Melbourne. As many clergymen upon the Restoration of their churches have introduced new and strange High Church forms and ceremonies into their churches, the Vicar drew together the leading members of his congregation in order to assure them that such would not be introduced into his church. He agreed:

1st   That no candles should ever be placed upon the communion table.
2nd   That the choir should never be clad in surplices.
3rd   That the clergyman should always preach in a black gown.
4th   That the services should not be intoned.

The parish church of St Michael, Melbourne was opened for Divine Service. Like all the other days fixed for the objects connected with the Restoration of this church, the weather was surpassingly beautiful : indeed Nov 3rd was the brightest which we have had this year. About 700, chiefly the nobility gentry and clergy attended divine service. The order of service was contained in the accompanying pamplet. The following is the account from the local papers -

THE ORDER FOR

Morning and Evening Prayer

TO BE USED AT THE

RE-OPENING SERVICES
OF

S. Michael's Church, Melbourne.

SATURDAY, NOVEMBER 3, 1860,
And the Seven Days next following.

Collections will be made in aid of the Church Restoration Fund on Saturday, Nov. 3, and Sunday, Nov. 4.
About £2,400 has been subscribed for the Restoration, but there still remains a large sum to be raised for works not included in the original estimate.

[Small engraving of west door of the church as restored, as used in the order of services for the reopening of the church, see below.]

[Newspaper cutting stating that Melbourne Church will reopen next Saturday, 3rd November. No provenance or date.]

[Another newspaper cutting, untitled, undated and unprovenanced, describing the proceedings of Saturday and Sunday 3rd and 4th November, in connection with the reopening of the Church.]

[An insert, being "The Order for Morning and Evening Prayer to be used at the re-opening services of S. Michael's Church, Melbourne, Saturday, November 3, 1860 and the seven days following". The leaflet notes that "About £2,400 has been subscribed for the Restoration, but there still remains a large sum to be raised for works not included in the original estimate". Morning prayer at 11am on November 3rd was to include the ministration of public baptism after the second lesson, and the newspaper account of the proceedings reveals that this comprised the baptism of Mr. and Mrs. Tasker's infant son. The service was also to include the administration of Holy Communion. "Those persons who do not intend to receive the Holy Communion are requested not to leave the Church until after the Prayer for CHRIST'S Church militant."]

1860

• *The Grange, Chapel Street, Melbourne, in an early photograph believed to date from c1874. This Georgian house with Victorian additions was the home of Mr. Tasker the surgeon, whose infant son was baptised during the reopening service of the parish church. The people in the photograph are no doubt members of the Tasker family.*

Nov 12   Since the Restoration of the Church it has been well attended. Between six and seven hundred [sic!] usually attend the evening service.

Nov 29   Corn harvest just finished in the parish. Hay and corn harvests have lasted 16 weeks : they are the latest since 1816.

Dec 1   Within the last year or eighteen months a custom has prevailed of wearing a beard or mustache [sic] or both. Some years ago an individual with a beard was a very remarkable person as contrasted with the barely-shaved faces which were everywhere to be met with : but now the habit of shaving the face is fast dying away and the day may come when a razor may be shewn as [173] household curiosity and the office of the Barber become obsolete [174] [sic].

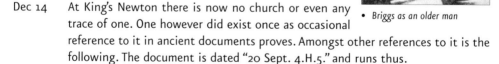

• *Briggs as an older man*

Dec 14   At King's Newton there is now no church or even any trace of one. One however did exist once as occasional reference to it in ancient documents proves. Amongst other references to it is the following. The document is dated "20 Sept. 4.H.5." and runs thus.

"Will. Chilcots p'sona ecclesiæ de King's Newton et alii confirmant Joh. Cockayne de Ashbourne militi, filio Elizabethæ, que fuit uxor Edmundi Cockayne ac filia et hæres Ricd de Herthull militis et Margaretæ <u>uxori</u> (not <u>uroris</u>) ejus." (Archaeological Journal Vol 7. page 381)

This church at Newton certainly existed about 123 years i.e from the 22nd [i.e. year of] Edward 1st about 1294 to 4th year of Henry 5th about 1417 as is proved by the foregoing and other ancient records. The only two priests which I can find as having officiated there are William Birley & William Chilcots.

---

173 sic. Presumably Briggs meant to write "as a"
174 Briggs himself sported a beard, at least in his later years!

In the possession of the Officiating Minister at Swarkeston [sic] for the time being is a very old parchment book much worn by time which contains several curious entries. Thomas Bancroft the "Small Poet" was born at Swarkeston in whose church his parents were buried but of whom there is no memorial. In the parchment deed before referred to are several entries to the family of Bancroft amongst which are the following.

Dec 15

- Bancroft was buried the 28th day of – 1699.
Mary Bancroft was buried 6th of April 1700.
James Bancroft and son to Thos Bancroft bapt. April 26 - 1708.
" - Bancroft daug. of Thos Bancroft was born 21st Nov. baptized Dec 20, 1712.
"The Right Honble the Countess Bellamont was buried 4th day of June 1714. [175]
"William Cantrell was byred 10th day of Nov. 1678 and affidavit within the time appointed by the act was brought to sygnify the corps was not byred in any shirt, shift, or shroud made or mingled with flax, hemp, silk, gold or silver or other then what is made of sheeps wool only, nor in any coffin lined or furrd with other material than sheeps wool only."

Snow ankle-deep : the first this season.

Dec 19

The Guizers came.

Christmas Eve

Within my memory companies of plough bullocks and morrice [sic]-dancers used to come: the former had a plough with them. They were dressed in ribbons and ornaments and used to go begging from door to door. The morris[sic]-dancers were the most attractive and the whole village turned out to see them. They were all men. One was decked as a harlequin or fool in a dress covered with shreds and ribbons of scarlet, blue, yellow & all showy colours. The others were dressed as men and women very gaily and they used to dance at peoples doors and afterwards ask for money. They have now ceased coming.

A Christmas Day as of the olden time. Intensely cold. Thermometer stands at 3. Ground covered with snow: trees thickly incrusted [sic] with hoar frost. Last night, thousands of birds perished.

Christmas Day

The "Derby Mercury" of to day says "The current year will be remarkable for many meteorological events and ends with a frost greater than has ever been recorded in this county since regular observations have been taken. On Sunday the 23rd the thermometer fell to 18° and on Xmas Eve it went down to 2°, or 30° lower than the freezing point: on the 25th at 10 O'clock a.m. it stood at 4°. The lowest point reached by the thermometer during the last 20 years was on Jan 3rd 1854 when it fell to 4°, still 2 degrees higher than the 24th last."

Dec 26

The milk in dairies was frozen into a solid block of ice:- meat froze on the kitchen table :- in one instance which I saw a cloth put to dry before a good fire to dry froze on the side which was from the fire:- dung froze close behind horses in the stable and certainly the cold was more intensive than it ever was within my memory. It seemed impossible even with the assistance of capital fires to keep the body even tolerably warm.

---

175 sic. The inverted commas to this entry and the preceding one are not closed.

1860/1861

Dec 28   Frost still very severe. I saw some horses at work and the cold had condensed their breath which hung in ice-icles [sic] from beneath their chins as long and thick as mens fingers. Eggs freeze even when covered closely up : potatoes freeze a few yards from a fire :– the milk is a block – beef is hard - and to add to the discomfort of a house the cold up chimneys is so intense that the smoke from fires is impeded and fills the rooms with smoke. Were it not that great expence [sic] is had recourse to in providing artificial food for stock upon farms a vast number must perish. Food however is neither so scarce nor so dear as was anticipated for people expecting a hard winter provided for it in time in the best way they could.

1861

Jan 1   During the night, a rapid thaw took place : meadows upon which yesterday men and horses were carting soil, on ground hard as a pavement are now a yard deep in water. Very high floods on the brook and Trent.

Jan 2   Frost again.

• *High Street, Melbourne, c1900. John Earp's shop was the one on the right.*

1861

Jan 4

Mr John Earp, High Street better known by the name of "Earp: the Grocer" died. He was a very thoughtful, painstaking, man in all matters of buisiness [sic] and rendered important services not only to many private individuals, but to the town of Melbourne. The public were not unmindful of his services and on Jan 26th 1848 presented him with a service of plate : value £50"0"0 an account of which will be seen at page 38 of this volume [i.e. entry for 26/1/48]. His legal knowledge was extensive and was often of great service to his neighbours who consulted him when placed in positions of difficulty. As one of the men of mark in Melbourne his loss will be much felt.

Jan 5

In a work like this pleasing traits of character ought to be recorded of those who from their exalted position command our attention. There is a fact which I wish to chronicle respecting the last Lord Melbourne – not William, usually called the great Lord – but his brother who was Ambassador at Vienna and eventually succeeded to the title and estates. In 1850, the times bore hard upon the farmer – corn was low – stock was low. indeed the present and future both looked gloomy. The tenants upon the Melbourne estate, in a very temperate, sensible, and convincing document addressed his Lordship upon the subject and the following was his answer: a letter, so kindly, so considerately and so feelingly worded that it deserves a permanent niche in my Melbourne Annals and I hope will long remain there an humble tribute to his honor.

"Gentlemen. "It is with much regret I learn from your letter of the 11th instant (Feb 11 1860) [176] that the circumstances of the times have materially affected your circumstances and prospects, a regret which is only tempered by the assurance it conveys of your determination to meet the difficulties of your situation by your own exertions.

Feeling as I do that our interests are inseperably united, I need hardly assure you that the assistance you require from me, shall as far as lies in my power be given to you. The nature and extent of it requires consideration and the late division in the House of Commons gives an expectation that the interests of Agriculture be henceforth so overlooked as they were during the legislation from which all these difficulties have arisen [177]. This consideration joined to the uncertainty which exists as to the scale of prices which may be permanently reckoned upon, render any final settlement between us inexpedient for the moment but before the next Rent Day comes I will determine after consideration with Mr Fox what amount of relief may benefit you and what it may be in my power to accord. In the meantime he has already received orders to comply with your request as to the period of the Rent Days. I am obliged to you for having made this application early enough to give time for its full consideration and I take the opportunity of assuring you that under all circumstances you will always find me disposed to co-operate with you for the advancement of your interests which I consider identical with my own." I have the honor [sic] &c.

176 sic. The correct year must be 1850, as the previous part of the journal entry suggests. The 3rd and last Lord Melbourne died in 1853.

177 sic. This sentence seems to require the word "not" in it somewhere, to make sense.

1861

In accordance with the spirit of this letter a reduction of 10 per cent. was made and a very beneficial change in the date of rent days made. In <u>Spring</u> to be payable the 2nd Monday in June In <u>Autumn</u> do *[i.e. "ditto"]* the <u>3rd</u> Monday in December.

• *Weston Church, from a Victorian stereoscope slide.*

Jan 5   Lying close to the exterior of Weston Church, in the Church-yard is an old moss-covered stone, whereon are inscribed letters of the alphabet. From early years this stone has always been pointed out to me as covering the remains of those soldiers who fell during the Parliamentarian Wars in an attack on Kings Mills. This may be [178] case - probably is (for tradition is often correct) but the letters on the stone certainly afford no clue to solving the question. With much trouble I have made them out as follows.

REMEMBER ALSO WELL TO LIVE
    THEN YOU'L THE BETTER DIE

AND HAVE THE BEST ACCOUNT TO GIVE
    AT THE GREAT JUDGMENT DAY.

Jan 5   The Verger of Melbourne Church when collecting for a new wig comes round with a paper with the following rather droll heading "John Bartram (Verger of the Church) has been bald from his infancy and has no means of providing himself with a new wig, the old one being worn out : the cost he says is 35s/-." The Verger's pate seemed likely to be thatched anew for he had collected a considerable sum towards the expence *[sic]*.

Jan 6   During the last Autumn a Government Commission has been visiting the chief rivers of England and Wales for the purpose of making enquiries into the state of the Salmon Fisheries with a view to their improvement. During the last week in Dec 1860 the Commission sat at Burton-on-Trent.

---

178 sic. Presumably Briggs meant to write "may be the case"

No very important information was elicited : but it may be well to chronicle the following remarks as more particularly applicable to our locality. It appears that King's Mills is about 50 miles from the source of the Trent and about 135 from Spurn Head at the mouth of the Humber. King's Mills is the fishering [sic] at which the Marquis of Hastings takes Salmon. That fish was formerly most abundant there but seems gradually to have decreased and yearly becomes more scarce. Mr Thomas Bradley, gamekeeper for the Hastings, stated from 1840 to 1860, during the first ten years the take was 845 : the last ten years 355 and for the last few years very few indeed. The season commenced on Nov. 12 and closed on Aug. 12 : fishing rarely commenced before February. The best month was April. The Marquis had exclusive right of using traps on the river from the point where his traps were fixed (King's Mills) to the tidal waters. The Marquis had a right to examine any wears [sic] situated between King's Mills and the Humber in order to see that no obstacles existed to impede the ascent of the Salmon. There were more than 20 Salmon nets used below the Marquis [i.e. his stretch of river, presumably] but these could not be used at night.

Jan 6

Trent still frozen over. The Trent freezes over in a somewhat remarkable way and different from most other rivers. Upon the appearance of very severe weather small masses of ice begin to form in the upper part of the river (it is said in the bed of the river) : these floating down amalgamate with other masses and eventually lodge in the stiller parts of the river. In these part [sic] they gradually [sic] collect and the frost congeals them together and thus a rough surface of ice is formed. The formation of this "ground ice" has long been a sore puzzle to the investigator into natural phenomena. Many theories have been propounded but we doubt whether the true one has yet been arrived at : we subjoin a few accounts from various sources. The Thames freezes over in the same way as the Trent. The following remarks are from the "Illustrated London News" Feb 24, 1855.

[Newspaper cutting entitled "THE FROST. – THE THAMES AT BILLINGSGATE" , explaining the theory that the ice on the frozen river forms on the bed of the river, and can be seen to incorporate material from the river bed.]

From "Illustrated News" [Newspaper cutting entitled "GROUND ICE", being the term given by Germans to the ice sometimes found at the bottom of rivers.]

From the "Field" Sep. 8. 1860. [Article entitled "THE FORMATION OF GROUND OR "ANCHOR" ICE" by C. F. Walsh, in response to John Joseph Briggs' request for an explanation of the phenomenon.]

Mr John Earp "The Grocer" buried in the New Cemetry [sic]. He was in his 70th year. Much respect was paid to him by the principal inhabitants of the parish who assembled at the Athenaeum Room and accompanied the corpse to the grave. About 100 were present. An address was delivered in the Cemetry Chapel by the Rev T. Gill, Baptist Minister [179], in which he gave some biographical details of the deceased.

Jan 9

179 i.e. the Rev. Thomas Gill, the popular minister of Melbourne Baptist Church 1847-1861
    (Melbourne Baptists by Rev. T. J. Budge, 1951, pp 37-40).

1861

Jan 9   The Trent now presents an extraordinary appearance : being completely frozen up from King's Mills to Swarkeston [sic]. It is about 15 inches thick. A bon-fire was made upon the Trent at Swarkeston. People pass and re-pass upon the ice at Weston constantly. Owing to the meadows being overflowed previous to the frost and now iced over a person can go upon the ice from the Marsh Gate to Weston Cliff which I never saw before.

Jan 20   The frost has now nearly broken up. Its severity has been intense. At Weston Cliff large masses of ice are visible and piled up as it is here and there six or seven sheets high has [180] a thoroughly Arctic appearance. The severe weather has killed the laurel and lauristinus plants. Larks, pipets and buntings entirely disappeared. Numbers of Rooks, blackbirds and thrushes have died. Grouse have been driven from the moors into towns and villages. Near Swarkeston Bridge a salmon was found embedded in the ice, 17 lbs in weight. The greatest amount of distress prevails.

A new disease called "Diptheria" [sic] is very rife. At the village of Milton, near Repton, a family named Somers lost four children of it. Numbers of hares and rabbits perished or have been picked up exhausted. In Chatsworth Park deer died from sheer starvation. The trees there have been a good deal damaged by being barked by deer, hares, and rabbits. If the game had not been well attended to it would have become extinct.

Jan 26   The severe weather is over : fine genial weather prevails : the Thermometer stands 86 degrees higher than on Christmas Day. The great variation in the weather has caused disease to be very rife : many too, have died from actual starvation. Being at Burton-upon-Trent today I saw the effects of a singular accident. The Bridge over the Trent is very old and very narrow. A boy in a cart was passing another cart and got too near the side of the Bridge, when the wheel touched it. Being tender with the late severe frost several yards of the bridge gave way and into the river went cart, horse and boy. The boy and cart were got out, the former alive but the horse was drowned.

• The old bridge at Burton.

---

180 sic. Presumably Briggs meant to write "and has"

170

1861

It appears that the harvest of 1860 is the most deficient gathered in for the last 25 years. The grain is wanting in bulk and weight and the total loss is not less than 4,000,000 quarters. In this district the yield of barley has been has been [*sic, repeated words*] from 2 $^1/_2$ quarters to 3 qrs less than usual : wheat from 1 $^1/_2$ to 2 qrs.

A man named John Shaw was found dead in a hovel near Wilson situated on some land formerly occupied by James Dolman Esqre. It appears that deceased had been suffering mentally and physically and expressed his intention of putting an end to his existence. He went from home on Saturday last and for many days was not heard of. To day search was made and thinking that he had drowned himself Melbourne Pool was dragged without effect. At last he was found accidentally we believe by some boys, whose attention was arrested by seeing a hat in a loft above the barn. They climbed up to it and to their astonishment found deceased standing on his legs in the rigidity of death, having round his neck a rope by which he had hung himself. The fright of the boys may be well imagined. He had been dead about 3 days and what was somewhat remarkable several children had been playing in the hovel for some time without discovering him.

The foundation stone of Mr John Hemsley's new factory laid at Melbourne [181]. The work-people presented him with a silver trowel on a velvet cushion [182]. There was also a procession and music. Many people considered it an un-necessary and foolish affair and some wags issued humorous [*sic*] squibs about it in the town : and sent 5 fools' caps to the New Inn to be presented to the 5 principal actors in the scene.

• *John Hemsley's enormous new factory was less than thirty years old when it was destroyed by fire in 1890.*

181 This factory was on Derby Road, where Budgen's Supermarket now stands. It was designed by Benjamin Wilson as "a building in which ornamentation will be combined with utility." The architect and contractors took part in the procession. After Mr. Hemsley laid the stone, the doxology was sung and the proceedings finished with a dinner at the New Inn (<u>Derby Mercury</u>, February 27th, 1861). The factory burnt down in 1890, although its remains remained visible for many years afterwards. The last fragment was only pulled down when Budgen's was built in the 1990s.
182 This trowel came to light again in 2003, when it was sold at auction by Neale's Auctioneers in Nottingham.

1861

Mar 2   Nathaniel Warren was recently buried in the Cemetry [sic] at Melbourne. For more than 30 years he was landlord of the Old Ship Tavern, Pelham Street, Nottingham. He died rather suddenly. He was a native of Melbourne where his mother is still living. He went to reside at Nottingham when quite a youth and was some time tap-lad at the Postern Gate, Middle Pavement then kept by Mr Johnson. During Nat's tenantcy [sic] the Ship tavern acquired a more than local popularity. Years ago his little bar parlour was often visited by "poor authors" a fact of which he was very proud. The Ship, the captain and his tap are laudably mentioned in "Gideon Giles" a novel written by Thomas Miller, the Nottingham basket maker, to whom Nat had shown many acts of kindness.

The deceased himself was a man of literary tastes and for many years he possessed an extensive library, containing numerous standard works on theology, history &c most of which, however, he disposed of about three years ago. Increasing age and failing health induced him a few weeks ago to decide upon retiring from his house of buisness [sic] with which his name had been so long associated and spending the remainder of his days in his native place (Melbourne.) Although arrangements had been made for that purpose he did not live to carry them out. He was 67 years of age and had been twice married. A son and two daughters, the issue of his first marriage and his second wife survive.

Mar 4   Bredon[sic]-on-the Hill Dr Hook has recently published a work [183] "Lives of the Archbishops of Canterbury." The "Critic" when reviewing it remarks "as a chapter on social progress and the cultivation of the arts, as far as then known, we may refer to the state of learning under Tatwine who was consecrated in 731, and who before that event left Canterbury, at that time the Athens of England and retired from all literary society to a remote monastery of Breodone (Bredon). It is believed that he there became the instructor of youth the master of the schools and carried on the system of education adopted already at St Augustine's college under the patronage of Theodorus."

Mar 6   "Old Thomas Taft" as he was usually called of King's Newton died at Newton in his 93 year being the 8th old person who has died in the village within 12 months. It is supposed he was the oldest man in the parish of Melbourne at the time of his death. He could remember the time when the roads in Melbourne parish were knee deep in mud – so deep as to be almost impassable, and on one occasion the carriage of a neighbouring squire stuck fast between Melbourne and Stanton and had to be drawn out by a team of wagon horses from Newton. He could remember the first stage coach being started – the country before it was enclosed - when the parish was undrained and only partly cultivated and only a few sheep kept where now there are hundreds and one quarter of corn grown where now there are four, and when the produce of the parish was carried to Derby market in sacks upon the backs of pack horses.

---

183 Altered from "Dr. Hook in his recently-published work on "Lives of the Archbishops of Canterbury" remarks: "...."

• *The "Hardinge Arms", King's Newton, formerly a farmhouse and later the wheelwright's premises of the Taft family.*

One of those distressing circumstances which occasionally occur to break the **April 8** peaceful quietude of a village took place at King's Newton this morning. Mrs Crampton the wife of a labourer of that name, being within a day or two of her confinement of a child, drowned herself. She lodged at Mrs Ward's house in the Hollow [184]. About 4, 0, clock this morning she got out of bed and with no clothes upon her (save a small flannel round the waist) no bonnet, stockings or shoes, went to a small field of Mrs Wards in Wards Lane and drowned herself in a small pool at the end of it: There was very little water in it and when found the body was in the water and the bare feet and ankles sticking out. The Husband of the woman found her himself, who communicated it to two neighbours who brought her to the Pack Horse Inn to await the verdict of the Coroner's jury. It is supposed that her death arose from temporary insanity.

• *Mrs. Ward's house, demolished in 1863, on Ward's Lane near the Holy Well.*

---

184 This was an old thatched cottage of stone and brick where the Ward family had lived since at least the 1770s, hence "Wards Lane", the alternative name for Holywell Lane. Mrs. Ann Ward gave up the tenancy in 1861, and the new tenant was William Hemsley. He had no need for the cottage, which was demolished during October and November, 1863 (Melbourne Hall Estate Accounts; MHMR Parish Surveys 1790 and 1840).

1861

April 8   A Census taken. The Rev. Gervase Wasse preached a Sermon upon the subject in the Church.

> "Pack Horses – In ancient times, merchandise of various kinds was conveyed upon the backs of pack horses – The first horse had round his neck a ring of bells, so that, at night, they might indicate the course which he was taking. The author of these notes, has one in his possession which was used between Derby and Leicester. It is about 200 years old, is made of stout leather and has seven bells, round in shape and each having a pea of metal in the inside to produce the sound"
> J. J. Briggs, written in a "Grangerised" copy of Glover's History of Derbyshire (1831-3) after page 218 (DLS). King's Newton's pubs once included a "Ring of Bells" on Main Street as well as the surviving "Pack Horse".

• The Packhorse Inn, c1952.

April 9   An Inquest held at the Pack Horse Inn Kings Newton on the body of Mary Anne Crampton. It appeared in evidence that she was about 8 months gone in pregnancy and that for some time she had been nervous and depressed in spirit partly perhaps brought on by her situation and partly by the anxiety of removing to another situation. Her husband and she lived upon good terms and they had had no quarrel.

On the night of the 6th she went to Melbourne, bought a pair of slippers and brought home some baby-linnen [sic], went to bed – rose a time or two in the night and at last went down stairs, apparently to the privy came again into the house and sat down – Her husband who was in bed called to her to go up stairs but she said she was not coming. He went to sleep she then must have left the house having on no shoes, but a pair of stockings, flannel jacket and shawl. She went to the pool, put off her shawl and threw herself in. Her husband found her first. She was a pretty, well-behaved young woman, much respected by all who knew her and her sad fate has caused a great sensation in the parish.

[A marginal note alongside this entry says: Verdict : "temporary insanity".]

- *Wards Lane was an alternative route from Kings Newton to Swarkestone Bridge, and is still a public bridleway. It emerges at Stanton by Hollow Farm, seen here in a postcard by Edward Martin [died 1921].*

At the request of the Rate-payers of Melbourne, expressed at a public meeting held in the Athenaeum Room a Committee of gentlemen was appointed to examine the Parish Chest and see if any of the papers which it contained were of importance and to take a list of them and report upon their character. This was done to day the following members of the Committee being present ([185] Richard T. Tasker Esqre, Mr King (Churchwarden) Mr Thomas Hollins and Mr John Joseph Briggs (myself). We found nothing of importance and nothing very curious. The following is a List of the Books and papers contained in the Chest.

April 9

4to Parchment-covered book entitled "Certificates received : Examinations taken"

Packet of Documents related to an enquiry instituted in the year 1834 concerning an alteration illegally made in the Enclosure Award by some person or persons unknown.

Many Packets of Certificates of settlements – Orders of Removal – Indentures of Apprenticeship and Documents and Orders in Bastardy Cases.

Parish Papers for the years 1841-2-3-4.

A Copy of the Commissioners valuation made upon the Melbourne Enclosure of all the properties in the Parish of Melbourne, except those which were and are the properties of the Earl of Moira. 4to. From this Book it would appear that in many instances (since the Enclosure) agricultural land has more than doubled in value and garden land increased to 4-5-6- and 7 times its value at that time.

A Certificate of the Redemption of Tithe.

Blank Book entitled "Register of Freeholders"

A Book containing a Register of Apprentices in the 42nd year of George 3rd

---

185 these brackets are not closed

1861

An account of the Expences [sic] incurred in the case of William Taylor the Constable [186].

The accounts of James Moss, Overseer from 1809 to 1814. 4to Book.

Folio Book Do from 1814 to 1818.
Do – Do - Do from 1809 to 1814.
Do – Do – Do from 1805 to 1809.
4to Book of Assessments for 1828.

Amongst the papers was nothing important. There was one item however which that [187] the custom of having a demonstration on the 5th November was much encouraged formerly as it discouraged now [188]. In 1777 there was the sum of £1"9"1 allowed to purchase gunpowder with.

It also appears that the cost of prosecuting some men who killed William Taylor, the Constable in a scuffle was £130"12"8.

Amongst the payments in the year 1809 are "Three hedgehogs 1^{S}/-" "Paid for sparrow [singular, sic] 3/2" 1808 "By one years Greens Charity due from Lord Melbourne £2"0"0" : "By half years Rent of Grays Charity land due March 1808 £3"10"0.

- *Exchange House, Potter Street, 1992. A previous house on this site was the home of Henry Green, shoemaker, who founded one of the Melbourne charities in 1679. Another charity was set up twelve years later by the will of Mr. Gray, so the charities were neatly known as "Grays and Greens"! It is fitting that the current secretary of the charities lives on the site of Mr. Green's house.*

---

186 William Taylor of Blanch Croft was one of the Melbourne parish constables. He was attacked and fatally wounded in a savage brawl at the Roebuck in May 1828 and died the next morning. His attackers, Ince and Cartwright, were locked up in the Melbourne roundhouse where no. 38 Potter Street now stands. They were transported to Australia and were never seen in Melbourne again. William Taylor is buried in the Baptist graveyard.
187 sic. Briggs presumably meant to write "which shews that"
188 sic. Briggs presumably meant to write "was as much encouraged formerly as it is discouraged now."

1861

At a Parish Meeting in the Athenaeum Room the Overseers of the Poor and Church-wardens were requested to enquire into the property connected with "Grays Charity" [189].

April 11

A very singular circumstance took place in connection with the recent death of Mary Anne Crampton. To say the least, it was a remarkable coincidence : a believer in spiritualism might consider it of importance. On the morning of April 8th, about the same time as the unfortunate woman committed the act of self-destruction, her brother was in bed at Melbourne with his wife - He was suddenly seized with an indescribable feeling = a kind of restlessness and feeling of frenzy as he himself expressed it "he felt like a madman" - He continued in this excited state about 2 hours when he was as well as before. He had had no intimation of the occurrence : indeed her death and his being seized in that extraordinary way occurred about the same time.

April 11

The effect of last winter's extraordinarily severe frost is now strikingly visible on plants and trees. Thousands of rose-trees have perished. The lauristinus, jasmine, pirus japonica's [sic] are killed. The ivy and privet are long in recovering. The Deodara and Aurocaria pines are much damaged generally : many are past recovery.

May 2

A circumstance is causing much excitement in the parish of Melbourne. Mr John Campion about 15 years ago was appointed Rate Collector for the parish under the Seal of the Board of Poor Law Commissioners in London. In course of time he received another appointment in addition to the first viz: that of Assistant Overseer. He has discharged the duties of both offices to the satisfaction of the Auditor, the Clerk of the Shardlow Board of Guardians and a large portion of the rate-payers of Melbourne.

May 6

A certain portion of the smaller rate-payers from some personal feeling called a Vestry Meeting and voted him out of his office by the number of 75 to 15 votes. Many of the Ratepayers thought this proceeding unjust and got up a Memorial to the Shardlow Board of Guardians in his favour.* [marginal note reads: " * signed by 160 persons paying more than half of the poor rate of the parish of Melbourne"] It was sent this day (May 6th) the resolutions passed at the Parish Meeting having been sent previously. The Shardlow Board considered the case: a point of law arose as to whether having been appointed Rate Collector by the Commissioners in London the second appointment was not of necessity engrafted upon it and subject to the same law and controul [sic] : which being the case the power to recind [sic] Mr Campion's appointment was taken out of the hands of the Melbourne Vestry and vested in the hands of the London Board of Commissioners.

---

189 The "Grays, Greens and Adcocks" Charities still survive, now all rolled into one. A small sum of money for the poor is available for distribution each year, but in the absence of any individual cases of hardship the money is generally given to an organisation that does good work in the community. The inquiry referred to by Briggs probably related to the alleged misuse of the charity funds by the trustees. See footnote to diary entry dated 23/3/1857.

1861

• *A view of the back of John Campion's house, 49, Derby Road, Melbourne, probably photographed in 1874. The title deeds show that Campion owned the house from 1867-75 and occupied it himself.*

When the Melbourne Memorial was presented at the Shardlow Board they considered the case and the opinion of the Board was taken when that opinion was found to be in favour of retaining Mr Campion without one dissenting voice. Upon referring to the books of the Board however Mr Campion's appointment could not be found registered in them and consequently they declined to interfere in the matter. The people of Melbourne thereupon considered it within their province to turn him out of his office and in accordance with that opinion, called a Vestry Meeting in the Athenaeum Room on May 16th in order to recind [sic] his appointment. The Vestry recinded his appointment and ordered him to deliver up his books. He refused to do so on two grounds:

1st Because he considered that the Vestry had not the power to cancel his appointment, the power being in the hands of the London Board of Poor-Law Commissioners.

2ndly. Because the books were necessary in order to properly perform the duties of his first appointment.

June 17 Mr Orton sold the property (which he purchased in 1848 of Mr Archer of Ashbourne) to day at the New Inn Melbourne. It has all risen in value since he purchased it 12 years ago. It was bought for £100 per acre. The prices attached to the various lots will shew the increase in value.

The House in Newton , Malt Office stable
&c orchard, garden 1 acre 0 roods 32 perches
For this lot there was bid   £600"0"0

Seven cottages and gardens, part freehold and part copyhold 1^a 0^r 11^p
No bid at the sale

The Chantry Close 8 acres 1 rood 27 perches per acre	£120"0"0
The Near Cross Flat 3 acres 0 roods 16 p	£130"0"0
The Far Cross Flat 2 do 3 do 15 do	£127:0:0
The Hill Close 2 do 1 do 10 do	£146:0:0
The Smithy Green 4 do 2 do 17 do	£127:0:0

July 2

A Comet, very brilliant, has made its appearance in the heavens. It is visible about 12' O clock on most nights. The nucleus is larger and more brilliant than "Donate's Comet" the tail particularly beautiful. The tail nearly reached the Poll [sic] Star. It was quite unexpected by astronomers.

[Cutting from the Derby Reporter, being a letter from "Investigator" of Shardlow dated July 10th 1861, about the Trent Navigation. The writer notes that "the Trent from Cavendish Bridge to Gainsborough belongs to an incorporated company, and is kept open and in an excellent state for navigable purposes for barges of 40 to 50 tons burthen, upon which an extensive trade is conducted".

From Burton on Trent to Cavendish Bridge the river is the private property of the Marquis of Anglesey, having been granted to Lord Paget by Acts of Parliament in 1698 and 1780. It has been useless for navigable purposes since the death of the late Mr. Lloyd, banker, of Birmingham, in 1855 or 1856. Mr. Lloyd was the lessee of the river from Burton to Cavendish Bridge, and the lease lapsed on his decease.

Mr. Lloyd's executors were called upon by the Marquis of Anglesey to pay £2,600 for dilapidations on the river navigation to put the locks, weirs, bridges and hauling paths etc. in repair. It is said that although a figure of £2,000 was agreed upon, the Marquis has not spent a farthing of the money on the work necessary.

The Marquis is obliged to keep the river navigable, and the writer is surprised that the uselessness of this part of the river has not excited the attention of the Burton brewers, whose trade is now so important. The writer further says that their indifference may be due to the availability of rail transport as an alternative, but in his opinion river transport would be cheaper to London, Hull, and the northern and eastern parts of the kingdom, by between 10 and 20%.]

1861

[Simple drawing of a Comet, in relation to "The Plough".]

[Two small newspaper articles concerning a proposal to publish private letters written by Sir Henry Crewe, Sir George Crewe, Lady Frances Harpur and the late Dowager Lady Crewe and others, to the late William Smith of Foremark Park. The letters are now in the hands of Dr. Massey of Melbourne, whose mother was the daughter of William Smith.

The working title of the publication was "Sketches of Private Life", "Compiled and Edited by a writer of eminence" who is not named. Arthur Smith of Edgeworthstown, Ireland, another grandson of William Smith, greatly objects to the proposed publication: "My Mother and I are aware that the fact of the Letters having come into the possession of Mrs. Massey (daughter of W. Smith Esq., and mother of Dr. Massey) was deeply regretted by my Father, who urged that they should be burnt unread in the presence of one of the Crewe family". It would be interesting to know whether anything ever came of this proposal, and whether or not the letters are still in existence.]

[NB. The index to Volume 1 starts here, but for this transcription a new index has been made, and moved to the end of the book.]

Aug 28   Several people have finished harvest. The weather this harvest has been magnificent. The days have been extremely hot with a light rustling wind and dry nights consequently the corn has been harvested in first rate condition.

Aug 28   This day Thomas Thompson died, and on this day we finished harvest. He worked with my father for 40 years. When we began to sow barley Mary Anne Crampton the wife of the man who drilled it was found drowned and on the last day of getting it Thos Thompson died so that at the beginning and ending of barley harvest a death occurred.

Dec 21   The Rev. G. Wasse preached the funeral sermon upon the death of His Royal Highness Prince Albert. Almost the whole of the congregation appeared in deep mourning. The Prince was universally respected

Dec 25   Christmas Day – The Church is decorated most beautifully with evergreens. The pillars are wreathed and various parts of the church are ornamented with stars and texts of Scripture. (next page) [190]

---

[190] sic. It is unclear what "next page" means here. Perhaps Briggs inserted, or intended to insert, an illustration?

1862

Saturday. About six O'clock this evening the whole neighbourhood was thrown into a state of great alarm by seeing a great fire not far from Melbourne. It proved to be at Mr Hasard's farm, Lodge Hill in Melbourne Park. In the rick yard two stacks were on fire, burning between a long range of other stacks and the farm-buildings. The Melbourne, Calke, and Derby Fire Engines were shortly on the spot but water being scarce there was great difficulty in getting out the flames which were not entirely got out until eleven O'clock the next day. Fortunately the fire was prevented extending to either the other ricks or the buildings although both were in great danger. The loss probably is about £100. The origin of the fire is involved in obscurity. Hundreds of people were immediately on the spot and gave ready assistance.
Jan 4

Primroses in full bloom. Violets peeping. Weather remarkably beautiful.
Feb 1

There are few persons who are not acquainted with the beautiful song called "Alice Gray." The author formerly lived at Kegworth, but falling into reduced circumstances was obliged to become an inmate of the Shardlow Union Workhouse – He died there this day aged 74 years. His name was William Mee. He was kindly treated by the Master and inmates of the house, for which he frequently expressed himself very grateful.[191]
May 29

A Bull upon Mr Scott's farm attacked a man named Taylor and nearly killed him.
June 10

---

191 NB. In the original manuscript, this entry is written on the back of the title page at the beginning. Its insertion here is an editorial decision.

1862

Melbourne.

Observations having reference to the

Parish of Melbourne:

Vol 2.

Commenced June 17th

1862

by

John Joseph Briggs

June 17   Wheat in ear.

June 20   An Act was passed some months ago, the object of which was to amend the Salmon Laws of England. It repealed certain other Acts relating to various rivers but did not repeal any Act with reference to the Salmon Fishery of the Trent. It appears that the family of Hastings of Donington Park have and have had the fishery of King's Mills from time immemorial and having the exclusive fishing for Salmon in the Trent and have the power of examining and having kept open all fish-gaps between King's Mills and the Humber.

These rights are very stringently provided for and protected by Act of Parliament - the Act giving the Hastings these rights was passed in the Reign of Queen Elizabeth and were [sic] afterwards zealously protected when the River Trent was made navigable from Wiln [sic] to Gainsbororough. In the year 1794 in 34th [i.e. year of] of George 3rd an Act was passed entitled "An Act to alter and amend an act of the 23rd year of His present Majesty for Improving the navigation of the river Trent and for making and maintaining a Navigable canal from the said river in the parish of Beeston, to join the Nottingham Canal in the parish of Lenton in the County of Nottingham and also certain cuts on the side of the said river".

This Act secures to the Hastings Family

1. All the rights of fishery which they had before the Act was passed.

2. The Navigation Company were not to erect dams or weirs to the injury of the fishery, especially at King's Mills. They were to leave proper outlets or openings in such weirs for the passage of salmon.

3. No person shall use these openings to catch the fish nor shall put nets into them.

4. The Navigation Company shall at their own cost within one month after a Requisition is made to them by the Earl of Moira his heirs or assigns to the Clerk or Agent of the said Company erect and set up and maintain at a distance considered proper by an Engineer appointed by the Earl of Moira &c substantial and sufficient piles and stakes in order as much as possible to prevent any nets from being set near or at such dams or weirs.

5. If the Company do not within the space of one month after requisition is made erect such piles, the representative of the Hastings family can set up and keep good such piles, charging the expence [sic] to the Company , and if they are not paid the Representative of Hastings can recover them by action at law in the Court of Record at Westminster.

6. If within four years after the erection of dams the value and quantity of salmon taken at King's Mills be less than in the four preceding years before the Act was passed and that such decrease appears to be consequent upon the erection of such dams &c the Company shall pay to the representative of Hastings according to his rights and interest therein at the time of such decrease happening, such compensation for the injury done to the fishery to be paid in a gross sum or by an annual rent as may be determined by an award of three persons as arbitrators, or any two of them, one to be nominated the representative of Hastings and another by the Company and the third by both.

7. The award of the arbitrators to be final: if they cannot agree in such reference or if the Company for ten days after a notice in writing of a reference by the representative of Hastings' to nominate a person as one of the arbitrators or that a third person shall not be chosen by the other two, or in case of delay in making such award beyond three calendar months from the date of such appointment of reference, then the compensation shall be determined and fixed by a special Jury of the County of Derby to be empannelled [sic] in the same manner as other Juries are according to the Act.

8. If after four years injury result to the fishery by the Company's work annual compensation to be made.

9. How the compensation is to be recovered.

10. A Penalty of £10 for destroying Salmon.

11. A Penalty of £20 for destroying Salmon below King's Mills.

12. A Penalty against catching Salmon by night.

1862

July 27   There is a strong belief amongst rural people that if St Swithen's Day be wet, it will rain for forty days afterwards - This is most ridiculous. This year it rained heavily but we have this year had one of the finest seasons since ever known. The weather is now remarkably beautiful.

Aug 1   The "Night Poaching Prevention Bill" now before the House of Commons is creating a good deal of discussion. Gangs of Poachers go about the country at night and take rabbits and game in any quantity they like and if they are not actually taken by the gamekeeper on the land, in the very act, they escape. This Act is to enable the Police of Town and County to search these poachers on the highways or upon entering a town and if they are laden with game to make them give a satisfactory account of it, and if they cannot do so to forfeit it and incur a heavy penalty.

Aug 6   This has been one of the finest hay-harvests ever known. The crops have been abundant and weather beautiful. Mangold Wurzel is a failure. Sweede [sic] turnips good.

• *King's Newton House.*

1862

"The Illustrated London News" of this day contains an account of the will of Joseph Thomas Cantrell Esqre Judge of the Derby County Court - His property is disposed of as follows

Aug 2

Trustees
&
Trustees
{
The Rev. Wm Cantrell

Robt W. M. Nesfield Esqr.

Will proved July 19th Ult.
The personalty sworn under £35,000.
Left his only daughter Cecilia his heiress
He died in April last aged 60.
His will made in 1860
His estates real and personal left to his daughter
The Trustees under this will will [sic, repeated word] are also Trustees under the marriage settlement
He confirms that deed subject to limitations in favour of the brothers and sisters of the testators last wife.
Tokens of remembrances left to friend [sic]
Legacies to Godchildren -
£500 to Rev. H. Cantrell : £200 to Mr Nesfield the Trustees -
His daughter to select such of his books as she wished to have, the remainder to the Treasurer for the time being of Derby County Court for the use of the Judge and officers.

About 9 O'clock on clear nights is visible a Comet the 3rd which has appeared within the last few years. It was seen in a position between Ursa Major and the Pole Star and was of peculiar shape.

Aug 25

[Simple drawing of comet.]

It was visible for some time but has now disappeared.

An extraordinary Storm occurred. Its greatest force was felt at Stanton - About 4 O'clock p.m. a peculiar haziness came over the atmosphere which deepened into a thick fog. This in some measure cleared off and the heavens were black as midnight - Peals of thunder shook the sky and down came rain in torrents - At Stanton the rain was mixed with large hailstones or pieces of ice more than 2 inches long - The storm passed away about six O clock and the sun broke out and it was a lovely evening.

Sep 2

Mr Thomas Hemsley of High Fields died at High Fields. He was originally a working man but by steadiness, industry and enterprise succeeding [sic] in establishing a manufacturing concern in Melbourne for silk gloves &c by which he amassed a large fortune - He bought the farm and house at High Fields on Melbourne Common for £10,000 of Mr Beard and lived there. His sons William and John have both manufactures in Melbourne -

Sep 13

1862

• The humble cottage on Quick Close, Melbourne, where Thomas Cook the travel agent was born of poor parents in 1808. It is interesting that Briggs' diary has nothing to say about Melbourne's most famous son, probably because Thomas Cook left Melbourne while Briggs was still a child, and did not build his memorial cottages on High Street until 1890-91, by which time Briggs was dead.

Sep 14   Mrs Taylor, the wife of Mr William Taylor of King's Newton died.

Sep 15   Long, wet, cold protracted harvest

Figure of a shield and ornament which were engraved upon a piece of copper (not a coin or medal). This piece of copper was found at the time of the Restoration of Melbourne Church, behind a figure of a Crusader which is on the south side of it - What the piece was intended or used for, it is difficult to say - The crescent is a bearing of the Cokes of Melbourne but the Crusader near [192] the piece was found is the effigy of a Hardinge -

Sep 28   Sunday. Such a torrent of rain fell as few persons ever saw before. It lasted about an hour - It came so copiously that it came through the roof of Melbourne [193] which has only just been leaded and poured from the roof until the spouting could not half carry it away. There is much corn out yet about Ashby, Castle Donington, and in even our own early parish few farmers have finished harvest. The late ones have corn yet standing which will not be ready to cut for a fortnight. It is a melancholy sight to see fine fields of corn lie soaking in the wet. Still it rains -

192 sic. Presumably Briggs meant to write "near where", or something similar
193 sic. Presumably Briggs meant to write "Melbourne Church"

An important Meeting was held in Derby to day in order to elect a Provisional   Oct 3
Committee to carry out a Railway from Derby to Nuneaton via Melbourne. The
Mayor of Derby in the Chair. The gentlemen elected upon the Provisional
Committee were as follows:

Mr J.P. Bainbrigge	(Derby)	Rev. J. Deans, Melbourne	
Mr Pegg	Do.	Mr W Hemsley	
Mr T [194]. Roe	Do.	" J. Hemsley	*[The two Hemsleys, Haimes*
" J.B. Forman	Do.	" T. Haimes	*and the two Earps were all*
" J. Clarke	Do.	" John Earp	*Melbourne men]*
" E. Barnet	Do.	" Webster Earp	
" W. Alton	Do.		
" Devenport	Do.		

It is proposed that this line shall leave Derby by Osmaston, run below Chellaston,
near Cuttle-Bridge, cross the Trent above Weston Cliff, cross the Trent valley, run up
the valley of the Brook Course by King's Newton and have a Station for Melbourne
at the New Bridge upon the Donington Road - Thence it proceeds to Wilson, Bredon
[sic], through the district of the coal-fields to the Ashby Line which it crosses and
on to Nuneaton.

There is no doubt that, independently of the passenger traffic, the country through
which the line passes is first rate for minerals - as the gypsum at Chellaston, the
lime of Calke of Tickenhall [sic], the lime at Bredon [sic], the vast beds of coal about

Worthington and Coleorton abundantly
testify. Added to this about 700 Tons of
vegetables are sent from Melbourne weekly
[sic!], during the Summer months and a large
proportion of manure brought back. Then as
regards the passenger traffic the Tolls
between Melbourne and Derby now let for
£12,00 [sic] per annum.

Rough memorandum of plumber's mark (1708) on the top of the lantern tower
Melbourne Church. About 18 inches across. The letters &c in high relief.

It appears from the papers that at the International Exhibition of roots and vegetables   Oct 10
open to all nations, Mr Samuel Robinson of the Shaw House, Melbourne, gained the
1st prize in 3 classes viz- Ox-cabbage, Sweede [sic] Turnips and potatoes.

---

194 Briggs does not always write capital Js in the same way. Sometimes they are like Ts. It is therefore difficult to decide
upon the correct initials of Messrs. Roe, Forman and Clarke in this list. The transcription is a considered guess.

1862

Oct 10 Barley harvest just finished. Some few patches of oats and beans to get - Harvest in this district about six weeks later than usual. A good deal of corn carried in bad condition and cut too green. To those who have been careful and taken advantage of favourable weather the harvest has been a good [195] and, I think the yield will be found large -

Oct 27 Edmonds (late Wombwells) establishment of Wild Beasts visited Melbourne - About 1500 people went to see it. Amongst other natural curiosities, it contained 2 large Elephants, one dwarf elephant, panthers leopards, tygers [sic], lions and cubs, polar bear Black bear rhynoseros [sic], river cow, Japanese pig - a multitude of monkeys, zebras and many other curious creatures -

Nov 13 Numerous parties of Surveyors and Levellers have been about Newton and Melbourne surveying for the Derby, Ashby and Nuneaton Line of Railway. The line fixed upon crosses the Trent between the Kincham Eve [196] and the Stone Wall and comes close up to King's Newton, running up the Brook Course valley to Bredon [sic]. The line is advertized [sic] in the "Derby Reporter" of to day. Sir John Harpur Crewe Bt, Sir George Beaumont Bt, Lady Edith Hastings, Lady Ferrers, and others have had large parties of watchers out day and night to prevent the land being surveyed and are deeply opposed to it.

Dec 10 It appears by notices which have been issued by the "Derby and Ashby Railway Company" that the line is to run through the Trent valley on an embankment about 14 feet high, up to near Mr Briggs's house at King's Newton near which it dives into the hilly ground to the depth of 43 feet gradually declining to 6 feet as it enters the Smither Green near the spot where Mr Orton had his brickyard.

Dec 13 This day was discovered by a man upon some high ground, upon our* [marginal note says:" * Mr Briggs's"] farm lying between Stanton and King's Newton a British Quern or handmill for grinding or rather pounding corn - It was found rather curiously - The field had been ploughed probably thousands of times. At one particular part was an extremely hard piece of stone which the ploughmen had frequently noticed and which had proved than once [197] an impediment to the plough.

On this occasion having four horses on his plough in order to break up the ground deeper than usual he determined to rip up the obnoxious stone and consequently when he came to it, set the horses to it - It resisted for some time the strength of the horses but a [sic] last gave way bent the coulter nearly double and knocked the man down at the Stilts - The stone came out however which proved a British handmill which had probably lain embedded there for 2000 years. It is very rude but in perfect preservation, having a hole at the top to put in the corn, from which there is a hole at the side to let out the corn when finished. In this mill (or perhaps rude stone mortar) the corn was not ground with a rotary motion but pounded as drugs are in modern times -

---

195 sic. Presumably Briggs meant to write "a good one".
196 Kincham or "King's Holme" is the name of a field adjoining the river. "Eve" or "Eave" is an old term relating to the river.
197 sic. Presumably Briggs meant to write "more than once"

This is the only one of the kind I have ever seen - In British handmills which I have seen, the upper mill-stone works upon the nether, but this is not so and I conceive it to be of very ancient date and made before the rotatory [sic] stone mill was found out. This mill or mortar too is of an unusual shape, being somewhat square in shape with the angles rounded off.

Very high wind – It un-roofed large portions of ricks and thatched buildings. Five chimneys and nearly all the roof of Mr Archer's new house on Mount Pleasant [198] were blown down.

Dec 19

- *Mr. Archer's house on Commerce Street, still known as the Mount House. It remained in use as a school for many years, and some older residents of Melbourne still recall attending it.*

MOUNT HOUSE, MELBOURNE, DERBY.
PREPARATORY SCHOOL FOR BOYS.

MR. & MRS. ARCHER

Receive YOUNG GENTLEMEN UNDER TWELVE to BOARD and EDUCATE. Accommodation superior. Domestic arrangements replete with every comfort. The aim of the Principal is to prepare Pupils thoroughly for the large Public Schools.

Terms and References on application.

- *An advertisement from Wright's Directory of Derbyshire, 1874.*

[*Newspaper article from the "Derby & Chesterfield Reporter", July 24th 1863, about the majority of the Marquis of Hastings. Donington Hall has been restored, altered and new buildings added during the last 18 months, under the superintendence of Messrs. Stevens and Robinson, architects, of Derby.*]

[*Newspaper cutting, no provenance or date, containing a comment by J. J. Briggs about the relative merits of dressing pasture land with night soil, lime or salt.*]

Xmas Day. One of the most beautiful days ever remembered. The sun is bright - the air clear and warm and were the leaves on the [199] it would be an April day.

Dec 25

---

198 This will be the "Mount House", which Mr. Archer built on Commerce Street. It is a very large house, reflecting the fact that the Archers used it as a boarding school, and probably built it with that use in mind.

199 sic. Presumably Briggs meant to write "were the leaves on the trees"

1863

[**1863** *change of year not indicated*]

April 17   Remarkably fine seed-time. Very dry for many months past but the country is most lovely.

April 26   Sunday. At half-past four O'clock this afternoon expired rather suddenly Henry W. Fox Esqre brother of F.F. Fox Esqre Agent to Lady Palmerston. Brought up to the profession of the Law, he attained an extensive knowledge of it, his opinion being particularly valuable upon curious and intricate points. Possessing a remarkably retentive memory he stored up the information which he obtained by reading, and the amount of anecdotes, choice scraps and bits of out-of-the way kind of knowledge which he possessed was remarkable. He was an excellent classical scholar. As a public speaker he was always listened to with attention and his remarks were frequently very humourous and gave rise to much amusement.

He had great aptitude for construing difficult ancient documents and would read without hesitation such as would have puzzled very excellent scholars. The writer of this once published a local history. He had occasion to have construed a document temp. King John written in abreviated [*sic*] Norman French. So abreviated [*sic*] were the words that frequently one single letter would represent a word: the letter T for instance stood for "Teste". After much perplexity and attention he could not make out the meaning of the document and he applied to several men learned in such matters. It foiled all their attempts at construction - At last it was taken to Mr. Fox. He construed it at once and gave a most excellent translation of the original.

Mr. Fox was peculiarly modest in manner and retiring in his habits. He was one of those individuals whom the world generally misunderstood, but he was much esteemed by the circle in which he moved as a kind-hearted man and very pleasant companion.

April 30   Mr H. Fox buried in the Melbourne Cemetry [*sic*].

May 12   Up to this period the weather has been remarkably dry, scarcely any rain having fallen for some months. The waters of the Trent have diminished, one third in quantity. Pools have dried up which have never been dry before, within memory. Still, cattle have done well and the growing crops have suffered but little.

Oct 6   The shock of an earthquake felt in this parish and neighbourhood. A sad accident has occurred at California Coal pits, it is supposed thro' the shock. A fissure is supposed to have been made by it underneath the ground and let an immense body of water out of a used up coal pit into one which was in work and drowned three men a boy and thirty horses - California is about 6 miles from Melbourne just beyond Staunton Harold.

- *Framework Knitting was a prominent cottage industry in Melbourne in the late 18th & early 19th centuries. This original workshop of 1795 at 47, Blanch Croft, now a bathroom, became a knitting shop again for one weekend only in September 2001, for Heritage Open Days. See page 11.*

• *J.J. Briggs, painted around the time that his first History of Melbourne was published in 1839. See pages 22-23.*

- *The front cover of Briggs' guide to Melbourne & King's Newton, 1870. Briggs had been apprenticed as a teenager to Bemrose the printers in Derby. He never completed his apprenticeship but remained on good terms with the Bemrose family, who printed all three of his histories of Melbourne in 1839, 1852 and 1870. See pages 21-25.*

• It was common for 19th century farmers to occupy rented farms while owning property elsewhere. This was J.J.Briggs' own house, where he spent the last months of his life in 1875-6. See page 26.

• The Mount House on Commerce Street, built by Mr. Archer, originally enjoyed a fine view of the Trent Valley. Its large size suggests that it was intended as a boarding school from the start. See page 189.

- William Lamb, second Viscount Melbourne (1779-1848) stayed at Melbourne Hall often during the 1840s. The Lamb family had inherited the Melbourne Estate via William's grandmother Charlotte (née Coke), who became the heiress when her brother George Lewis died childless in 1750.

- The hall and church at Staunton Harold. Staunton Harold is mentioned by Briggs in the entries for February 21st and December 14th 1846; January 25th, 1848 and December 25th, 1870.

- Park Farm, in the old royal hunting park at Melbourne, was built in the 1830s to replace the old home farm buildings of Melbourne Hall near the parish church. It is one of the farmsteads that Briggs had in mind in his diary entry for December 18th, 1848.

- The Melbourne Athenaeum was a proud addition to the town when it was built in 1853. It was designed by well-known Derby architect H.I. Stevens in the Italian style which was fashionable at the time. 150 years later, the tower or campanile is still waiting for its clock! See pages 87-89.

• *A mid 19th century embroidered silk glove, produced by Thomas Haimes & Co. A hallmark product of Victorian Melbourne. See pages 11 and 94.*

THE CROSS TREE
KINGS NEWTON,
PEACE REJOICINGS, 1856.

- A lime tree was planted in the cross steps at King's Newton by Thomas Scott around 1780. The artist of this painting, showing the tree decorated to mark the end of the Crimean War, is unrecorded. The tree was replaced by a modern cross to commemorate the accession of King Edward VIII in 1936. See page 107.

The Trent

AND OTHER

POEMS.

By

JOHN JOSEPH BRIGGS,

F.R.S.L.

1859.

- *The front cover of Briggs'"The Trent and Other Poems", published in 1859. The profits of the book were given to the fund for the restoration of Melbourne Parish Church (See pages 27, 130 and 160).*

• This wall painting was discovered in the parish church in 1859, while the church was being restored. Its subject remains a matter of debate. The editor believes that the two women may be crystal ball gazing or "scrying". Fortune telling, linked to superstition, was condemned by the Church. See pages 152-153.

- We cannot form much idea of George Lewis Coke's character and personality from the little we know of him. He is portrayed on the "Grand Tour", with the Coliseum in the background. His chief legacy to Melbourne was in commissioning the rebuilding of the garden front and east wing of Melbourne Hall by William Smith in 1742-5. George Lewis thus completed the Georgian remodelling of Melbourne Hall that had been begun by his father. See page 158.

• The early 17th century date of this monument in the parish church is given away by its characteristic "strapwork" ornament. Until the restoration of the church, it was fixed to a pillar in the nave. See pages 129 and 160.

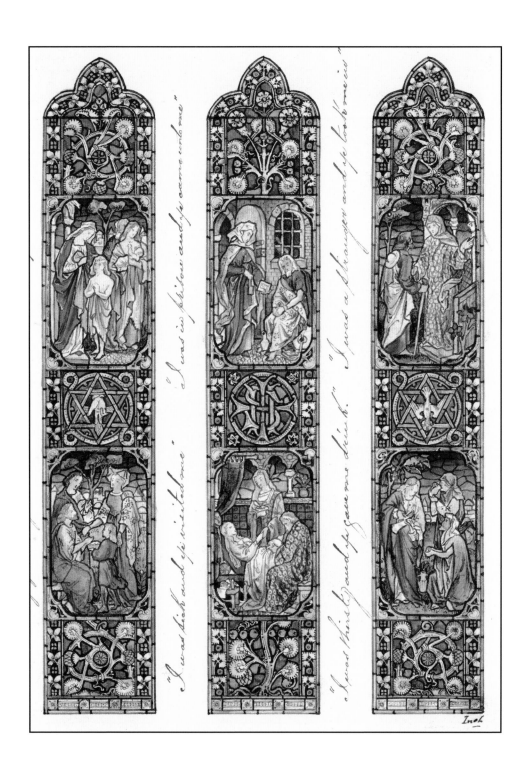

• *A coloured sketch or "cartoon" for the Haimes memorial window in the south aisle of Melbourne Parish Church. Briggs does not explain how he came into possession of it. See page 229.*

- This photograph, despite its grainy quality, is significant for several reasons. It was taken by pioneering Melbourne photographer James Earp and is of a very early date, taken within a few years either side of 1868. It captures the banks of Melbourne Pool off Penn Lane part way through the process of "gentrification". Cliff Cottage, on the right, built in 1862, is there, but only as a small summerhouse. "The Hollow", halfway up the bank on the left, is captured before the substantial Victorian alterations and extensions were made to it. Behind Cliff Cottage, Huntingdon House is seen in its original guise as Melbourne's Independent Chapel, built in 1779. See pages 211-212.

- Elms Farm, Trent Lane, home of the Briggs family. The house was rebuilt in 1802 following an arson attack which destroyed the previous one in 1800. See pages 13-19.

• *Sir John Harpur Crewe, 9th Baronet of Calke (1824–1886), standing outside Calke Abbey. See pages 222–224.*

The last harvest was very prolific. Barley yielded in most cases a quarter or 12 bushels more than in ordinary years.

Oct 12

Another Railway Company (The Midland) has been measuring through this Parish for a line of Railway. The following is the advertized [sic] route which it will take.

Nov 16

[Newspaper cutting on the proposed route of the railway. No date or provenance.]

After a series of very mild and beautiful weather, the Barometer fell this morning with surprizing [sic] rapidity and a tremendous gale sprung [sic] up - Stacks and thatched buildings were un-roofed, trees uprooted and blown down – houses un-tiled and great injury done.

Dec 3

[The caption on these sketches reads:

"This Vault, now used as a cellar, is under the Chapel at Welbeck, the floor of which is supported by a group of eight pillars, four square and four octagon from whence the arches spring, height of the pillars 5 feet circum. 2 feet 9 in:".]

[Note written on printed Memorandum slip of Bemrose & Sons, Printers etc., Iron Gate and Midland Place, Derby, as follows: "Aug 1 1878 Dr Mrs Briggs The two drawings herewith are I feel sure belonging to the Rooke's drawings – why they were left out I do not know but have been found in clearing some old papers away – They had better be put inside the book of drawings although they may have been intended to have been made other use of in some other way –

Mrs. Wm. is suffering from a gathering in her ear, All well else hope you & yr family are well".]

1864

Jan 1	For some years it has been customary here to pay considerable attention to the Christmas decoration of the Church, but this year it is very beautiful. The pillars are wreathed with holly: the pulpit and lectern are also trimmed: over the screen is a star in the centre of which are the letters IHS in holly-berries: over the tower archway in evergreens are the words "Glory to God in the highest" – at the east end a rich pattern in diaper work and the words "God with us": at the west end IHS in medalion [sic] and the words "On earth peace" -
Jan 11	On New Years Eve commenced a severe frost without snow which has just passed away. The Thermometer fell to 11 below freezing point within 9 of the temperature experienced on the memorable Xmas Eve of 1860. The Trent froze over: dung froze behind horses in the stable and many birds perished but the effects were nothing like so remarkable as in 1860.
March 6	It ceased raining about 2' O clock having rained 25 hours without ceasing.
April 6	The Curfew Bell is still ring [sic] during the winter months at Melbourne, most of the principal inhabitants paying the Verger 1/- each for ringing it. It begins on the 29th of September and ends on the 6th of April. It is rung at 8' O clock on every week day night except Saturday when 7' O clock is the hour.
May 16	Temperature in the shade 83.2 degrees. The weather has been intensely hot: the hottest with the exception of 1847 ever known. The earth is most luxuriant – blossom abundant and verdure and grass of a wonderful richness of green.
May 18	Thermometer in the shade rose to 87.7 degrees: in the sun to 110 degrees a higher altitude than has ever been reached in the month of May since the year 1794.
May 20	The best sheep's wool is now at the extraordinary price of 70s/- shillings per tod.
June 1	Last night an unusually sharp frost and cut off acres of potatoes, kidney beans and spoiled much fruit – The potatoes were nearly ready for getting up. Damage estimated at £1000 -
June 8	Wheat in ear - Very dry season -
July 17	Exceedingly dry summer. The brook nearly dried up - The grass on the pastures very short and embrowned like hay.
	[Two newspaper articles, no date or provenance, one entitled "MARRIAGE EXTRAORDINARY", and both concerning the marriage of the Marquis of Hastings with Lady Florence Cecilia Paget, youngest daughter of the Marquis of Anglesey.]

1864/1865

[Another article on the same subject entitled "THE RECENT ELOPEMENT AND MARRIAGE IN HIGH LIFE". This article relates the story of Lady Florence Paget's engagement to Mr. Chaplin of Lincolnshire, a gentleman with estates that brought in nearly £40,000 of rent per year. It was known that the Marquis of Hastings had intended to propose to Lady Florence had Chaplin not beaten him to it. Lady Florence sensationally changed her mind and married the Marquis of Hastings at St. George's, Hanover Square.]

Intense drought. Since March 6th no rain of any consequence has fallen: so the drought has now continued five months. Several crops of corn have been sown and harvested and have scarcely had a shower upon them - Cattle are being foddered in the fields and eat pea straw greedily - Many wells and pools are dried up - The Trent is dry three parts across. In many instances cattle are being driven for miles.

Aug 5

1865

[Newspaper article dated Feb 17, 1865, no provenance, concerning the proposal to convert the Midland Railway Company's Ashby tramway between Breedon and Ashby into a locomotive railway. Length 5 3/4 miles. Estimated cost £40,709.]

The railway from Derby to Ashby being marked out.

Feb 1

Heavy fall of snow one of a series of falls which have marked this winter. It has occasionally fallen to nearly two feet in thickness and in some places drifted to the depth of seven or eight feet. A few weeks ago travelling was seriously interfered with – Coals could not be obtained from the pits and people burnt wood instead.

Feb 17

Probably the last summer (1864) was the dryest [sic] ever known – Many farmers began last July to fodder their cattle and have continued to do so up to this present May; a period of ten months – The yield of wheat about 2 qrs per acre: barley 3 qrs – Hay about £8 - 0 - 0 pr ton.

May 1

The "Burton and Nottingham Railway" fight commenced in the Committee of House of Commons and the Bill was thrown out on the 16th. The Bill had passed the Committee of Standing Orders and the Court of Referees and then went into Committee of the House of Commons. The Line proposed to be made ran by by [sic, repeated word] Repton, Stanton, Kings Newton, Melbourne Donington Kegworth Gotham Bridgeford [sic] to Nottingham – Messrs Bass and Jennings of Burton Solicitors to the Bill –

May 3

The proceedings had gone on several days in Committee and several witnesses in favour of the Bill had been examined when Mr Bass, the Solicitor of the Bill was examined - It came out in examination that £44,630 " 8 " 2 had been raised from the Marine Insurance Company in London wherewith to pay the deposit upon the Bill, and the controul [sic] over the Bill passed away from the promoters by agrement [sic] signed on the part of the Insurance Company by B. M. Nicholas and on the part of the Railway Company by Saml Robinson of Melbourne.

1865

The Committee of the House of Commons having enquired minutely into this transaction, reported to the whole House that in their opinion "the Deposit in the Court of Chancery in the case of the said Railway Bill <u>constitutes an evasion of the security</u> provided by Parliament to ensure the <u>bona fide</u> character of such undertaking, and they have resolved to submit the case to the House"

The case was brought forward in the House by Mr Perry ["*Worthington*"?] and the House sent it to the Committee of ["*Standing*"?] for their opinion, who threw out the Bill.

Sep 24   The Derby and Ashby Railway began to be staked out from the Trent towards Melbourne.

Oct 1   An extraordinary dry time. It is now as hot as at Midsummer – very little grass for cattle – the fields as bare as a high road – This year following the last dry summer of 1864 will be very disastrous.

Oct 9   Bessy Holt of Kings Newton - a promising young woman – was asked [200] in Church last Sunday (yesterday) and died this morning.

Oct 17   A Terrific thunderstorm occurred on the afternoon of to-day. Some cows upon my farm (Mr Briggs's) were lying in a group, under an ash tree ready to be milked, about 4 'o clock when an aweful [sic] stroke of lightening [sic] came [next short word deleted] seemed to pass through the shed, flung the door of it back with great violence and almost stunned the men who had just entered the shed. At the same time the lightening [sic] struck the ash tree – before alluded to – and apparently killed two fine cows lying underneath it. When milking was over the men went to get the two dead cows away when only one was really killed and the other was thrown several yards with great violence into a ditch, legs upwards - With some difficulty she was got out alive, restoratives applied and she seems recovering.

Oct 18   Lord Palmerston, Prime Minister of England, died at Brocket Hall Herts.

Oct 27   Lord Palmerston buried in Westminster Abbey.

200Perhaps Briggs' use of the word "asked" means that her banns of marriage had been read?

1865/1866

[Printed notice issued by J. J. Briggs, containing a copy of a letter of condolence addressed to Lady Palmerston, and a lithographed copy of her reply to Briggs dated December 31st, 1865. It seems likely that Briggs wrote the letter of condolence on behalf of Lady Palmerston's Melbourne tenantry. The text of Lady Palmerston's letter, on letter paper with a heavy black border, is as follows:

Dear Mr. Briggs,

I am very much obliged to you for your kind Letter, and am very much touched by this Expression of good will, and Sympathy, from all my Tenants and Old Friends of myself and my Family. It is Indeed an Overwhelming and deep Affliction, to lose such an Excellent & devoted Husband who was the Happiness of my Life – but it is some Consolation to my Heart under this great trial, to find him so appreciated by all the world, and to see the Universal regret which his loss has occasioned in all parts of our own Country.

Pray express to all those who have so kindly signed their Names to this Address of Condolence, my very Sincere thanks and Gratitude, for this proof of regard & Sympathy in my very deep Affliction.

Believe me my dear Sir,

Yours very Sin^y,
E Palmerston
Decr 31st / 65]

1866

The Cattle Plague broke out here. The first case occured [sic] on High Fields farm belonging to Mrs Hemsley – A cow was attacked with it and died in two hours. Another began and was instantly killed. 4 more healthy ones were killed to prevent them having it.
    Jan 10

The Cattle Plague raging dreadfully in some parts of England. From 9,000 to 10,000 a week carried off.
    Jan 11

Trade in Cattle and sheep almost suspended. No cattle can be removed from one part of the farm to another without magistrates order -
    Jan 13

Mr John Dearman Dunnicliff died. He was a native of Melbourne went to Nottingham and amassed considerable property – settled again at Melbourne and built an ornamental cottage on the south bank of the Pool [201] and died there aged 56 years. Buried at [blank].
    Feb 1

---

201 Briggs means the north bank of the pool. Mr. Dunnicliff's ornamental cottage was built in 1862 on a garden which he began renting from the Melbourne Estate in the previous year (MHMR Estate Accounts; MHMR 54/5 - notebook on estate cottages). It survives today as "Cliff Cottage", but is no longer a small summerhouse. It was extended in 1879 (MHMR Estate Accounts) and has been further altered since.

1866

• *The Hollow, Penn Lane, seen over Melbourne Pool in an early photograph of c1868. Cliff Cottage is on the right with the old Independent Chapel behind it. The chapel was converted into a house in 1874.*

Feb 18   The Cattle Plague still rife in many parts: this parish so far with the one exception recorded has escaped. But its existence causes great fear and alarm. No remedies to stop its progress seem to avail.

Feb 19   The Derby Melbourne and Trent Railway begun. The Contractor commenced at Chellaston.

March 2   Very stringent measures are being adopted for staying the progress of the Cattle Plague. No straw, manure, skins hides may be carted along a public road without a magistrates order. No cattle of any kind can be moved along any public road (not even from a homestead to a distant part of the farm) without a magistrates order. If the disease attacks a cow in a shed where there are more cows not attacked, the healthy cows are immediately slaughtered. As many as thirty healthy cows have been slaughtered on a single farm.

May 2   The Cattle Plague greatly on the decline - About one fourth of the number only are now attacked as were attacked some time ago.

May 2   Heavy snow. Very cold.

          [Article from "Derby Mercury" November 15th, 1865, concerning the construction of a railway from Findern to Swarkestone.]

July 30   The Derby, Melbourne & Ashby Railway commenced this day on this side of the Trent: the first step being for the Contractors to bring railway waggons [sic] near the Hall Close.

July 30   The Cattle Plague in this country greatly on the decline the numbers dying weekly in this country having decreased from about 16,000 to about 350.

When digging out the foundations of arches for the Railway near Weston Cliff a short time ago the workmen found some red deers [sic] horns and some small round substances, apparently nuts from a hazel nuts [sic] which altho they must have lain for centuries were tolerably sound.

Aug 6

Drawing of an ancient Key which was found some time ago at Bredon [sic] on the Hill : supposed to be Roman.

Aug 11

Rain has fallen heavily for nearly 28 hours. Floods on the Trent and brook. The Trent rose so rapidly that some person [sic] had their cattle penned up by the flood in the meadows – Mr. Robinson had to swim his milking cows over the water and get out his sheep over planks.

Aug 29

The corn damaging and wasting very much by the heavy rains. The rains in some cases have gone quite thro stacks which were harvested and they have been taken back to the fields – if possible – to dry

Sep 1

[Article from "BOW BELLS" dated July 4th 1866, titled "MELBOURNE CHURCH, DERBYSHIRE", with a crude engraving of the interior as it then was, but omitting the pews etc. Only a short part of this short article is actually about the church. The remainder is about the manor and castle of Melbourne, and literary figures of King's Newton. It seems heavily influenced by, if not actually written by, Briggs.]

Heavy rains still continue to fall. Most farmers have a great deal of their corn down which is much sprouted and grown. Even growing corn is much sprouted – The loss will be very great.

Sep 5

One of the wettest seasons ever known. It still rains - Corn housed in bad condition. Harvest just finished here. Too wet for wheat sowing – Good barley has fetched 53 shillings per quarter.

Oct 22

1867

Jan 7   This year is ushered in with a frost too remarkable not to be long remembered. It began about the 2nd after much rain and the weather was fearfully cold and numbers of birds perished. The thermometer fell to 13 degrees. It vanished suddenly about 7th and was succeeded by a [sic] immense flood on the Trent.

Jan 8   An immense flood upon the Trent but not so large as that in [blank] The flood however came to its height more rapidly than was ever remembered: it is supposed on account of the snow disappearing very quickly from hills around.

Jan 17   In the night between the 17th & 18th died Colonel Gooch at Melbourne Hall

[Newspaper article on the death of Colonel H. E. Gooch, no provenance or date. Text as follows:" We regret to announce the death of Colonel H. E. Gooch, formerly of the Coldstream Guards, and a Waterloo officer, who expired on Friday, at Melbourne Hall, Derbyshire. The late Colonel Gooch served in Holland, in 1814, and commanded an advanced party in protection of the ladders at the attack on Bergen-op-Zoom. He was also present with the light companies of the 2nd Brigade of Guards at the battle of Quatre Bras, and assisted in the defence of Hougoumont at the battle of Waterloo. He retired from the army in 1832. He was an ardent lover of field sports, and a very warm friend to the poor."]

Jan 24   A second long and exceedingly severe frost this year broke up - slight snow fell. Neither of these frosts were so severe as that which occurred a few years ago.

[Newspaper article on the burial of Colonel Gooch, no date or provenance. It begins as follows: "The remains of the deceased gallant Colonel were interred in the Cemetery of Melbourne on Thursday last. The spot chosen for the vault was on the north side, very near the spot where the late Judge Cantrell was buried, and immediately underneath the window of the church side of the cemetery chapel. As the gallant colonel was much esteemed by all classes in Melbourne, they desired to be allowed to show him every mark of respect. Consequently about 12 o'clock all the principal inhabitants, or portions of their families, began to assemble near the hall, and when the funeral cortege started placed themselves in front and walked at the head of the procession to the Cemetery." Shops were closed in Melbourne as a mark of respect.]

[Newspaper article dated December 26th, 1868 [sic], recording the death of Sir Thomas Gresley, one of the Conservative members for South Derbyshire, at Mr. Mundy's Shipley Hall. He was in the 36th year of his age and had been ill for a few days. He left a widow and young children.]

Mar 22   A deep fall of snow. It snowed incessantly for 8 hours: the snow lay 6 inches on the ground: a remarkable circumstance at this period of the year.

April 9 About 3,'0 clock in the afternoon an extraordinary storm occurred of wind, hail, rain lightening [sic] and thunder.

1867

A child from Melbourne named Beardsley drowned in the brook near the Plank Bridge. It is supposed that she was playing on the bank of the brook and was blown into the water during the storm.

April 9

Men very busy now making the Railway to Melbourne. The piles of the Trent Bridge are driven the King's Newton cutting (33 feet deep) nearly through and tipping going on in various parts.

April 9

Mr Bernard Dolman, Surgeon died at Melbourne.

April 9

Drawing of an iron instrument supposed to be a spur found recently at Bredon [sic].

April 10

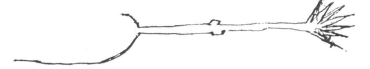

It is rather singular that during the Railway excavations and operations, so few antiquities of any kind have been found. In the Hall close several ancient handmills or Querns have been found and in the Coopers Orchard a curious kind of Spoon of which the following is a rude figure, the size of the original: the bowl of the spoon having a kind of lid or tongue in the middle.

April 10

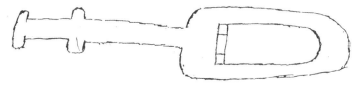

"Bob", the tipper who was at work near King's Newton cutting, met with an accident the horse knocking him down and the soil-waggons [sic] running over him.

May 20

- *There are no features to give away the location of this photograph, which shows a steam shovel at work on a railway cutting. It is believed to show the construction of the Derby-Ashby line in the Melbourne area in 1867.*

1867

Aug 20   This morning there was a most extraordinary storm or fall of rain. The lightening [sic] was magnificent and the thunder grand in the extreme. The rain measured 2.11. in [i.e. inches] an amount only exceeded 3 times in 27 years and about one 12th of the annual rainfall for Derby.

Sep 3   Another tremendous fall of rain. Lightening [sic] and thunder incessant. The storm lasted about 5 hours.

Sep 6   At various times during the last week the excavators at the cutting between Kings Newton and Melbourne, on the new line of Railway now making have found a considerable number of vases containing calcined bones: probably in all 20 – Seven were placed in a row together with the mouth upwards and some of the tops were covered with small flat stones to keep out the earth from the bones inside. They were of dark black clay, burnt and deposited from 2 to 3 feet beneath the surface of the ground. Only one was got out whole and it is in possession of Dr Massey of Melbourne. I have the broken remains of several. Most of them would have stood about 7 inches high. They had a little ornamentation about the neck the body of the vase being quite plain. The following are sketches of some of the pattern [sic] drawn from the broken fragments.

[Newspaper cutting, being a letter to the editor of the Derby Reporter from Wm. Massey, dated Melbourne, Sept 4th, 1867. It notes the discovery of the urns, which Dr. Massey thinks are Celtic. The bones are blanched and warped and have evidently undergone the process of partial combustion. " One perfect urn with its contents undisturbed, and several fragments of others obtained from the same spot, are in my possession, and I shall be very happy to show these relics to any one interested in British antiquities. "]

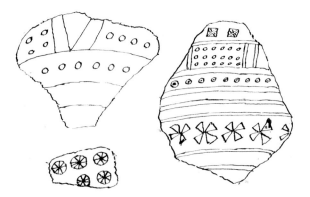

The surface of the ground where these remains were found was cut into hollows and dumbles and it was supposed by many that stone had been got out, but it was evedent [sic] from the perfect condition of the urns found that the soil had not been disturbed since they were deposited there.

In my opinion the spot was a miltary [sic] outpost, as the situation was high and commanded a good view of the river Trent so that any persons crossing it were readily perceptible. On the hill opposite to that on which the urns were found are rude entrenchments also commanding a view of the river whilst a brook runs between them and would supply the soldiers at the outposts. Both these outposts are about 2 miles from Bredon [sic] Hill on the summit of which the Romans had a large camp covering about 20 acres encircled by a fosse and vallum of earth, the remains of which may be seen to this day - The urns found at King's Newton contained the calcined bones of such soldiers as died at the outpost and were deposited there

Fig 1.

Another Urn found near the spot where the others were discovered containing a large number of calcined bones. It was the size and shape of the following drawing [NB reduced].

Sep 7

Four more urns found by Dr Massey in good preservation - In one case there was an urn within an urn. All the urns contain calcined and small broken bones - They are usually placed with the mouth upwards the bottom resting upon a flat stone. As yet no coin or implements were found with them or on the spot. The urns found to day were chiefly of dark coloured clay with a slight crust or covering of red on the outside and were of various sizes from a few inches high to a [sic] 10 or 12.

Sep 8

Three more urns found to day but in a delapidated [sic] state about 8 inches high and globular in shape. Also pieces of 8 more - Altogether there must have been 50 urns or more deposited.

Sep 11

The spot where these urns were found is on the crest of a hill near King's Newton overlooking the valley of the Trent and upon examining the spot minutely, I have no doubt that I have discovered the traces of a Roman Camp, the fosse on the north side being very perfect : that on the south side partly filled up, in order to plant an orchard - It was originally an oblong square about 165 yards long and 30 yards wide, with a deep fosse and vallum : the latter having been carried away and spread over the surface of the inside [202] the camp - The burial place where the urns were found was just outside the south ditch of the camp and I believe that there was a road to

Sep 11

---

202 sic. Presumably Briggs meant to write "of the inside of the"

1867

it from Derventio (now Little Chester) crossing the Trent at Weston Cliff by a ford which still remains and running by King's Newton to the camp - There was evidently another road from the direction of Repton. There was a road which left it in the direction of Bredon [sic] in the direction of Ratae (now Leicester). The following sketch gives some idea of what remains of the fosse. [The words "south" and "north" at the top of the sketch have been altered in the manuscript to "north" and "south".]

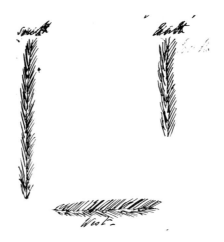

One urn was found within or at the bottom of the southern fosse

Sep 12 Another urn found, but in fragments. Unfortunately these urns cannot be got from the earth entire, for although the shape is distinctly visible and well defined the roots of trees growing near have got into each vase and fed upon the bones, then swelled out and burst the shell of the urn into fragments. Pieces of pottery of a red colour have been found. Sometimes the centre of the clay composing the urn is black and the inside and outside seem to have been coated with red colouring matter : in a few instances the urn is rudely ornamented in the inside.

[Newspaper cutting, being a letter from John Joseph Briggs to the editor of the Derby Mercury, dated King's Newton, Sept 14th, 1867 and entitled " INTERESTING DISCOVERY OF ANTIQUARIAN REMAINS AT KING'S NEWTON". Briggs thinks there is little doubt that the urns are Roman, because they are of a Roman shape and were found just outside the earthworks which Briggs believed to be the remains of a Roman camp, enclosing an area about 166 yards long and 65 wide. Briggs suggests that it was a military outpost connected with the "great camp at Bredon", i.e. the hillfort, which Briggs thought was also Roman.

Briggs notes that the urns were sometimes placed singly, sometimes two or three together, and in one case seven were found. Many were unornamented, and on each of the ornamented examples the ornamentation was different. Briggs suggests that from first to last about 100 specimens may have been discovered, but not more than six or seven were tolerably perfect.]

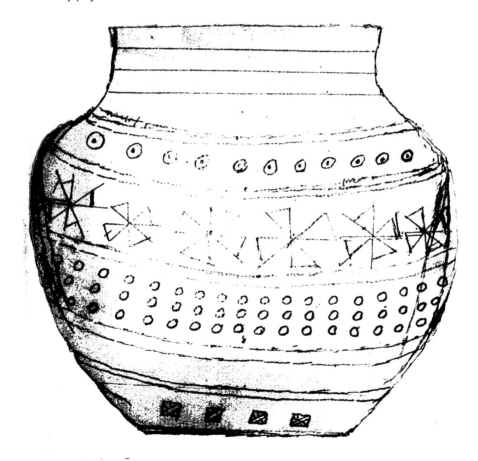

[In the manuscript, the illustration above [NB reduced] is labelled "original size Fig 2."]

[Three more sketches of urns at original size follow, labelled figs. 3, 4 and 5.]

1867

• Some of the cremation urns found at King's Newton in 1867, from a photograph inserted by Harriet Georgiana Mundy into a Grangerised copy of Lyson's "Derbyshire".

Sep 16 A very beautiful, and one of the most highly ornamented urns that have yet been exposed was found to day. Although broken into small fragments the outline was visible and I am enabled, from one of the larger pieces saved to give the character of the ornamentation.

[Sketch of piece of an urn, labelled "Fig 6"]

This vessel was very remarkable for having a large admixture of small, pure white quartz pebbles thickly intermixed with the paste of which it was composed.

Sep 16 In addition to the urns a remarkably shaped horse-shoe was found : also a flattened bullet, silver coin (inscription invisible) and a small bronze bell. I am not sure that any of these articles have any connection with the urns, without it may be the bell. The bell is prettily ornamented - Fig 1 represents its side : Fig 2 the bottom.

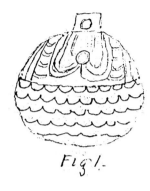

Fig 1.

Fig 2.

In shape it is nearly round, with a pea of metal to make the sound and holes in the side for the sound to escape - In speaking of deposits "undoubtedly Roman [203] Mr Bateman our best authority says "At Bakewell in the year 1808 in digging in Church Row an urn having handles like an amphora, and partly covered with a green glaze was found and destroyed. It contained, in addition to the usual deposit of calcined human bones a small bronze bell, with a ring at the top, much corroded." Probably the bell in my possession was originally contained in an urn afterwards broken and destroyed as numbers were by the workmen.

There has long been a tradition that in the valley on the south-east of Bredon [sic] near a spot now called "Wooffer" bridge a great battle was fought between the Saxons and the Danes - The place is most likely for such a battle and the name of the bridge seems somewhat to confirm the account of tradition - "Wooffer" is merely a corruption of Wulfur, and was spelt in old Saxon Chronicles in a dozen different ways, and is probably derived in some way or another from the name of the great Mercian King of that name. Recent excavations by railway navies [sic, i.e. navvies = navigators] when making a line of railway near the spot have found several skulls (two of which are in my possession) and other remains corroborating to a great extent the story of a great battle having been fought there and I have no doubt whatever that such did take place there between the Danes and Saxons one army occupying the entrenched camp at Bredon [sic] and the other occupying the hill opposite which bears some traces of rude fortification.

Dec 26

[small outline drawing of a flint, not referred to in the text]

[The following seems to be a new entry, date not given:]

I went this day to the spot where the skeletons were found. It is on a gentle knowl which runs down to a rivulet which tradition says "ran down with blood" on the day of battle. I disinterred several of the skeletons : some were without skulls : some buried straight some crooked : some with the knees drawn up others on their sides, but one thing was observable in all the skeletons, that whenever the skull was on the skeleton it always lay due north. The skulls were all of persons grown

---

203 sic. Inverted commas not closed.

up to manhood. They seemed to me to be remarkably thick, very similar in character being very broad at the back of the head and very narrow over the forehead. The hill seemed full of skeletons, many thousands must be there : indeed some hundreds must already have been carted away with the soil in making the Railway - The hill seemed quite full of animal matter and cut with a spade like butter. Before the surface was disturbed, the grass upon it grew long and rank, three times as high as the surrounding herbage and cattle did not seem to care to graze it. The skeletons were buried about 18 inches beneath the surface. No bones of horses have as yet been found and no implements of warfare or utensils of domestic use [204].

[**1868** - *change of year not indicated*]

Feb 28   The Railway is now made on one line from Derby to Melbourne and a train of luggage ran for the first time through to day.

Feb 29   This day (Saturday) is a remarkable day in the Calendar and forms a circumstance which only occurs only [*sic, repeated use of "only"*] once or twice in a lifetime - It is the 5th Saturday which has occurred in this month. The last occurrence of one was in 1840 or 28 years since the next will be in 1896.

June 9   Wheat barley and oats in ear. One of the most forward seasons ever known.

June 12   A remarkable summer excelling in dryness the summer of 1864 and it is said equalling that of 1826. It seems wonderful how cattle exist at all. Mangel crop a failure – turnips too – cabbage poor -

[*Newspaper article on the Melbourne address given to Sir John Harpur Crewe on the occasion of his son Mr. Vauncey Harpur Crewe reaching his majority, from the " Derby & Chesterfield Reporter " of January 3rd, 1868. The illuminated address was prepared by Messrs. Bemrose of Derby, and was presented on 23rd December 1847 by a deputation of about 20 people representing the various interests of Melbourne. The address was read by F. F. Fox, who preceded it with some remarks of his own. It was signed by about 400 inhabitants of Melbourne.*]

[*Sir John explained that he was weak and unwell, and had therefore pre-written a response to the address, which he read out. He notes that he has bought an estate in Melbourne some years since, late the property of Mr. B. Cheatle, for Vauncey so that he would have a vote upon his coming of age.*]

---

204 F. Taylor in his History of Breedon-on-the-Hill: Church & Village (1906) page 7, says: "It is most probable that a battle was fought near where Tonge and Breedon Station now stands, and a small hill there has always borne the name of "Woeful Bridge Hill", because of the great slaughter which took place. The word bridge refers to a bridge which probably crossed the small stream which flows at the foot of the hill".

• Sir J. H. Crewe, 9th Baronet of Calke.

The Melbourne deputation was shown around the house before returning to Melbourne, where they joined others for a meal provided by Mr. Warren at the New Inn. "The dinner was enriched by a handsome present of game from Calke, amongst which was a pair of noble cygnets weighing about 50lbs. They were in splendid condition, and were cooked ... in the true Norfolk fashion ..." During the toasts, Mr. Tasker noted that Sir J. Crewe's health had been very indifferent for many years, which prevented him from taking part in public affairs. But his address to the Melbourne deputation had "shown how gifted he was in the best qualities of head and heart."

• Calke Church, from a Victorian stereoscope slide.

1868

Mr. Haimes, in the course of his speech, "hoped that the cloud which had overshadowed the trade of the place and commercial interests generally, would soon pass away – indeed he thought he saw symptoms of a healthier state of things."]

[Page of illustrations from the "Illustrated Midland News" comprising head and shoulder portraits of Lord and Lady Palmerston, a view of Broadlands, a bridge in Brocket Park and the gardens at Melbourne.]

June 18   About 9 o clock p.m. this day occurred a large fire at Derby Railway Station which was seen burning here for hours. It proved to be some cheese warehouses and the toasted or roasted cheese was smelt four miles off. The fire caused damage to the amount of £20,000.

July 28   Harvest ended. Remarkably dry forward season. Harvest earlier by at least two months than in 1864 - Excessively dry - People foddering their cattle with straw and hay.

• *The gates of the old Hardinge family home at King's Newton Hall, photographed shortly after the house was rebuilt in 1910.*

July 30   The Inscription on the Holy Well at King's Newton re-cut under the direction and at the expence [sic] of Captain Hardinge R.N. [205]

---

[205] This work is undoubtedly the subject of a letter from Edward Hardinge to J. J. Briggs dated 13th July, 1868 (Derbyshire Record Office D4627/1/38): "My dear Sir I enclose herewith a P. O. Order for £1 ,, 6 the amount of my agreement with Barton & Dunnicliff. Will you oblige me by holding the same until the work is completed? If it is convenient & agreeable to you to see how the work is going on from time to time, it might add to their attention to details. The stone is to be faced & the inscription cut anew..." The Holywell was pulled down by vandals in 1948 (Derbyshire Advertiser, June 4th, 1948) and the inscribed lintel disappeared. It was rebuilt, more plainly than the original, by the Melbourne Civic Society in 1984.

• *The Holy Well at King's Newton.*

An extraordinary dry time - Many trees and shrubs have been killed by the excessive heat.

Sep 1

The Railway to Derby from Melbourne opened as far as Melbourne.

Sep 1

Melbourne Railway Station, opened in 1868.

The Marquis of Hastings died in London

Nov 10

The Marquis of Hastings buried in Kensal Green Cemetry [sic] London.

Nov 14

1870

July 1   One of the most extraordinary dry seasons ever known. The Heat has been intense : yet strange to say on this day came a sharp <u>hail storm</u>.

[Two articles, one from "Queen" November 14th 1868 and the other from the "Derby Mercury" of November 20th 1868, on the death of the Marquis of Hastings.]

[Newspaper article, no date or provenance, on the sword of William Wallace, 58 inches long. It was preserved at Loudon Castle and brought to Donington in 1866 by the late Marquis of Hastings.]

[Newspaper article from " Queen" reporting the funeral of the late Marquis of Hastings in Kensal Green Cemetery. " The funeral was far more numerously attended than could have been anticipated, the crowd being evidently stimulated by some other motive than curiosity, for there was nothing whatever in the cortege to attract attention". *]*

[Newspaper article, unprovenanced, dated November 17th, 1868, entitled " FUNERAL OF THE MARQUIS OF HASTINGS". *The article notes that the Marquis's illness culminated in* "Bright's disease", *from which he had suffered more or less since he was fourteen years old, and which had accelerated the deaths of his father and aunt. The Marchioness was devoted to her husband throughout his illness.]*

[Newspaper article, no date or provenance, about the Marquis of Hastings' winnings by his horses in the past racing season. The article notes that it " was not owing to a want of luck that he was compelled to break up his stud ", *as his winnings had been very handsome.]*

[Newspaper article, no date or provenance, being a highly critical account of the late Marquis of Hastings' wasted life. " He had done a vast amount of mischief in six years, and mischief of a much more vulgar kind than those who write sermons about him seem to suspect.." *]*

[An article, no provenance or date, being another critical account of the Marquis of Hastings and his fortunes on the racecourse. " There should surely be some moral attached to the career of such a man as the Marquis of Hastings. In a few brief seasons he contrived to sacrifice "health, fortune, friends, and fame," by a course of conduct that can only be characterised as utterly reckless ". *The article also notes that "* The Marquis of Hastings ... lived to sell or mortgage everything he could touch. "*]*

[*The Marquis of Hastings, from* The Field *]*

[*Small newspaper article about the tenantry's festivities at Moorgreen, Notts, to celebrate Earl Cowper's marriage.*]

Oct 25

Lord and Lady Cooper [*sic, i.e. Cowper*] married.
[*Article from the "Derby Mercury" of November 2nd 1870 on the marriage of Earl Cowper to Katrine Cecilia, eldest daughter of Lord and Lady William Maclean Compton. After the wedding lunch, the Earl and Countess left to spend their honeymoon at Compton Wynyates in Warwickshire. In Melbourne, the marriage was celebrated with a dinner at the Athenaeum rooms, provided by Mr. S. Warren of the New Inn and presided over by Mr. F. F. Fox. " A number of ladies occupied seats in the gallery ", says the article, indicating that the dinner must have been held in the front room upstairs.*]

There appeared in the heavens an Aurora Borealis of remarkable beauty. The sky was illumined by red and fiery streamers, striped with rays of white. These presented an extraordinary & somewhat teriffic [*sic*] appearance but in some parts very beautiful.

Oct 25

Tremendously severe frost. Trent frozen over and persons passing over it on the ice. It freezes in bed-rooms and under beds : also in stables the dung behind horses.

Dec 25

1870

Earl Cowper requests the pleasure of

Mr & Mrs Briggs'

Company at a Tea and Soirée to be held
at the Athenæum Room Melbourne, on
Friday November 4th 1870

Tea at half past 5.

[Newspaper article, no date or provenance, containing a quotation from a work called "Old Stories Re-Told", describing in some detail the hanging of Laurence Earl Ferrers at Tyburn fields in May, 1760.]

[Newspaper article, no date or provenance, about the marriage of Earl Cowper and the dinner to mark the occasion at the Athenaeum Rooms in Melbourne.]

[Newspaper article, no date or provenance, about an angling match at Weston-Cliff between Mr. J. W. Bailey of Nottingham and Mr. J. Woodard of London.]

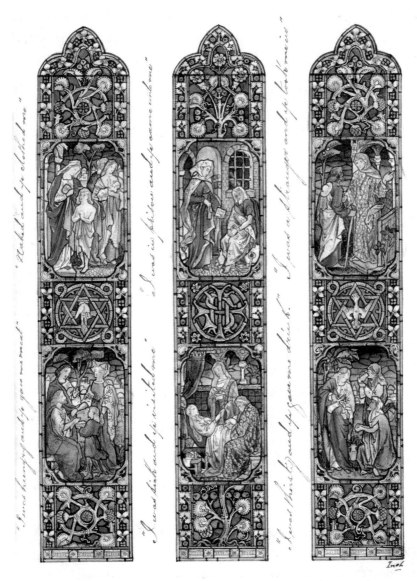

[Coloured sketch or "cartoon" entitled: "The Haimes Memorial Window In Melbourne Church". The window has three lights, with two scenes represented in each, as follows (left to right):

"I was hungry and ye gave me meat"
"Naked and ye clothed me"
"I was sick and ye visited me"
"I was in prison and ye came unto me"
"I was thirsty and ye gave me drink"
"I was a stranger and ye took me in"]

1870/1872

A key found near the Chantry of St. Katherine Melbourne and supposed to have belonged to it.

[*Newspaper article, no date or provenance, on Samuel Robinson's prize produce, particularly his enormous ox cabbages.*]

[*Newspaper article, no provenance but dated June 25th, 1872, recording the sale of Lot 1 of the Lockington Estate (2193 acres, 3 roods and 15 perches) by auction on Thursday 20th June in London. It was knocked down to Mr. John Shaw of Derby on behalf of Nathaniel Curzon Esq. of Etwall Hall, for £190,000 exclusive of timber.*]

1872

July 9 A coin of Flavius Vespatian found in a field, alongside the West-field Lane in Kings Newton. Near the same lane, coins of Tetricus, Constantine and other Emperors have at times been picked up -

[*Two unprovenanced newspaper articles, one dated April 30th 1873 and the other undated, regarding the Countess of Loudoun's petition for the revival of ancient peerages.*]

[*Small unprovenanced and undated clipping, text as follows: "But Sydney Smith's character had its serious and even solemn side. Lord Houghton tells us that he heard Lord Melbourne say "Sydney Smith had done more for the Whigs than all the clergy put together, and our not making him a bishop was mere cowardice". This was blunt honesty, characteristic of Lord Melbourne."*]

[*Proof page, with engraved illustration of bird and plants etc., entitled "The Natural History of Melbourne", in diary form. The entries cover Oct 13th and 14th, 1843. Reproduced in the Introduction to this book, page 27.*]

1872/1873

The body of a poor weaver of Melbourne, named Kersley, was found in the Trent below Weston Cliff. It is supposed that being depressed in spirits he had thrown himself into the river on the 7th ult.

Oct 11

[Another newspaper article, no provenance or date, about the revival of the Hastings Baronies.]

[A six-page article by Joseph Jones of Derby, being pages 193-198 of an unidentified work. Jones had been given permission to visit Donington Hall on a quest to discover more about the mansion as it had been in the Countess of Huntingdon's day. It was said that the oaks in the park appeared mutilated because they had been lopped in the Countess of Huntingdon's time to build Methodist chapels. It was also said that two large patches of arable land, which once formed part of the park, had been ploughed up so that they might be sowed with corn, to supply some of the Countess's preachers with bread. The article includes an engraving of the house.]

[Newscutting from the Derby Mercury Nov 5th, 1873, being a letter dated Nov. 3rd, 1873, to the editor from F. F. Fox of Melbourne, concerning Mr. Samuel Robinson of the Shaw Farm, Melbourne. Mr. Robinson has been given notice to quit his farm, and the Derby Mercury has implied that the treatment of Mr. Robinson is unfair. Fox therefore has sent in Mr. George Benjamin Brownson's general report on the farm, which is published in the article.

Mr. Brownson asked Mr. William Tomlinson of Bradley near Ashbourne to accompany him on his visit. Both thought the farm cruelly used and in a filthy state, and agreed that a notice to quit was fully justified.

In his defence, Mr. Robinson had sought the comments of W. Wright, Land Agent, of Sandiacre. In a short note dated October 21st, 1873, also published in the article, Wright considered that the farm was in a fair state of cultivation, and far better than the bulk of farms he was asked to look at when tenants were given notice to quit.]

1873

Mr Robinson has notice to quit the "Shaw farm" which his family has much improved. There is a good deal of talk about it in the neighbourhood : some blaming the landlord (Earl Cowper) and some the tenant

Nov 5

[Editorial comment from the Derby Mercury of November 5th, 1873, on the dispute between Earl Cowper and Samuel Robinson. Mr. Fox has demonstrated that there are two sides to every argument, but the Derby Mercury had only wished "to defend a well-known and respected agriculturalist from an amount of pressure which will, if not modified, end in his ruin."]

1873

THE TENANTRY of an ESTATE, whose boast it is that TWO PRIME MINISTERS OF ENGLAND have been connected with it.

Before your *Landlord's* awful throne,
  Ye *tenants* bow with humble joy;
Know that YOUR Steward's God alone,
  HE can create, or he destroy.

HIS mighty power has, with YOUR aid,
  Made "SERFS" of you, instead of MEN;
And when *Rack-rent* by you is paid,
  HE sends you back to work again.

YE are his TOOLS, and YE his CARE,
  Your *goods,* and *all your mortal frame;*
What lasting honours shall ye rear,
  Almighty fools, to THIS MAN'S name?

You'll crowd his door with thankful songs,
  High as the roof your voices raise,
And when your *"noble Landlord"* comes,
  You fill th' "REPORTER" with his praise.

Wide as the estate is HIS command,
  Vast as HIS MIND, you'll find HIS LOVE,
Firm as a rock *the truth will stand,*
  When all such TYRANTS CEASE TO MOVE.

[This fly sheet is a bitter verse about the tyrannical authority of the Melbourne land agent (i.e. F. F. Fox) over the tenantry, despite the fact that two Prime Ministers of England have been connected with the estate. It is based on the words of a well-known hymn.]

[Newscutting, being a long letter to the editor of the Derby Mercury from Samuel Robinson, dated November 8th, 1873. As Mr. Fox has publicised his side of the story, Mr. Robinson gladly avails himself of the same medium to vindicate his cause.]

1873/1874

The bulk of the article comprises two reports on Robinson's farm, the first by W. Wright of Sandiacre and the second by Messrs. Greatorex (of Stretton near Burton on Trent), Cartwight (of Drakelow), Chappell junr. (of Breaston), Goodall (of Milton) and Asher (of Stanton). The reports are far more favourable than Mr. Brownson's, and take into account the naturally poor quality of the farmland and the fact that much of it was formerly wasteland.

Robinson concludes with some comments of his own. He believes that he would have had nothing to fear if his landlord had judged his case from personal inspection. As it is, he will leave the farm with the general sympathy of the public "which I would not exchange for any pecuniary advantage which could be offered me".]

[Newspaper article from the Derby and Chesterfield Reporter September (14th?) 1875, suggesting that Lady Loudoun's request to have her hand cut off may have been connected to the wish of a previous Marquis of Hastings, mentioned in an old volume of the Mirror from 1827. In a letter, he asked that on his death his right hand be cut off, and preserved until the death of the Marchioness, when it should be buried with her in her coffin. The cutting also includes the next article in the newspaper, being a brief description of the Ashover area, noting that the writers Dr. Spencer T. Hall and the Howitts once lived there.]

[Four newspaper articles, all without date or provenance, concerning the death of the countess of Loudoun. She died on the 23rd January, supposedly by " lesion of one of the blood-vessels of the brain". She succeeded her brother, 4th Marquis of Hastings, at his death in 1868. In her will she asked that her right hand be cut off and buried in the park at Donington at the bend of the hill to the Trent, under a cross inscribed "I byde my tyme".]

[Article from the "Illustrated London News" August (1st?) 1871 about Coggia's Comet, including a diagram.]

1874

Coggia's Comet. This beautiful visitant is now nightly seen in the Northern heavens. It appears in its greatest brilliancy about 11, O'clock p.m. The tail of the Comet appears to the naked Eye, about 4 feet long. During the same Evening it moves its position considerably in an easterly direction. Remarkably dry summer -

July 9

[Letter to Briggs dated 22nd April 1874 from "J. W. Pycroft"?, written at the Temple Club, London. The writer has heard of Briggs' interest in the Topography of Derbyshire, and wishes to bring to his notice a rental of Melbourne made on 5th April in the 7th year of Henry V (1419), of which the heading is transcribed and translated in the letter.]

The rental is made on the oaths of Robert Tillot, Richard Parker, Thomas Ward, William at the Cross, Simon of the Pool, Robert of Neuton, William Wilne, John Ragge, Thomas Day, John of Wilne and John Ryvet.

1874/1875

The writer offers to obtain an estimate of a full transcript and translation for Briggs, and suggests that it might be printed and published in "The Reliquary". In a long PS, the writer notes that he was present when the barrow at Barrowash [sic] was opened during the construction of the Derby & Nottingham line. Many skulls were found, of people aged from 18 to 60 according to Mr. Douglass [sic] Fox, cloven by Danish battle axes. The writer believes that a few of them were presented to Derby Museum.]

1875

Jan 4   There has been a hard long continued frost : thermometer standing at 10°. Trent & Melbourne Pool thick with ice. The snow has also been very deep. It broke up about the 4th A good deal of wild-fowl about amongst which was a splendid Goosander shot by the Earl of Loudoun. The Birds have had a terrible, hard, time of it. Almost all kinds of work have been suspended.

[Long newspaper article from the "Loughborough Monitor" dated Thursday, June 25th 1863, about the conviction of the Marquis of Hastings and three keepers (James Domilow/Domelow, Edward Platts and Joseph Fairbrother/Farebrother) for cock fighting.]

• *A promotional photograph taken on the market garden of O. J. Hatton, Melbourne. Samuel Robinson's glorious career may have had an unglorious and abrupt end, but he has remained an honourable and legendary character among the Melbourne market gardeners ever since.*

Selective index of persons and places

Briggs compiled his own index to his diary, which is placed halfway through the year 1861. The subsequent part of his diary was not indexed. The index published here is entirely new, with an emphasis on the names of people and places. Briggs' own index has been omitted. The introduction to the diary is not indexed.

This index uses date references instead of page numbers. Some entries are followed by the letters f, i, or n, and by numbers in brackets. When using the index, please bear in mind that Briggs' diary entries are not always in strict chronological order, and there may be more than one entry for a single date.

f   means that the information, or additional information, is contained in the footnotes.

i   denotes an illustration or the inclusion of illustrative material such as an invitation or letter, inserted with the diary entry as listed in the index.

n   denotes a cutting from a newspaper, book etc, inserted with the diary entry as listed in the index.

(2) or (3) after a date means that there are two or three separate relevant diary entries with the same date.

Cowper, Earl, marriage of	1/7/70n; 25/10/70n; 25/12/70ni
Cox, Rev. H., curate	5/8/50; 1/5/51; 18/9/51f
Crampton, Mary Anne, apparent suicide of	8/4/61; 9/4/61; 11/4/61; 28/8/61
Crewe family, proposed publication of private letters	2/7/61n
Crimean War	28/3/54; 2/4/54; 26/4/54; 15/5/54(2); 18/7/54; 15/9/54; 24/9/54; 17/10/54; 13/11/54; 14/11/54; 21/3/55; 5/4/55; 10/9/55; 31/3/56; 5/1856; 3/6/56n; 10/6/56
Dawson, Bryan, Isabelle and William (early 17th cent)	2/3/60
Deans, Anne	15/6/56
Deans, Rev. Joseph	22/8/51; 27/8/53n
• publishes a history of the church	10/1843
• vicarage built for	1843
Derby, railway station, fire at cheese warehouses	18/6/68
Derby Hills House Farm	20/3/48f
Derby Road	
• John Hemsley's new factory on	25/2/61f
• New Inn (now Melbourne Hotel) on	26/2/49; 28/10/51; 6/11/52; 11/1853; 25/2/61; 12/6/68n
Diphtheria, a new disease	20/1/61
Dolman, deaths of brothers Alfred and James on same day	11/10/58i; 14/12/58; 18/12/58
Dolman, Bernard, surgeon, death of	9/4/67
Dolman, Hugh, killed by lightning	19/6/46
Donington Park	
• birds, scarcity of	4/6/55
• Bradley, Thomas, gamekeeper	6/1/61
• Daniel, Colonel, of	29&30/7/59
• deer, thinning of fallow	22/4/45
• gamekeeper killed	31/7/50
• hounds at	3/1/46
• Huntingdon, Countess of	11/10/72n
• felling of trees in	7/1/45
• Loudoun, Countess of,	5/11/73n
• mesmerism at	3/4/45
• Wallace, William, sword of at	1/7/70n
Drownings	
• in brook	9/4/67
• of Mary Anne Crampton	8/4/61; 9/4/61; 11/4/61; 28/8/61
• in Melbourne Pool	28/12/53
• in shipwreck of the "Dalhousie"	19/10/53
• in Trent, at Burton Bridge	26/1/61
• in Trent, of - Davidson	15/7/47
• in Trent, in a flood	13/11/52
• in Trent, below Weston Cliff	11/10/72
• at Weston Cliff Ferry	10/1846
Dugmore, Thomas, innkeeper	1820
Dunnicliff, Mr. John Dearman	1/2/66

Earl, John
    • introduces a steam thrashing machine   2/9/56
    • superintends road works at Woodhouse   30/1/55
Earp, John
    • of High Street, death and burial of   4/1/61; 9/1/61
    • presentation of a service of plate   26/1/48
Elections / Members for South Derbyshire   15/3/49; 17/3/57; 23/3/57;
                                     23/4/59ni; 26/4/59; 27/4/59;
                                     7/5/59; 24/1/67

Ferrers, Earl, of Staunton Harold
    • trial and execution of (1760)   25/12/70n
    • trial for Breach of Promise of Marriage   21/2/46; 14/12/46
Fire Engine (Melbourne)   17/4/59; 20/4/59; 4/1/62
Foresters, order of   30/7/45
Forty Foot Lane   4/8/45
Fox, Frederick F.   13/9/45; 6/3/60; 26/4/63;
                                     12/6/68n; 11/10/72n; 5/11/73n
Fox, Henry   1836; 21/4/57;
Fox, Henry W.   26/4/63; 30/4/63
Fox, Mrs., burial of   21/4/57
Gasworks – see Castle Street
Gill, Rev. T.   9/1/61f
Gooch, Colonel H. E., death and burial of   17/1/67; 24/1/67n
Grays Charity   9/4/61; 11/4/61f
Greens Charity   9/4/61
Green, Robert Esq., of King's Newton Hall   17/4/59n; 18/4/59; 23/4/59;
                                     26/4/59; 30/4/59; 11/5/59;
                                   29&30/7/59; 8/8/59
Greaves, Miss   13/6/45
Guisers   24/12/60
Haimes
    • Mr., starts silk hosiery branch   5/12/48
    • builds a new factory   24/10/51
    • Haimes and Hancock's warehouse robbed   5/11/52
    • Mr., erects Melbourne's first steam engine   4/1/54
    • death of Mr. William   21/8/54f
    • Mr., comments on trade   12/6/68n
    • Memorial window in parish church   25/12/70i
Han(d)cock, Mr.   5/11/52; 14/2/60
Hardinge, Captain, recuts inscription on Holywell   30/7/68
Hardinge family vault opened in parish church   12/1/60
Hardinge memorial slabs lifted in parish church   25/1/60
Hardinge, Sir Robert   26/1/46
Hardinge, Sir Henry, created Baron Hardinge of   13/4/46
  King's Newton
Hardwick Hall   14/10/45
Harpur, burial at Hemington / Lockington   21/11/45
Harpur-Crewe, Sir John   20/9/45; 14/11/45; 20/11/45;
                                     13/11/62; 12/6/68n

King's Newton Hall
- bazaar picnic in gardens   2/8/59
- tradition of visit by King Charles II   26/1/46
- destruction of, by fire   15/4/59n; 17/4/59; 18/4/59; 19/4/59; 20/4/59; 23/4/59(3)i; 30/4/59(2)ni; 11/5/59; 29&30/7/59; 8/8/59

Lamb, Sir Mathew   23/12/45
Langley Priory   19/12/58n
Lockington   21/11/45; 25/12/70n
Loudoun, death of Countess of   5/11/73n
Main Street, King's Newton
- Chantry House   12/2/48; 13/3/48; 27/10/51
- Church House   18/9/51f
- King's Newton House   2/5/59f
- lime trees planted   2/4/56; 16/5/56; 16/6/56
Market Gardening   1/11/51; 7/4/59
Marston on Dove   1820f
Massey, Dr., of Melbourne   2/7/61n; 6/9/67n; 8/9/67
Matthews, gamekeeper, death of 5 children of   8/4/59; 9/4/59; 10/4/59
Mechanics   24/11/54
Mechanics Institute   30/7/50; 1/6/53n; 27/8/53
Mee, William   29/5/62
Meeting Lane – see Chapel Street
Melbourne Agricultural Society   27/12/55
Melbourne "Association for Killing Sparrows"   10/1/48
Melbourne, 1st Lord   1820
Melbourne, 2nd Lord   23/8/45f; 3/9/45; 1/10/45; 13/11/45i; 24/11/48; 1/12/48; 3/12/48; 18/12/48; 5/1/49; 9/7/72n

Melbourne, 3rd Lord (previously Lord Beauvale)   24/11/48; 16/6/56f; 5/1/61
Melbourne Hall Gardens
- bazaar in, for church restoration   23/6/58n; 29&30/7/59ni
- grand fete in, for Mechanics Institute   30/7/50
- planting by Mr. Pontey   20/3/48
- visit by George Stevenson   5/7/45
- visit by Wordsworth   1843
Melbourne Horticultural and Floricultural Society   31/7/45
Melbourne "Mechanics Organ"   25/11/47; 1/2/48; 20/2/48
Melbourne Mill, miller killed at   26/2/49
Melbourne Parish Church
- article (brief)   1/9/66n
- baptisms, large number of in 1837   1837
- curfew rung at   21/11/45; 6/4/64
- decorated for Christmas   25/12/55; 25/12/61
- fire scare at   3/4/59
- history of, by Rev. J. Deans   10/1843
- parish chest, contents of   9/4/61

Police Force	6/4/58; 1/8/62
Pontey, Mr., landscape gardener	23/8/45; 20/3/48f
Poor Law	1836; 1837
Postal Service	18/5/47; 25/1/48; 5/1/54
Potato Disease	8/10/45; 14/11/45; 29/3/46; 20/8/46; 6/8/48; 18/11/48; 17/10/51
Potter Street	
• Athenaeum, concert at	5/4/59
• Athenaeum, foundation stone laid	1/6/52ni; 27/8/53f
• Athenaeum, lectures at	16/1/56; 17/3/57; 2/1/58
• Athenaeum, vestry meeting at	6/5/61
• black flag hoisted on	10/6/56
• Bulls Head Inn	1820
• chemist's shop on	23/3/57f
• deaths by lightning strike	19/6/46
• gas lit to celebrate opening of gasworks	5/11/53
Querns, discovery of	13/12/62; 10/4/67
Railway, construction of, through parish of Melbourne	1/2/65; 24/9/65; 19/2/66; 30/7/66; 6/8/66; 9/4/67; 10/4/67; 20/5/6728/2/68; 1/9/68. See also King's Newton, cremation cemetery discovered at.
Railways, projected, in locality	8/9/45; 13/9/45; 20/9/45; 22/9/45; 1/10/45; 8/10/45(2); 14/11/45; 20/11/45; 22/12/45; 7/4/59; 15/4/59n; 20/10/59; 3/10/62; 13/11/62; 10/12/62; 16/11/63n; 1/2/65n; 3/5/65; 15/11/65
Roads, dispute between Melbourne and King's Newton	1832f; 4/8/45; 5/4/59
Roads, complicated method of levying rates for repair	5/4/59
Robinson, Samuel	23/4/59; 10/10/62; 25/12/70n; 11/10/72n; 5/11/73n
Robinson, Mr. Thomas, death of	14/1/51
Robinson's Hill	
• Bleak House	14/2/60
• The Shaw	14/1/51; 23/4/59; 10/10/62; 11/10/72n; 5/11/73n
Roman Roads (supposed) in neighbourhood	5/5/60
Schools	18/9/51; 23/10/51; 1/6/53n; 27/8/53; 19/12/62f
Scott, G. G., architect	19/11/58; 10/12/58; 4/4/59n
Scott, Mr., of King's Newton	
• loses five cows	7/10/45
• leaves farm	16/3/48; 20/3/48
Scott, Mr. Thomas, loses three cart horses	11/1/57
Shardlow Union Workhouse	1836; 29/5/62
Shaw, John, suicide of	5/2/61
Silk glove trade	18/5/45
Silk hosiery branch started by Mr. Haimes	5/12/48

Sinfin Moor, encaustic tile found on	2/1/59i	
Smith, Francis (miller) killed	26/2/49	
Smith, Miss, of Austrey	21/2/46; 14/12/46	
Smith, William, of Foremark Park	2/7/61n	
Stanton by Bridge, St. Brides Farm at	5/5/60	
Stanton Barns, Mr. Newbold of	28/3/46	
Staunton Harold, California coal pit near	6/10/63	
Staunton Harold Hall, visit of Patrick Byrne the blind harper	25/1/48f	
Stevens of Derby, architect	27/10/51; 27/8/53f	
Sunday Schools, Independent	1/10/45	
Swarkestone		
• bloodhound experiment	19/4/45	
• book kept by minister, re Bancroft family etc	15/12/60	
• steeplechases	10/3/46; 15/4/48	
"Table moving"	1/6/53(2)	
Taft, John, first burial in new cemetery	3/6/60	
Taft, old Thomas, death of	6/3/61	
Tasker, Mr.	2/9/59f; 3/11/60; 12/6/68n	
Taylor, Mrs, wife of William, death of	14/9/62	
Taylor, William, fatal wounding of	9/4/61f	
Thompson, Elizabeth, of King's Newton, death of	22/7/57	
Thompson, Thomas, of King's Newton, death of	13/7/45	
Thompson, Thomas, death of	28/8/61	
Tomlinson - , estate of	23/3/57f	
Trent Navigation and Fishery	30/7/45; 6/1/61; 2/7/61n; 20/6/62	
Underwood, Mr., and family	19/10/53	
Union Street	23/3/57f	
Vicarage, rebuilding of	1843	
Ward, Ann	8/4/61f	
Wards Lane	8/4/61f	
Warren, Mr.	28/10/51	
Warren, Nathaniel, life of	2/3/61	
Wasse, Rev. Gervase, curate	15/6/56; 10/4/59; 2/9/59f; 8/4/61; 21/12/61	
Wells, dryness of	28/3/45; 26/3/55; 20/12/55; 7/4/58	
Weston Cliff		
• angling match at	25/12/70n	
• ferry at	10/1846; 31/10/51	
• nightingale at	20/5/59	
• river frozen at	4/1/54; 23/3/55	
Weston on Trent, supposed burial of soldiers in churchyard	5/1/61	
Wilson (parish of Breedon)	4/8/45; 20/8/45; 7/1/48; 1/6/53	
Wilson, Benjamin, architect	28/3/59	
Wombwell's (later Edmond's) Menagerie, visits of	29/4/45; 24/10/51; 27/10/62	
Wood, J. H., teacher and minister	23/3/57f	
Woodhouses		
• causeway and cutting made	24/11/54; 30/1/55	
• death of Matthews children of	8/4/59f; 9/4/59f; 10/4/59	
• inquest into death of George Black of	23/9/45	

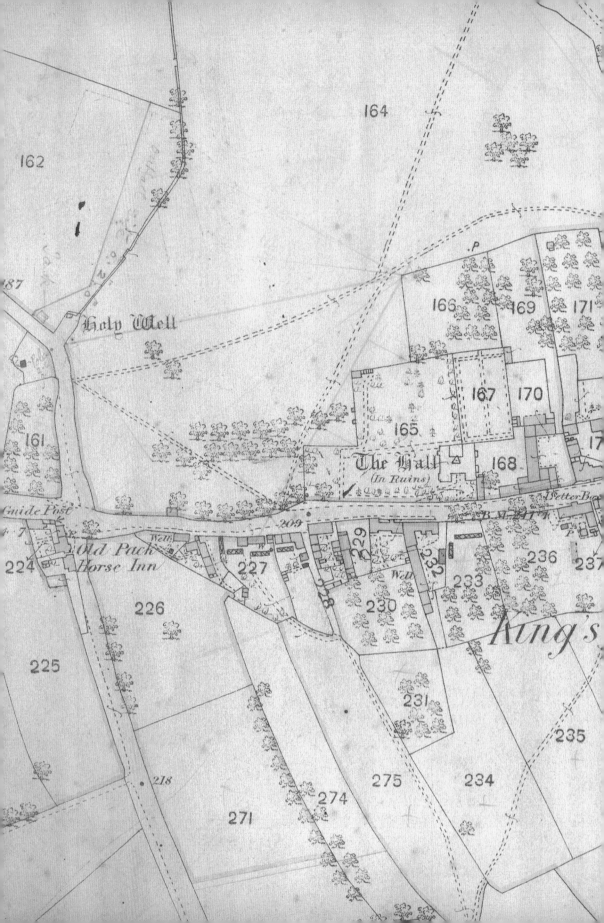